鑪峰古今

珠海學院香港歷史文化研究中心 出版

香港歷史文化論集 2017

蕭國健　游子安　主編

鑪峰古今
香港歷史文化論集2017

主 編
蕭國健　游子安

出 版
珠海學院香港歷史文化研究中心

責任編輯
危丁明

製 作
書作坊出版社
香港沙田美田路33號康松閣1405室

版 次
2018年7月初版

ISBN 978-988-12530-5-7
Printed in Hong Kong

謹誌

珠海學院香港歷史文化研究中心成立十周年

◎目錄

009　序言　　　　　　　　　　　　　　　　　蕭國健

專題論文

011　Sha Tin as a Suburban District　　　　　　P.H. Hase

110　見步行步：殖民地時期
　　　鯉魚門地區的防禦工事　　　　　　　鄺智文

130　香港科學工藝教育的源頭：以李陞格致
　　　工藝學堂和香港實業專科學院為例　馬冠堯

174　冷戰初期兩岸的僑教政策——
　　　對香港中學畢業生升學的影響　　　周正偉

197　道行佛緣——扶乩選址
　　　與建設而成的圓玄學院　　　　　　游子安

214　亡者的告退：民國時期
　　　廣州喪葬儀式與空間的重構　　　　潘淑華

234 客家人遷莞歷史以及遷徙原因初探　　麥淑賢

270 深圳廖氏源流及村莊分布簡況　廖虹雷 廖顯軍

280 深圳坪山打醮　　楊耀林

學人傳略

283 敬悼蘇師景坡瑩輝教授 (1915-2011)　　蘇慶華

地區考察

292 赤柱歷史考察　　蕭國健

295 香港歷史文化研究中心
2017年9月-2018年6月活動簡介

302 編後語　　游子安

序 言

「香港歷史文化研究中心」之成立，目的除於校內為學梓介紹香港歷史外，更向社會人士推廣香港及華南之歷史與文化，多年來與香港歷史博物館、及屯門長者學苑合辦香港歷史文化專題講座及田野考察；又多次與嗇色園、香港中文大學、香港浸會大學、香港歷史博物館、及非物質文化遺產辦事處舉辦國際學術研討會，會後且出版論文集，並出版《鑪峰古今》專刊，以推廣香港及華南之歷史與文化。

今年適逢創會十週年，本會更將論集內容擴充，以輯錄海內外友好學者之鴻文。本期《鑪峰古今2017》，內容除有關香港歷史文化專文多篇外，且收錄馬來亞大學蘇慶華之〈敬悼蘇師景坡瑩輝教授（1915-2011）〉，東莞博物館麥淑賢之〈客家人遷莞歷史以及遷徙原因初探〉、深圳博物館楊耀林之〈深圳坪山打醮〉、及廖虹雷與廖顯軍之〈深圳廖氏源流及村莊分佈簡況〉等大作。

本書蒙各講者及友好學者惠賜鴻文，及各界好友之幫助，始得完成，特此致謝。

蕭國健教授
珠海學院 香港歷史文化研究中心主任
2018年仲夏

Sha Tin as a Suburban District[*]

Patrick H. Hase

皇家亞洲學會香港分會

Most academic studies of the New Territories concentrate either on the history of the area before development, that is, the history of the area as a traditional rural area, or else on the post-development, contemporary period, the period of the New Towns. Relatively little work has, however, been done on the period between the two, the period of suburban development. This period is, however, not only vital to the history of the New Territories, and to Hong Kong as a whole, but is of the greatest interest in itself. This paper, therefore, studies the history of Sha Tin between 1910 and 1972, to give a flavor of the post-traditional, pre-New Town period of the district.

Sha Tin, so close to the urban area, was a natural suburban district. Before development of the New Town began in 1972, there was a phase of suburban development which was important in its time, and which needs to be considered in the history of the district as a whole. This discussion of Sha Tin as suburban district falls into four parts. The first discusses the land, and the transformation of Sha Tin from an intensely farmed rice monoculture basin, surrounded by bare and denuded hills, to an equally intensely farmed vegetable market-garden area, surrounded by heavily afforested hills. The second part discusses the people, and the transformation of the district from one where the population almost entirely comprised indigenous Punti and Hakka villagers to one where newcomers from the City and China came to form the majority population. This part also considers the social changes which came to the district as the result of these

*   An earlier version of this paper was prepared for the Leisure and Cultural Services Department (Hong Kong Heritage Museum), 1998. The author is indebted to Mr.Tim Ko Tim-keung for assistance with the plates.

changes in population makeup, including the formation of the new market town, and the coming of modern industry to Sha Tin. The third part discusses services and infrastructure, and how a completely traditional, self-sufficient, subsistence community was brought into contact with the City by new roads, railway and telephones and became accustomed to modern educational, medical, police, and other services. Finally, a section discusses the long evolution of the New Town proposals for Sha Tin, between 1910 and 1967.

Land

The Kowloon Peak Villages: Traditional Market Satellites

Suburban development in Sha Tin in fact begins before the coming of the British. This early suburban development was centred on market gardening and associated activity for the market at Kowloon City. Every significant market town in the wider Hong Kong region was traditionally supported by a few villages which were satellites of the market town. These satellite villages were either market garden villages, or industrial villages. Kowloon City was a relatively large and important market, and thus supported several such satellite villages. Hoklo Tsuen and Sha Po were such satellites, immediately adjacent to the market town: the Lok Sin Tong (樂善堂) which was a charitable organisation and hospital, was at Sha Po, immediately east of the market.

Kowloon City, however, lies at the foot of Kowloon Peak. In the broader Hong Kong region, market towns close to the mountains tended to specialize in "mountain goods". In the case of Kowloon City, six satellite villages were established in the mountains near the market, which lived by producing "mountain goods" for sale in the market there. These six villages were on the northern slopes of Kowloon Peak, on the Sha Tin side of the ridge, and were, from west to east, Shap Yi Wat, Mau Tat, Kwun Yam Shan (with its dependednt hamlets of Kong Pui and Tso Tui Ha), Fu Yung Pit, Mau Tso Ngam, and Lo Shue Tin. As Map 1 shows, their dependence on Kowloon City can be seen from their access paths, which are very clearly oriented on Kowloon City, rather than the Sha Tin lowlands.

The oldest of these villages was Kwun Yam Shan, which was probably founded in the late eighteenth century.[1] According to the traditions of the villages (including their Tsuk Po, were they have one), Mau Tso Ngam and Lo Shue Tin followed in the second quarter of the nineteenth century, and Fu Yung Pit, Mau Tat, and Shap Yi Wat were established in the later nineteenth century. Certainly Kwun Yam Shan, and probably Mau Tso Ngam, predate the coming of the British to Hong Kong in 1841. All these villages lie between 750 feet and 1,000 feet above sea-level (except Mau Tso Ngam, which lies between 1,000 and 1,250 feet above sea-level), and all lie in the upper valleys of the mountain streams which flow down to the sea at Sha Tin. All have only very tiny areas of land able to be used for growing rice: this is especially so of Shap Yi Wat, which has scarcely any. More importantly, all the villages lie close to extensive woods – the whole area between the villages and the line of the main mountain ridge was well wooded (Shap Yi Wat was established close to an extensive area of bamboos).

The economy of these villages was based on the sale of "mountain goods", and the purchase of rice with the income thus gained. The agricultural land of the villages was predominantly not used for rice, but for vegetables, and for goods which could be sold in the market. The "mountain goods" which these villages produced consisted of flowers, rattan products, tea, herbs, honey, fruit, firewood, game, and cattle.

Mau Tat and Mau Tso Ngam grew flowers in pots, and the green slips which can be grown in water: these were carried on shoulder poles to the market for sale. Shap Yi Wat lived off the stands of rattan and bamboo near the village. The households there sold bamboo poles. They also made rattan sieves and baskets, and rattan stools, and so forth, for sale in the market. Village women from all these mountain-side villages also made brooms for sale from the twigs of certain bushes.

All these villages had tea-trees. These were owned by individual households, who would each have three or four or more. These trees were not gathered into plantations, but were scattered here and there on the edges of plots of land owned by the family, or on the hill-slopes nearby. New trees were established by cutting slips from the ancient, communally owned, trees which grew near the main ridge, and setting them on field baulks. They would be productive after a few years. The villagers would allow the trees to grow naturally, plucking them each year, until they grew leggy and spindly, when they cut them for fuel. Every household would plant two or three, and cut for fuel one or two each year.

The tea produced, therefore, came from a mixture of young and old trees, and was not regular in size, but a mixture of larger and coarser leaves from older trees, and smaller and finer ones from younger ones.[2] Tea was plucked in the late Spring and early Summer, and was dried over slow fires in the family wok, each household drying its own, a long and time-consuming job (it was the work required to dry the tea which in practice limited the family's capacity to grow tea - the trees themselves were easy to propagate and needed little attention). Each family could sell "several catties" of tea a year, in addition to the tea they dried for their own use. The tea produced was "Mountain Tea" (山茶), astringent and clean-tasting, but the hand-drying left it coarse, with twigs and dust. The market town tea merchants would raddle it to remove the coarsest parts, although the villagers usually did not bother for the tea they drank themselves. The villagers did prepare a higher quality tea as well, from the first plucking of the year (usually at or near the Ching Ming Festival, and often from trees growing near the family tombs), when only the best leaves were taken, which were then carefully picked over to avoid any twigs or coarse leaves being included. This tea was carefully raddled by the villagers. It was sold at a higher price for use in festivals and at the New Year: the villagers always kept a catty or so of this higher quality tea back for their own use at festivals. These villages supplied most of the tea sold in Kowloon City. Some of these villages still produce some tea for their own consumption each year.

Medicinal herbs ("Mountain Drugs", 山藥, or 生藥) were a recognised part of the local pharmacopoeia. The market-town doctors knew and kept the classic drugs ("Known Drugs", 熟藥) , but used the Mountain Drugs as well, either instead of, or alongside, the Known Drugs. Many local housewives also used Mountain Drugs to prepare tonics of various kinds, without prescription from a doctor. Not every family knew how to find and prepare medicinal herbs: this was knowledge passed from father to son in certain households only, who guarded their secrets jealously. It was not just a question of finding the herbs, but of recognising good specimens, and giving them the required drying, cutting, or other preparation as demanded by the doctors. Drugs were either sold to the market-town doctors in this ready-to-use form, or were sold raw and green to housewives in the street, although, in this last case, only the commoner Mountain Drugs were usually involved.

Allied to the trade in medicinal herbs was the gathering for sale of pomelo leaves and rushes for boiling up to make sweetsmelling water to bathe in, and the gathering of the Mountain Tuber (山薯), which after maceration, was used by the boat-people to water-proof their nets with. Also sold was hair-lacquer for women. This was the juice of a certain mountain bush boiled up into a sticky paste, and the women of the market-town district often preferred to buy it ready-made than pound and boil it themselves, especially since the juice was highly poisonous, and the manufacture rather dangerous.

Honey was produced in most villages, but was a speciality of the mountainside villages. The large numbers of fruit trees in these villages allowed relatively large quantities of honey to be produced. This honey was usually sold to doctors, for it was a vital ingredient in many prescriptions. The fruit which allowed more than the normal number of beehives was mostly tangerines. The whole valley behind Mau Tso Ngam is a mass of tangerine trees - several hundred at least. The fruit was cut and sold branch by branch at the New Year. The tangerines were not usually sold in pots, since the weight made the carriage to the market, over footpaths, and with shoulder poles, impossible except for a few each year. Some of the tangerines were sweet and edible, and were sold for eating. Also at the New Year, villagers sold branches of Bell Flower (吊鐘花, also known as Chinese New Year Flower), cut from the trees which most villagers owned, high in the mountains.

Firewood was something which was gathered by women from every village for sale in the market, and these mountainside villages had no monopoly of this trade. However, the ready access of these villages to their woods gave them a definite advantage over other villages, and the production for sale of firewood was more of a full-time occupation there than elsewhere. These villages always had to keep a sharp look-out for people coming from the lowland villages to cut in their woods: although there is no memory of fighting in the

Kowloon Peak villages, there can be little doubt that, as at Wong Chuk Yeung, the villagers would have fought to prevent poaching of this, their most important asset. [3] Knowledgeable villagers state that this trade continued until about 1950 or a little later.

There was always a market for game. The market towns in this area had a reputation for game well before the coming of the British. Wild boar was the most important game, but porcupine meat, wild duck, pangolin, venison, and snake meat were also important. Hui Wing-hing (許永興), a famous local scholar and poet in the later nineteenth century, refers in his poems (1880-1890) to the hunting of wild boar, deer, and pythons in the general area of Sha Tin. [4] The Kowloon Peak villages had hunting dogs, and set traps and nets, and were regular sellers of game in the market. The villagers claim to have set traps for tigers as well, although none were caught within living memory.

Cattle-breeding was a speciality in particular of Mau Tso Ngam. Few villages could afford breeding stock, and villagers from the lowland villages needing a new plough-beast would usually buy a young animal from a village which specialised in breeding them. Mau Tso Ngam had plenty of grazing land, on those slopes behind the village not covered in trees, and were one of these specialist villages.

These unusual ways of life were noted by Hui Wing-hing. He has this to say of Mau Tso Ngam and Fu Yung Pit:

> 茂草岩前栽萬卉，芙蓉壁愛種花園
>
> At Mau Tso Ngam there are thousands of flowers in front of the village.
>
> At Fu Yung Pit, too, they love to plant flower gardens.

Another version of the poem has a different line for Mau Tso Ngam, referring to the cattle at the village:

> 吊草岩前堪畜牧
>
> The land in front of Tiu Tso Ngam [the old name for Mau Tso Ngam] is fit for pasturing animals.

The villagers of these six mountainside villages which were

satellite to Kowloon City normally managed to live lives no less comfortable than those who lived in the poorer lowland villages. Their lives were hard, but no more so than those of the other Sha Tin Hakka villages. They were able to support a common school (at Kwun Yam Shan), and they had a full ritual life, taking part with the other Siu Lek Yuen Yeuk villages in the She ritual, and with the rest of the Kau Yeuk in the decennial Ta Tsiu.[5] However, when the War came, and famine with it, they suffered very badly. No-one wanted to buy flowers, or rattan-work, or even tea or herbs, and the villages did not have enough rice-land to survive without the income from what they sold in the market. Shap Yi Wat was, by the end of the War, reduced to only three persons left alive, the others having died of starvation. The other villages were not so badly off, but all of them suffered.

Interestingly, these mountainside villages, which had been founded as satellites to Kowloon City, remained dependent on Kowloon City, in some ways to the present day, and never became suburban to the City as a whole, even when the rest of Sha Tin did. These villages continued to live by selling "mountain goods" at Kowloon City down to the 1970s, and a few families in them still trade in this traditional way even today. Kwun Yam Shan, Mau Tso Ngam, Mau Tat, and Shap Yi Wat are still fully inhabited today, although Fu Yung Pit and Lo Shue Tin are now uninhabited.

Pre-War Market Gardening

Modern market gardening, that is, growing vegetables or flowers, or rearing pigs or poultry, for the main urban markets of Hong Kong (as opposed to the traditional market-town relationships of the Kowloon Peak villages), began in Sha Tin essentially in the mid 1920s. There is little evidence of any significant market gardening of this sort in Sha Tin before 1926, when there is a record of large flocks of ducks being kept on the marshy land near the station in Sha Tin for sale in the City.

An area of Crown Land was sold in 1920 for a Camphor Plantation near Tai Shui Hang Village, but nothing seems to have come of this venture. A very large area (143 acres) of Crown Land was sold to

"Messrs Donnelly and White" near Keng Hau Village ("near the entrance to the railway tunnel"), for a building and associated land, and this group of Westerners extended their holdings by purchase of additional Crown Land in 1924. This must have been a commercial venture: it is likely that it was another forestry project. Nothing further is heard of it, and the land probably eventually fell into the hands of the Hin Tin villagers in the mid 1930s. A substantial area (2 acres) of Crown Land near Keng Hau was sold to Chan Kim Kwan for development as an orchard in 1935: this was also probably a commercial venture. Donnelly and White and Chan Kim Kwan probably proposed to have their products carried to the City by lorry using the upper Keng Hau Road - this road had been built in 1906 to assist the building of the railway tunnel.

The Government had been urging the villagers to consider turning their land into market gardens ever since the takeover of the New Territories, as it seemed obvious to the Government that this was where the best agricultural profits were likely to be found. Village conservatism, however, responded very slowly to this urging, although there is a record of lychees being carried by the railway (probably from near Fanling) to the City as early as 1911. This tendency towards conservatism was despite the establishment of the Government Fan Ling Experimental Gardens in 1915, and of the private New Territories Agricultural Association in 1927, both essentially aimed at encouraging development of farming for the market.

The District Officer noted in 1925, however, that the boycott of trade with China instigated by the Chinese Government in that year had led to a fillip in market gardening in the New Territories, since the supplies of vegetables normally received from China dried up.[6] Numbers of professional market gardeners who had been dependent on the Hong Kong market moved into the New Territories from China at this time, as did other market gardeners who were being forced out of New Kowloon by development pressure there. In 1926 the District Officer reported that a good deal of farm land had been rented to these incomers, who were living in sheds built in their fields, for which matshed permits were being issued: 608 such permits had been issued by 1928. In 1928, the District Officer stated that most of this new market gardening development was "along the railway" and "along Castle Peak Road". Almost all of it seems to have been near Ping Shan (which was a major centre by then for both pig rearing and vegetable growing) and near Fanling and Sheung Shui. A further wave of matshed permits to Hakka pig-rearers came in 1935, and more again in 1939-1941, but, as before, very few were in Sha Tin.

Apart from the duck farms on the marshes, there is no record of anything very much happening in Sha Tin until well into the 1930s: Sha Tin seems to have missed out on this development almost entirely in these early years. Conservatism in what was, in these years, a relatively traditional district, with no market, must have played a part in this, but poor transport infrastructure also played a part (see Plate 1, showing the Valley in 1930, with all fields being used for rice). Market gardening cannot be successfully undertaken without the means of getting the produce to market: in Sha Tin that meant, essentially, that the site had to be close to the railway or road accessible.

The station at Sha Tin was not well located for this trade, as it was built away from the main areas of flat and usable agricultural land. The railway was always very conscious of the profits to be made by carrying local farm produce to the City. Up to 1930, the railway would attach goods wagons to any local train. Villagers wishing to carry goods would gather at the station and a goods van would be loaded and sent into the City. In 1930, because of the delays this practice caused to the scheduled services, the practice was stopped. Instead, two "mixed" trains (goods trains with a passenger carriage attached) would be scheduled each day, which would pick up goods at each station. Areas were set aside at each station for the storage of livestock and other goods, which would be loaded onto the mixed train when it arrived. It was not essential for the consignee to travel with the goods: the wholesale laans ("laan", 欄, means a wholesale dealer, and is the normal Hong Kong term for such a dealer) to whom it was to be assigned would meet the train and take their goods. At some stations (eg Tai Po Kau, 1919, and Tai Po Market, 1921), special shelters were built for this trade, fenced in, with a roof on pillars. Sha Tin did not get such a special shelter, but photographs of the station, and the memories of the villagers, show that, despite the poor location of the station, this trade was important at Sha Tin, too.

Thus, Wong Chuk Yeung village, although lying well over a mile from the railway station at Sha Tin, over a mountain pass, raised a few pigs for the market from well before the War. Village households there would raise two pigs at a time, one for themselves, and one to sell. They could do this because of the abundant rough grazing available near the village (few lowland families could manage to rear more than one pig at a time). Two men could carry a pig in a pig-basket strung on a pole from the village to the railway station in something over an hour, and have it consigned to the pig laan in the City.[7] Although costs were high, and the numbers of pigs able to be reared low, this trade kept Wong Chuk Yeung alive as a village until a road (albeit long, narrow, and very steep) was built to it in 1961 as a by-product of the Integrated Water Scheme. Other mountain villages within a mile or so of the railway (eg Kwai Tei, Shan Mei, and Au Pui Wan) also reared pigs in the same way.

The railway was also very important for the transport of tubs of live fish to the City (the importance of this for the fish trade at Tai Po, and presumably Sha Tin as well, is noted by the District Officer as early as 1916), and for the transport of poultry. The duck farms noted in Sha Tin in 1926 were close to the station, and it can be assumed that the ducks were shipped to the laans in poultry baskets by rail.

Before the War, the only road of significance in Sha Tin was the Tai Po Road, and that was, for most of its length within Sha Tin, either running over mountains far from any village, or else pinned between the railway immediately on the one side, and the sea on the other. Little of Sha Tin was, therefore, favourable to lorry-based market gardening in the modern way.

It was only in the Tai Wai area that the Tai Po Road ran through fields and near villages. Tai Wai was also within one mile of the station, and so within the zone which could use the railway. It is, therefore, no surprise that the best evidence for pre-War market gardening for the urban market in Sha Tin, apart from the duck farms on the marshes, comes from here. Tai Wai villagers interviewed in 1980 remembered "five or six" commercial pig-farms; "two or three" commercial poultry farms, and "half-a-dozen" commercial vegetable farms near this village before the War. One pig-farm was on a large scale for that date, with at least fifty pigs, housed in two large sheds. This was north of the village, on the lower slopes of Tung Lo Wan Shan. The villagers remember this farm well, because, during the fighting between the Japanese and the British for Kowloon, the Japanese Army made its base in Tai Wai, and the villagers fled, most of them taking shelter in these pig-sheds. Another commercial pig-farm, in this case on the other side of the Railway Station from Tai Wai, was the Tai Tei Farm. This bought Crown Land at Ha Wo Che for its farm-buildings and pig-sties in 1940.

Another farm near Tai Wai was the "Indian Farm". This was started by Azim Khan in 1939, north of Tai Wai, on the slopes above the Shing Mun River. He took partners and extended his holdings in 1940. He reared goats for the market, and grew specialist vegetables for the Indian community. This farm was quite prosperous, but was not restarted again after the War.

While the commercial vegetable farms were mostly being run at this date by villagers who used part of their fields for the purpose, there was at least one outsider who rented rice-land near Tai Wai in the 1930s and converted it to commercial market gardening use: he grew bananas and sugar-cane. One such outsider, however, is far from the 608 in Ping Shan and Sheung Shui! Of the Tai Wai poultry farms, one or two were duck farms, but there was at least one chicken farm. There were eight commercial chicken farms in the New Territories in 1936, five of which had opened in that year, and it is likely that one of them was at Tai Wai. Of the vegetable farms, a few were full time, but a number of villagers were, in the late 1930s, using their rice fields to grow vegetables during the Winter season, and were thus farming on a subsistence basis for the peak rice harvest, but growing for the market in the Winter (the District Officer noted this as an important factor in market gardening in the area in 1939).

Half a mile from the road at Tai Wai, at Tin Sam, there was much less. There the villagers can remember only one or two commercial farms before the War, and most were small scale. The Tung Tak Company, which bought Crown Land for agricultural use in the general Tin Sam area in 1933, was one of these commercial farms. Half a mile further from the road again, at Kak Tin, there were none.

By 1939, 25% of all vegetables in Hong Kong were being brought in from the New Territories (in 1925 there had been almost none, except from the New Kowloon area), and the Government was looking forward to a gradual transformation of agriculture to market gardening over the next years. This, however, did not happen. All these market gardens were, in the event, closed down, and reverted to rice cultivation under the Japanese. At that time, starvation was a very real threat. In many mountain villages in Sha Tin half the population died of starvation during the years of the Japanese Occupation; in the lowland villages like Tai Wai the percentages were much lower - perhaps 10% - but still significant. No-one could afford to use rice-land for anything other than rice. There were few people in the City who could afford to buy meat or vegetables then, and more people can be kept alive on a subsistence diet of rice, than if meat or vegetables are required as well. A few vegetables were grown, mostly sweet potatoes on land that could not grow rice, but very few of them were sold in the City. Lack of transport (no trains, and no lorries, were in operation under the Japanese), and the need to carry everything on shoulder poles or handcarts made sale in the City extremely difficult, although a few villagers remember pushing the occasional barrow-load of vegetables on a handcart along the Tai Po Road, in the hope of making a sale in Yaumatei in these years.

After the War it was several years before anyone again considered growing food for the market in Sha Tin. It was only in the early 1950s that the first tentative re-start of market gardening began. Because of this, the fact that suburban market gardening had made a start in Sha Tin during the 1930s, only to be crushed under the Japanese, tends to be forgotten.

Post-War Market Gardening

At the end of the War every inch of land that could used to grow rice, was. This even included some land that had not been cultivated when the British came to the New Territories. This remained the position as late as 1947. The District Officer notes in his Annual Report for 1948 that there had been an increase that year in the number of large poultry farms, and, in 1949, he noted the appearance of new squatter huts in various parts of the New Territories, mostly connected with the rental of rice-land to incomer market gardeners. In 1950, the large numbers of new poultry farms being run by refugees from Shanghai were noted, and this was noted again in 1951 and 1952, and again in every year from 1954 to 1956. By 1954, the Government was beginning to be concerned about the environmental damage being caused by these new farms in some places. Many of these new farms were, as in the pre-War period, at Ping Shan.

Government had taken steps immediately after the War to facilitate the return to market gardening in the New Territories, especially with the establishment of the Vegetable Marketing Scheme, and the introduction of district vegetable co-operatives (1946). There was a certain degree of opposition to the Vegetable Marketing Scheme at first ("fomented by interested middlemen"), but, by 1951, the scheme was well-received, and functioning without problems. From 1952, the Kadoorie Agricultural Advancement Association provided assistance to farmers wishing to start up in business as market gardeners or livestock rearers. Also from 1952, the annual Agricultural Show was resumed (it had functioned well in the years immediately before the War): this, too, encouraged farmers into the livestock and market gardening side of agriculture.

Thus, taking the New Territories as a whole, the rebirth of market gardening and livestock rearing began to be noticeable in the Ping Shan area in 1948, and was a major feature there by 1954. In Sha Tin, however, as before the War, the development of this cash farming came a little later. The first signs appear in 1950, but the main development came later, after about 1955.

In 1950, the Union Farm bought Crown Land for agricultural use near Keng Hau. In the same year a large orchard was established on Crown Land at Pat Tsz Wo, at the upper end of the Fo Tan Valley. The Pat Tsz Wo orchard was certainly a commercial venture: it was owned by a Tai Wai villager, and was of considerable size (1¼ acres). In 1952 two commercial pigeon and chicken farms were established, in the Shing Mun Valley north of Tai Wai, and in Pai Tau. It is from these 1952 establishments that Sha Tin began to get a reputation for pigeons.

The Sha Tin villagers say that a major factor in the return to market gardening in Sha Tin after the War was the Integrated Water Scheme. From 1960 onwards, all the streams in Sha Tin were diverted into catchwaters, and it was found that there was just not enough water in many parts of the lowlands of Sha Tin to allow rice-growing to continue. Very few of the Sha Tin rice-fields had been converted to other uses in 1960, but between 1960 and 1965 the majority of the Sha Tin lowland rice fields were converted to vegetable fields (see Plate 2, showing the Valley with all fields down to vegetables, and

Plate 3, a Vegetable farmer, believed to be in Sha Tin). Few Sha Tin indigenous villagers felt able to take part in this trade: they rented out the fields especially to incomers from Canton, who were used to market garden work. This was the pattern, as noted above, which had developed in the Ping Shan and Sheung Shui areas in the late 1920s and 1930s. The Sha Tin villagers themselves tended to leave to run restaurants in Britain, or to seek a better life in the City.

The lowland villages in Sha Tin, unable to grow rice on their fields, rented them, as noted above, to new incomers. But the incomers were not permitted by the villagers to settle in the villages. The lowland villagers hoped, for a number of years, that one day the Government would be able to give them their water back, and allow them to take up rice-farming again. They insisted on keeping the villages in the hands of the indigenous residents. The new incomers were to build sheds to live on in the middle of the fields they were renting.[8]

This is the forgotten period of Sha Tin society. For nearly a generation, before it was all swept away by the coming of the New Town, Sha Tin was marked by a double society: the old, indigenous villages, with their shrunken populations but fiercely conservative attitudes, and enjoying a monopoly of political power and contact with Government, and the vegetable farmers out in their huts in the fields. The vegetable farmers of Sha Tin had no political or social status, and few legal rights. Little is known of their lives or attitudes: the studies of Goran Aijmer and Judith Strauch provide almost all that is known.[9] What seems to have occurred was a steady increase in prosperity among the vegetable squatters. Initially there had been some disputes between indigenous landlords and immigrant tenants, which had been caused by left-wing agitators of the Hong Kong and Kowloon Chinese Farming and Agricultural Association, but this quietened down by 1951. After that year the tenant farmers showed a marked unwillingness to cause waves by quarrelling with their landlords' villages. In the years about 1970, Sha Tin vegetable tenant farmers were providing a significant percentage of Hong Kong's vegetables and fresh flowers.

Afforestation

When the British came to the New Territories, most of the hillslopes were bare of trees, and denuded of cover. Most were grass-covered, although in some places the denudation had led to the soil being eroded away, and the slopes left as gullied rocky badlands. There were still Fung Shui woods behind the villages, and woods on the higher slopes - those on the higher slopes of the northern face of Kowloon Peak, near the Kowloon Peak villages, and on the eastern face of Needle Hill, near Wong Chuk Yeung village were particularly important - and there were other, smaller, woods in the remote and inaccessible gullies on the higher slopes elsewhere, but, in general, the accessible woodlands had all been cut for fuel long before 1898.

Reafforestation, to prevent soil erosion, and with a view to providing a more stable fuel supply in the longer term, was treated as a high priority by the Hong Kong Government from as soon as the Government was fully established in the New Territories. The Annual Reports speak of afforestation along the line of the Tai Po Road (especially below it) in 1900, 1902, 1903, 1912, 1916, 1920, 1921, 1923, 1924, and 1926. This area had become "thickly forested" by 1920. This re-afforestation project included the development of the Tai Po Kau Forestry area (1925-1926). It also included large areas in the Kowloon Reservoir area, and elsewhere in Sha Tin. Afforestation on the slopes of the Kowloon Hills took place as well. Afforestation of these hills took place in 1911, 1912 (when 66,000 trees were planted here), 1913, 1914, 1915, 1918, and 1920. Most of this afforestation took place on the Kowloon slopes of the hills, but some took place on the Sha Tin side as well, since we are told that there was already a pine plantation there sufficiently advanced to be thinned in 1918, when a further area near Beacon Hill on the Sha Tin side was planted as well. Afforestation is also mentioned near Wu Kai Sha (1922), and Mui Tsz Lam (villagers were fined for cutting fuel in a planted area here in 1929). There was a good deal of further afforestation in this period which is not specifically mentioned in the Annual Reports: by 1941, the efforts of the · Government's forestry staff had achieved a major revolution: from bare denuded hillslopes, most of the Sha Tin hills had become thickly wooded.

This reafforestation programme was not universally welcomed by villagers. The areas planted were forbidden to be cut for fuel, to give the new trees time to establish themselves, and this meant that the villagers were deprived of access to areas that they had traditionally used as fuel-cutting grounds. Warnings and fines for illegal fuel cutting were the result. Outbreaks of illegal cutting sufficiently serious to get into the Annual Reports occurred at Tin Sam and Keng Hau in the Sha Tin Valley in 1915, at Tai Wai in 1916, again at Tin Sam and Keng Hau in 1918, and throughout Sha Tin, but especially at Mui Tsz Lam, in 1929. In 1922 there was "active hostility" to reafforestation at Wu Kai Sha.

The Government did not merely forbid villagers to use the hillslopes for cutting fuel, however. It wanted to get the villagers to take out Forestry Lots, areas of Crown Land granted on Permit which would be used to provide fuel on a rational basis. The villagers would be obliged to plant part of these Forestry Lots annually, and to cut them in rotation, so that the hills were always wooded, but the villagers still had access to fuel. But the villagers objected to the expenses of the planting, and the Permit Fee, and felt their traditional rights to cut fuel freely should not be interfered with. Few villages in Sha Tin seem to have been willing to take out Forestry Lots in the early years, although the Kowloon Peak villages, and Wong Chuk Shan, seem to have come to an agreement with Government as to the control and use of their traditional woods. The lowland villages on the whole did not. In 1919, the Government instituted a scheme whereby it paid financial incentives to villagers to plant trees, but this was not immediately successful. When the first of the Shing Mun villagers were re-sited to Hin Tin village in Sha Tin (1925), they were given a Forestry Lot free of Permit Fee as part of the terms of the compensation package. It would seem, however, that the system of Forestry Lots became more accepted during the 1930s, at least, there is no further mention of problems of illegal cutting after 1929 in Sha Tin. Thus, by 1930, the Government had not only succeeded in reafforesting most of the Sha Tin hillslopes, but had also managed to get the villagers to accept the new situation, under which their rights to cut the slopes were restricted.

Under the Japanese, when fuel was in seriously short supply, many of these newly-afforested areas were cut for fuel. Even many of the roadside trees were cut at this time. The Japanese did try to stop illegal cutting, especially of roadside trees, but their generally weak control of the New Territories made it difficult for them to enforce controls except sporadically, although the Tai Wai villagers remember Japanese raids on villagers trying to cut roadside trees. However, the relatively short period of the Japanese Occupation meant that most of the re-afforested areas retained enough trees for natural re-seeding to begin from 1946. Also, the Government started a new reafforestation programme in the late 1940s (this included a major re-afforestation programme for the Shing Mun Reservoir area, in 1951, and the establishment of the Government Forestry Nursery at Ping Kong in 1954).

This re-afforestation drive led to little opposition from villagers, since, by then, many villagers were switching to new fuels, especially kerosene, and scrap wood sold from building sites (ie used concrete cladding), and the firewood from the hills became less important to them. Only in the remoter areas of the New Territories (the Tolo Channel, and parts of Lantau), and where there were very large numbers of poor refugees (especially in the Tsuen Wan area) was illegal cutting of fuel a serious problem in the years 1950-1954. In 1951-1952, carpenters in search of good wood were trying to buy camphor trees in village Fung Shui woods. This was banned by the Government in 1952, but permitted from 1953 where the trees were dead or dying, and where the income from the sale was used for communal purposes. A considerable sum was raised by these sales during 1953-1954. By the end of the 1950s, the Sha Tin hillslopes were as densely wooded as they had been in 1941. Since 1965, with the abandonment of the mountainside villages, natural growth has led to these woods extending down into areas which were cultivated in 1941. There can be little doubt that Sha Tin is now more densely wooded than at any time in the last two hundred and fifty years.

People and Society

The Abandonment: of the Mountainside Villages

Many villages in the mountains of Sha Tin were not road accessible (the Kowloon City satellite villages mentioned above were connected to Kowloon City - although not to Sha Tin - during the 1960s). Most of the mountainside villages were fully inhabited during the War, when every inch of land usable for rice was occupied. There was no change to this position up until 1947, when the District Officer still noted that every inch of land that could be cultivated, was.

However, by 1954, the District Officer was noting that some "five or six square miles" of agricultural land had gone out of use since 1899 - probably most of it in the previous year or two. The Government was hopeful that it could get this land back into cultivation, but, although there was some success in reversing the abandonment trend for a few years, in the longer term this was not to be. The subsistence lifestyle of the remoter, non-roadaccessible villages (which were too far from the road to allow villagers to work outside, and too far, too, to carry goods for sale, or to bring in goods bought outside) became unacceptable. The villagers saw their friends and relatives in the lowland, road-accessible, villages getting more and more prosperous and objected to their own continuing poverty. Families drifted away, either moving to the City to work as labourers there, or trying to rent land in the lowlands for working as a vegetable market-garden, or they emigrated to the United Kingdom. After a few years, the villages started to become depopulated and abandoned.

It is not possible to date the abandonment of the Sha Tin mountainside villages exactly, but some points can be made. Generally it was the more marginal villages, and those furthest from the roads, which were abandoned first, and the smaller the village, the earlier it was likely to be abandoned. Some very marginal villages high on the mountain slopes were abandoned after only a generation of use. These tiny settlements, of just one or two families, were built at what was found to be above the effective limit of viable cultivation. The settlement at Ngau Au, which seems to have disappeared about 1910, was one such. Another was Wang Lo Ha (橫路下), also known as Wang Au (橫凹). This tiny village was built on the pass, where the old road from Sha Tin to Tai Po crossed the mountains.[10] As well as its few tiny fields, this village subsisted by selling drinks of tea to travellers who needed a rest after carrying heavy loads up to the pass.

This village seems to have been abandoned almost as soon as

the railway was opened (1910), since much of the Tai Po to Sha Tin traffic switched to the railway once it was available. The Tai Po Road (1903, but greatly improved 1920), on its much lower course, near the coast, also took away a good deal of traffic. Wang Lo Ha does not seem to have survived to 1920. No other Sha Tin village, however, seems to have been abandoned before the late 1950s.

Some villages were abandoned in the late 1950s (see Map 2). These were mostly the very tiny villages first founded only in the later nineteenth century on very marginal pockets of land, which, even in the 1950s, after perhaps three generations, were still only one or two households in size. Many were high on the mountainsides, at between 550 feet and 1000 feet above sea-level. Many of the early abandonments were in the area above the Fo Tan Valley. Here Cheung Lek Mei, Nim Au, Shek Lau Tung, Ngau Wu Tok, Yiu Tau Ping and Lo Sheung Tun were all abandoned early. For some of these settlements, even the sites cannot now be traced. In this area, the loss of trade when the Sha Tin to Tai Po traffic moved to the railway (1910) and to the Tai Po Road, especially after it had been widened and improved (1920) (all these villages were more or less close to the old path) was an added factor. It was critical to Wang Lo Ha, but it affected all these other villages to some degree. These villages were too far from the road to be able to act as satellite market villages like those on the slopes of Kowloon Peak. Shek Lung Tsai, above Siu Lek Yuen, was abandoned at about this date.

The larger villages of the area above Fo Tan, Au Pui Wan, Shan Mei, and Ho Lek Pui, were abandoned during the late 1960s, that is, some ten years later than the smaller villages nearby.[11] In 1954, villagers of Nim Au and Cheung Lek Mei were still sufficiently settled in their ancestral villages to buy Crown Land to open additional fields, but, a decade later, the villages were effectively abandoned. For some time the clans from these villages (the Laus, 劉, of Au Pui Wan, and the Hungs, 洪 of Shan Mei) sent representatives back to the village every year to worship at the Ancestral Hall, but later even this became less frequent.

This same decade, from the mid 1960s to the mid 1970s, also saw the abandonment of the villages high up in the saddle between Sha Tin and Sai Kung - Ngong Ping, Wong Chuk Shan and Mau Ping. The villagers of these villages began to drift down to live near Sai Kung

Market (many to Po Lo Che, where the Wong Chuk Shan New Village was established) in the late 1950s and the last active men left in the late 1960s, although some hopeful villagers bought Crown Land to build new houses as late as 1959 (Mau Ping) and 1960 (Wong Chuk Shan). However, by the end of the 1960s there were only one or two elderly people left. These villages, like those above Fo Tan, suffered by loosing the opportunity to trade with the people who used the old path from Sha Tin to Sai Kung: after the road to Sai Kung (Hiram's Highway) was opened to motor traffic in 1947 (it was originally built by the Japanese, but the road was not really motorable until after improvements were made to it in 1947, when a bus service to Sai Kung was initiated) people did the journey by lorry or bus, and the old path was deserted. Mui Tsz Lam, much lower down, survived a little longer: Crown Land was being bought by the villagers to build additional houses in 1955 and 1959, but the last families moved away here in the 1980s. A waterworks road was built to Mui Tsz Lam in 1961, but, in this case, this was not enough to keep the village alive (the road only went down to the pier at Tai Shui Hang, and did not, at that date, connect with the roads in Sha Tin).

At Ma On Shan, the iron mine, opened well before the War (the mine was in full active operation before 1936) and connected to the pier at Wu Kai Sha by road, brought, for a short time, a certain prosperity to the village there (the mine re-opened after the War in 1948, and employed up to 2,000 workers over the next few years). Crown Land was sold near here for four villas with gardens in 1958: these were rented to senior mine staff. The mine, however, closed in 1976, and, within the following three or four years, the village was effectively abandoned. A few of the miners remained behind, living in squatter huts near the old mine, but the old village was effectively abandoned by the early 1980s.

As noted above, the narrow thread of its steep, but motorable, road, kept Wong Chuk Yeung alive when the other villages in the hills above Fo Tan failed. Much the same was true of Ma Liu, which survived because of its narrow, but motorable, road linking it with the Tai Po Road at Hotung Lau: Crown Land was sold here in 1953 for an orchard, and in 1959 for a new house, and, in the later 1970s, there was a rush of development of a dozen or so villas, perched precariously on a narrow ridge near the end of the road.

In 1950, all the villages which existed in Sha Tin when the British came were still fully inhabited, except for Ngau Au and Wang Lo Ha. By 1980, all the mountainside villages were abandoned (and most were by 1970), except for Wong Chuk Yeung and Ma Liu with their threads of motorable road, and the Kowloon Peak villages.

There were two factors which made this abandonment easier. The first was the old United Kingdom Immigration Ordinance, which allowed free immigration and settlement rights in the United Kingdom to anyone who was a British Subject by descent, ie who had inherited that status by birth from parents who were British Subjects. In 1898, when the British took over the New Territories, all New Territories villagers were made British Subjects. By the 1950s, almost all New Territories heads of families were second or third generation British Subjects, and thus had the Right of Abode and citizenship in the United Kingdom. Few residents in the City could claim this. It was, therefore, easy for the villagers abandoning their old mountainside homes to move to the United Kingdom. Since the 1950s and 1960s were when every town in Britain started to want Chinese Restaurants, they were able to get jobs as waiters and cooks in Britain. But life as a poverty-stricken subsistence mountain farmer did not imply a wide knowledge of Chinese cuisine: one reason for some of the strange twists to Chinese food as sold in Britain even to this day!

The second factor, already mentioned, was the ending of rice-farming in the lowland villages after the water was cut for the Integrated Water Scheme from 1960. This led to a wave of emigration from the more prosperous lowland villages. These villagers did not emigrate without assistance. Sha Tin villagers tended to go to certain areas in Britain only, especially Liverpool and London. In Liverpool, the village of Tai Wai bought a tiny flat out of communal village funds. There any Tai Wai villager (or other Sha Tin villager if there was room) could live at a very low rent while they looked for work. Because of things such as this, the Chinese in this or that district of Britain tend, even today, to be from one district or even just one village of the New Territories, and often, therefore, are related. The villagers from the poor mountainside villages in Sha Tin were able to emigrate so easily in part because they were able to get help from the bigger lowland villages (who were "brothers of the same Heung") who were emigrating at the same time.

Thus, the period 1960-1970 saw the single largest social change to come to Sha Tin between the arrival of the Hakka in the late seventeenth century, and the coming of the New Town in 1972. The mountainside villages, with their fields cut with such labour from the hillslopes a century before, were abandoned, while the rich lowland villages stopped growing rice, with their fields rented out to incomers. Almost half the Hakka indigenous population of the district disappeared, and a sizeable percentage of the indigenous Punti left the district as well. All this was due in a large measure to the suburban situation of the district: while subsistence life in the mountainside villages became more and more unacceptable, at the same time, access to the City and overseas became easier and easier; and, when rice-farming became impossible, it was easy for families to move away.

Communications

The Tai Po Road

The first major change in the life of the villagers of Sha Tin after the leasing of the New Territories to Britain was caused by the construction of the first modern road over the mountains: the Tai Po Road. The British decided to build roads throughout the New Territories as soon as they acquired them. These roads were initially justified "by administrative and military needs", as the District Officer put it - essentially, they were roads for the military to march along, and for Government officers to ride on. There was no overall road plan at this early stage.

The first road to be built was the Tai Po Road, from Sham Shui Po to Tai Po. This road was built to a 14' width, without proper surfacing (1903). Because it was justified by military and official needs, it by-passed most of the villages (it came close to Tai Wai and Fo Tan in Sha Tin), and its course was deliberately kept quite high in the hills, to avoid expensive bridges over streams near the sea. The road also avoided expensive cuttings, and so twisted and bent around every tiny spur and valley. It was initially little used by villagers to travel between Sha Tin and Kowloon, since the villagers found the old paths more useful, as the new road took a much longer route to reach Kowloon City, which remained the destination of most villagers (see Plate 4, of 1910, showing the first Tai Po Road, and also the railway, shown just before it opened). This was especially so after the Government built roads from Kowloon City to Sha Tin Pass (the Shatin Pass Road, 9' wide), and to Customs Pass (this road was eventually extended to Tate's Pass, 6' wide), in 1907 and 1908 respectively, thus improving the old paths on the Kowloon City side of the hills. The new Tai Po road was used more intensively between Sha Tin and Tai Po, especially by drovers of cattle, for whom it was a much easier path than the old paths through the hills. The new road was much easier than the old path through Wang Lo Ha, and only a little longer. Several short lengths of 6' road were built during 1905 linking Tai Po and some of the more important villages near that town, especially Sheung Shui.

The second New Territories road was the Castle Peak Road, and it was built from Castle Peak pier at Tuen Mun to Fanling, and thence to Au Ha near Sha Tau Kok. It was built between 1908 and 1911, apart from the main bridge at Au Tau, which was not finished until 1915. The section from Fanling to Au Ha was closed as soon as it was opened, and used as the road-bed for the new light railway to Sha Tau Kok. This Castle Peak Road was begun at 6' width (Castle Peak to Ping Shan), and then widened to 8' (Ping Shan.to Fanling). An 8' wide spur was built to Kam Tin in 1910-1911.

In 1911, however, the decision was taken that the New Territories roads must be made motorable, and fit for use by commercial traffic. A proper network was to be built, based on a road which was to go right around the New Territories. This new New Territories Circular Road was built in stages. The first of the new motorable roads was the short spur linking Fanling station and the new Golf Course at Fanling (1911). The Tai Po to Fanling section of the main Circular Road was built in 1913-1914. Both this road and the Golf Course Road were initially 16' wide, but were a few years later widened to 20'. The Castle Peak Road from Castle Peak pier to Fanling was widened to 20' (except for the bridge at Au Tau, which was left at 14' wide) between 1914 and 1917. The Kowloon to Castle Peak sections were built between 1916 and 1917 (Sham Shui Po to Tsuen Wan), and 1917-1918 (Tsuen Wan to Castle Peak). These sections were built to 16' width · . The final section to be rebuilt was the original Kowloon to Tai Po section of the

Tai Po Road. This was rebuilt, eventually to 20' width, between 1916 and 1920, the rebuild involving many cuttings to remove tight bends to make the road easier to use for motor vehicles. Finally, the whole Circular Road was covered with Tarmac (this work was completed 1923), to provide an all-weather surface.

It was, then, only in 1920 that Sha Tin was connected by a fully motorable road with the City. By 1920, there were significant numbers of motor lorries available, and the lorries and the new road made an immediate impact on Sha Tin life. Almost as soon as the new road was open, lorries started to be hired by villagers wishing to sell in the City, and by City merchants wanting to buy in the New Territories. Nonetheless, the immediate impact, although significant, was less than might have been expected (and very much less than the District Officer expected). Market gardening in Sha Tin only began in a significant way, as noted above, in the 1930s, and was limited to the areas easy of access to the new road. The road did, however, permit the growth in weekend villas and small Buddhist monasteries which was a feature of Sha Tin life between the mid 1920s and the Japanese War: these all assumed that motor access was available. In 1937, there was a motorable road connecting the Tai Po Road with Canton as well: this increased the overall use of the Tai Po Road.

Apart from the short spur of the upper Keng Hau Road (built, as noted above, from the Tai Po Road down to the north entrance to the railway in 1906 to facilitate access to the tunnel while it was under construction, see Plate 1), and the Tao Fung Shan Road, which was built as part of the development of the Christian Mission to Buddhists by the Rev. C. Reichelt from 1930 on, there were no other motorable roads in Sha Tin until after the War. After the War and before the coming of the New Town three additional sections of important motorable road were added: the Lion Rock Tunnel Road (1967), the lower Keng Hau Road (1960-1961, but only connected to the main road system at Tai Wai by an unsurfaced track and timber bridge from 1964-1965, and by a surfaced road and concrete bridge only from 1969: this road was later replaced by the present Che Kung Miu Road in the early 1980s), and the Siu Lek Yuen Road (1967).

The Kowloon-Canton Railway

Preliminary agreement to survey a route for a railway from Kowloon to Canton was secured between the Hong Kong and Imperial Chinese Governments in 1899, but nothing was done about the proposal until 1905, when it was agreed that the section of the railway within Hong Kong would be built by the Hong Kong Government, and the section within China by the Chinese Government. The line was surveyed in 1905-1906, and construction began in 1906. The railway was opened to passenger traffic as far as Lo Wu in October 1910, and to Canton a year later (see Plate 4).

The railway had an immediate and profound effect on Sha Tin life: an effect much greater than the opening of the first road nine years earlier. It became easy for villagers to go into the City to do their shopping, and for market shop-keepers to go there to acquire foreign-made articles for sale in their shops. The Governor, Sir Henry May, said at the opening of the railway, "the administration will be greatly facilitated, trade will be stimulated, and the condition of the inhabitants must be improved by their being brought into close connection with the large market which Hong Kong affords ... The railway will enable some of us to take short holidays ... Others again will prefer to lead the simple life in the country, visiting Hong Kong daily for their business ... The railway will in short bring the inhabitants of the district greater ease and greater wealth".[12] The District Officer said six months later: "A taste has sprung up for many foreign luxuries, and aerated waters, cigarettes, clothes, caps, towels and kerosene oil are now common articles of sale in the small market towns ⋯ decent clothes, caps, and shoes, formerly luxuries, are now among the necessities of existence".[13] The first casualty of the railway was the locally woven hemp cloth, which had been the villagers' normal wear from time immemorial. This had been retted and spun by the villagers, and woven by travelling weavers who went from district to district, weaving the yarn prepared since the previous year. Now, villagers found they could buy foreign cloth easily, or, if they still wanted the tough hemp cloth, then they could have the cloth woven more easily and cheaply in the City: the last itinerant weavers came to Sha Tin in 1926 or 1927, and then they had been weaving only mosquito nets and similar crude pieces for a few years before they stopped coming. Similarly, wood-block print books, mostly made in Canton, which were the universal type used in the New Territories villages up until 1910, were entirely replaced by lithograph prints from Shanghai within a year or two of the opening of the railway.

Village life the New Territories market towns was significantly changed in just a few years after the coming of the railway.

There were emigratory pressures in traditional Sha Tin society from late in the nineteenth century.[14] The coming of the railway greatly accelerated this trend. It became easy to travel to the City to work, and many young villagers, unwilling to go overseas, took this route, the railway making it convenient to have both the income of working away from home, and the comfort of easy return home. The railway was welcomed unreservedly by the villagers.

More immediately, after the coming of the British, the building of the Tai Po Road, and the railway, and the construction of Government buildings, provided many job opportunities. The railway looked for navvies in part from the communities through which it passed, and the wages offered were far greater than any wage opportunities ever before known in Sha Tin. The Governor noted in 1900 that over $10,000 had been spent in wages paid to villagers in the New Territories within the first year of British administration - and this was before the beginning of work on the railway (it included the first few months of work on the Tai Po Road). Large numbers of villagers went to work on the railway in consequence of these high wages. At Wong Chuk Yeung, the village schoolmaster, a villager of that village, closed his school, and went to work on the digging of the Beacon Hill Tunnel, and was employed there throughout the period 1906-1910. Many of his brother villagers did the same. It has been noticed elsewhere in the New Territories that the huge wages offered by the railway and other construction projects in the first twenty years of the century led to at least a partial collapse in the traditional education system, as the wages were available to literate · and educated and illiterate equally, so that villages were prepared to see schools close and young men go to work before they had finished schooling, since the wages were so good.[15]

The railway works, of course, were not a permanent thing, but those villagers who had worked on the railway were able to get work on the construction of the Kowloon Reservoir (1909-1910), the rebuilding of the Tai Po Road and bridges (1917-1920), and on the work needed for the construction of the Police Stations and other Government buildings constructed during the same period, and often thereafter for work done in the City by the companies who had come to know them. For a whole generation, in fact, coolie labour at the high wages offered was the best work opportunity available, especially to the poorer mountainside villages. Most of those villagers who did this work were, in fact, Hakka from these poorer villages. It was this work, and remittances from villagers working overseas as seamen, which enabled the mountainside villages to survive, and even to prosper in a small way during the 1920s and 1930s. It was only the coming of the Japanese, when remittances could not be received, and there was no construction work available, and which thus threw the villages back on their very inadequate subsistence rice-lands, which spelled the end for these villages. A few years after the War, as we have noted above, the villagers had had enough, and abandoned their homes for the greater security of work elsewhere, especially in Britain.

A further effect of the railway was an increase in cash-based market gardening, also as noted above. The railway enabled villagers to sell products to the City. The railway, also as noted above, had an arrangement whereby pigs could be brought to the station, and then be transported to the City pig laans. Crates of chickens or ducks could be sent by rail, and baskets of fish, and village women could carry vegetables to the bigger City markets by rail, instead of over the mountains to their traditional markets, and this became an important social factor as well. As noted above, this became a steadily more important feature of life in the areas of Sha Tin within reach of the station during the 1930s in particular.

A downside of the coming of the railway was the ending of the vigorous commercial life at the ferry pier at Yuen Chau Kok. Much of the traffic here were passengers from Kowloon City travelling to Canton, or Waichow. As soon as the railway opened, it captured all the Canton trade. The railway also captured all the traffic from Sha Tin to Tai Po, and the old coastal sail ferry from Yuen Chau Kok to Tai Po closed immediately after the railway opened. The Waichow traffic was carried by a sail ferry to Sha Yue Chung on the northern coast of Mirs Bay. The railway replaced this ferry with a steam ferry from Tai Po Kau, which connected directly with the railway (this ferry was established before 1917, probably as soon as the railway itself opened). This left Yuen Chau Kok only the sampan ferry across the harbour to Lok Lo Ha, and even this ferry came close to closure. The villagers now wanted to go to the railway station rather than Lok Lo Ha, and a new footbridge (the Tai Chung Kiu Bridge) over the river opposite Tsang Tai Uk was built in 1914 to make it easy to walk to the station - this bridge was built by Government, but the Sha Tin rural community paid for half of its cost. The Lok Lo Ha pier was rebuilt and improved in 1917, and continued to be used, but it was never again as important as it had been.

The Sha Yue Chung Ferry continued as an important route from Hong Kong to Eastern Kwangtung. The Tai Po Kau Station was rebuilt in 1918 to make examination of the baggage of ferry passengers more convenient. The ferry was captured by pirates in 1921, and twice in 1922, which can probably be taken as showing its importance, and the large number of people using it then. The Tai Po Kau pier was destroyed by a typhoon in 1924, and rebuilt on a larger and stronger scale. A new, larger, ferry-boat was put on the route in 1924, and a second ferry-boat was added to the service in 1926, to allow two sailings a day. The Tai Po Kau railway station was again extensively remodelled to improve facilities for passengers coming to or from the ferry in 1927.

The ferry, however, began to loose traffic to buses operating on the road from Sham Chun to Waichow from 1933: by 1934 the ferry was running at a loss. In 1939 the ferry came back into its own, as the Sino-Japanese War made it the only usable method of transport between Hong Kong and Eastern Kwangtung. The ferry did not operate during the War, and, after the War was never fully reestablished. A Mirs Bay ferry was re-introduced, but it stopped at a number of places as well as Sha Yue Chung, and catered only for the local traffic. With the domination of the Chinese side of Mirs Bay by Communist guerillas from 1949, the operation of the ferry became "tricky", and it closed in 1950, only to reopen a few months later, and then close again for good in 1951. In 1955, the Tolo Harbour Ferry was inaugurated, which linked Tai Po Kau station with the villages within Tolo Harbour, that is, within the New Territories.

The station for the railway in Sha Tin was built half way between Tai Wai and Lok Lo Ha, because the railway wanted to capture the traffic of both the traditional roadway coming in to Lok Lo Ha, and the traffic from the largest village in the area, but did not want to build two stations. So the station was built out in the fields, with only the tiny village of Pai Tau nearby. This penny-pinching decision has had large and long-term consequences. Not only did the station, given its remote location, get given the district name as understood by City dwellers ("Shatin"), thus rivetting the name on the district for ever, but it became to a very real degree the centre of district life. When the Sha Tin market and market-town were built (1951-1955), they were built next to the Station, and the Rural Committee built its headquarters there as well (1949) (see Plate 5, showing a Lo Wu bound train leaving the station at Sha Tin about 1955, with the fields of Pai Tau village in the foreground, and the Market behind). When the New Town was planned, its centre was, again, planned for the land adjacent to the station. A more natural site for the centre would have been Tai Wai, at the junction of the valleys, and where there was plenty of flat land for development, but the decision on the siting of the station in 1910 made the present siting of the Town Centre inevitable. A station was built at Tai Wai in 1935, but it was closed again in 1936, and did not affect the predominance which the Shatin station had achieved by then.

Local traffic on the railway was heavy from the first. 277,800 local passengers were carried in 1916-1917 (the first year from which traffic figures survive), and this rose steadily to 1,177,234 in 1924-1925. In 1927-1928 this dropped to 835,240, but rose again steadily from that figure to 1,917,603 in 1939-1940. In the 1930s, there were "normally" 24 local trains a day (12 a day each way, with 13 each way on Sundays and Public Holidays), plus the two "mixed goods" trains which carried the local goods traffic.[16] In 1939 the Sha Tin station must have handled between 1000 and 1500 passengers a day.

Much of the passenger traffic from Sha Tin before the War consisted of city-based people commuting from a villa in Sha Tin, or villagers going to shop at either Tai Po or in the City. So many residents were travelling from Sha Tin to Yaumatei in 1932, in fact, that extra carriages had to be attached to all trains, which were detached at Sha Tin. When Cheap Day-Returns were introduced in 1934, they were an instant and huge success. The railway was concerned about competition from buses and lorries from 1933: the Government refused to allow buses along the Tai Po Road in direct competition with the railway, except between Tai Po and Fanling. The railway asked the Police to take action against lorries carrying passengers in 1934. In 1938 the railway succeeded in closing down the bus service between Tai Po and Fanling: they replaced it with a Railbus service with 14 trains a day (seven in each direction). A very special railway service was the provision of Special Trains from Tsimshatsui to Lok Lo Ha in 1915, to the "Aviation Display" which took place in that year on the mudflats at Lok Lo Ha.

The Sha Tin station was steadily improved, to cope with the very high numbers of people using it. It was double-tracked in 1919, to allow trains to pass in the station. Very soon, Sha Tin was used as the most common passing station. In 1921 the passing track was itself doubled (thus providing three tracks) to facilitate movement of locomotives. The original station of 1910 had only one, concrete, platform; but a second was added, of wood, in 1919: this was replaced in 1921, and, again, with a new concrete platform, in 1937.

The railway, with the steady growth in wage opportunities within the New Territories and in the City which it brought, led to a major increase in the cost of living. As the District Officer remarked in 1912, between 1900 and 1911, the cost of living in the New Territories approximately doubled, but wage rates had more than doubled, and the standard of living had appreciably improved. The New Territories in 1911 were noticeably more prosperous than before, and the railway had played a significant part in this. Sha Tin more than shared in this increase in prosperity: it was able to get a greater share in the new wage opportunities than elsewhere in the New Territories.

After the War, the railway was not able to stop the establishment of bus routes along the Tai Po Road, and thereafter the railway always faced direct competition. However, the steady increase in population along the railway was such that the railway remained extremely busy throughout the period. The electrification of the railway, and the double tracking of the entire system (1982-1983), which increased the capacity of the system many times over, however, is part of the New Town development phase of Sha Tin's history.

Telecommunications and Electricity

As early as 1899, improvements in communications had been noted as one of the most urgent requirements for the New Territories, and a telephone system was laid down within the first year of the British administration. The system was a Government system, not a public one. This system was run on poles from Kowloon over Sha Tin Pass to the Sha Tin Police Station, and from there to Tai Po, and so to all the other Police Stations. The telephone system was open as far as Tai Po by 1900, and had reached all the New Territories main Police Stations by 1901. Even the remote Sha Tin Gap Police Post was connected to the system in 1911. In 1913, this system was re-routed so that it followed the newly opened railway, as the line over Sha Tin Pass was too exposed to typhoon damage: at this date, the system in the New Territories consisted of "ten pairs of lines". The re-routing along the railway was also required since the railway also had a private telephone system linking all its stations, and this was carried on the same poles. In 1925-1926 the lines were laid underground in a conduit, initially as far as Sha Tin, again to avoid typhoon damage.

This system was a private Government system, designed to ensure that the Police Stations and other Government institutions in the New Territories were in close contact with the headquarters in the City. It became the custom, however, that the Police would send telephone messages for villagers in emergencies, but it was not possible, in these years, for private individuals in the New Territories to have telephones of their own. In 1930, however, it was agreed that the Hong Kong Telephone Co., and China Light and Power, could run cables through the Beacon Hill Tunnel, and, in 1931, electric light became available at Tai Po, and a telephone sub-exchange was set up there as well. There was a strong feeling that this development had been unduly delayed: the District Officer, when he reported the arrival of electric light at Tai Po, added "at last". Tai Po Market was lit with electric street-lamps in 1934, the first place in the New Territories to receive this modernisation. Tai Po was also the first place to have a public radio loudspeaker, on a pole in the market (1935), which was very popular.

Electricity was immediately welcomed, and widely used, in the market towns, but the high price of telephones meant that only a few New Territories residents subscribed. Relatively few villagers outside the market towns could afford electricity before the War. An electricity sub-station was built at Sheung Keng Hau at the northern entrance to the railway tunnel in 1930, and it was extended and improved in 1935 {it was replaced with a bigger one in 1968). The Sha Tin Police Station was wired for electric light in 1932, and a few private houses in Sha Tin were at about the same time. Tsang Tai Uk was certainly wired for electricity by 1937, since it was "illuminated" in honour of the Coronation in that year. It is not known when the first private telephones were installed in Sha Tin. It was probably in the mid 1930s, and very likely in one or other of the villas owned by rich merchants from the City. Sha Tin village elders state that there were a few village houses with both electricity and telephones by the time the Japanese came. Most were the village shops. The telephones here functioned as quasi-public telephones, being used by the whole village as needed. There were no public telephone kiosks in the New Territories until 1950.

After the War, improvements to the telephone system came quickly. In 1951, Government abandoned its private system in the New Territories, and switched to the Hong Kong Telephone Company system. The cost of both electricity and telephones was much lower after the War, and the result was an immediate surge in applications. At Sha Tin, so great was the interest in telephones that a new sub-exchange for Sha Tin was required in 1953 (it was at Tung Lo Wan). By the mid 1950s, village houses with electricity and telephones were no longer rare.

The Market

There had traditionally not been a market in Sha Tin. The population of the district was too small to support one. Before the War, the villagers had marketed either in Kowloon City or Tai Po, depending on which was the closer. A few villages also marketed in Sham Shui Po or Sai Kung. Each of these markets was separated from Sha Tin by a mountain pass, and access to the market was always difficult and troublesome.

By the late 1920s, the population in Sha Tin had risen to the point where a market was an economic possibility, but the coming of the railway and the improved Tai Po Road (1910, 1920) deferred any talk of establishing a new market in Sha Tin, since, for the time being, the greater ease of access to Tai Po, and to Yaumatei (which took the place of Kowloon City as the market of choice for a number of villages once the railway made access there easier) made the use of these external markets more acceptable.

It was immediately following the end of the War that a market in Sha Tin became a reality. Crowds of hawkers began to operate in the station forecourt at Sha Tin immediately after the end of the War. Because Sha Tin was, in consequence, seen as "a place for buying and selling" Sha Tin villagers were not allowed to participate in the bidding for stalls in the new Tai Po Government Market (1949). In 1950, because of the problems caused by this unauthorised market, which was spilling over onto the main road, and interfering with railway business, land was formed opposite the station for a market. A marshy area was filled by the land owner, and was to be made into a small town, to include a private market, which was to be run by the Rural Committee. The following year (1951) a Government plan for the market area was agreed with the landowner, and the new market town laid out, and the Rural Committee market at its heart opened (see Plate 6, showing the Market in 1960). Development of this new market town was broadly complete by 1955, when a piped water supply was provided to it, from a dam above the Fo Tan valley.

As can be seen from Map 3, the Sha Tin Market Town, as planned in 1951, and as built over the next few years, consisted of four streets running back at right angles to the Tai Po Road (First, Second, Third, and Fourth Streets), and two streets running parallel to Tai Po Road (Main Street and Back Street). In addition, there was a row of shop-houses built facing onto Tai Po Road itself. First Street and Fourth Street as planned were only developed on one frontage. Back Street was only partially developed on its rear frontage. The Market itself lay at the centre, between Second and Third Streets, and facing into Main Street. The town was originally envisaged as comprising 137 shop-houses, but, in the event, seven houses were changed into a cinema, and ten houses on Back Street were never built, and one house there occupied three house-sites. Thus, in the event, the town comprised 118 shop-houses, a market, and a cinema. By 1959 a row of illegal squatter shops had added, on the undeveloped south frontage of First Street: this added some fifteen commercial premises to the market town.

All the shop-houses of the 1951 plan were built as one, two or three-storey structures, with tiny back courtyards opening onto scavenging lanes. The streets were narrow (about twenty-five feet between house-fronts, except for Main Street, which was twice as wide), and with very narrow footpaths. Few vehicles, however, ever tried to enter the market town. The market town was, like most New

Territories market towns in the 1960s, lively and full of energy. Goods spilled out from the shops onto the streets. There were always crowds wandering about. Litter was a perennial problem.

The market town was an immediate success. Not only did the Sha Tin villagers react very positively to this market of their own, but large numbers of people came out from the City to enjoy themselves here. In 1950, the Annual Report notes "Sha Tin, which since the War has attracted great crowds from Kowloon at weekends". Very soon, many of the market town shops were changed into restaurants, especially selling the things Sha Tin had become famous for: beancurd (made in the district), clams (dredged from Sha Tin Harbour), sweet potato soup, and roast pigeons. With every train that came into the station there would be a flood of people crossing the road into the market town (latterly, as the traffic on the Tai Po Road grew, often at great risk to themselves, until a pedestrian footbridge was provided in 1967). Around the market town, entertainment stalls sprang up, renting out bicycles and rowing boats. In 1951 there was a proposal for an Entertainment Park here, although, in the event, this did not materialise. From the northern end of the station (just beyond the area shown on Map 3) a passageway passed under the railway tracks, and up to the still existing Lung Wah Hotel, which had been built on Crown Land sold for a hotel and restaurant in 1931. This passageway was also lined with stalls selling clams, biscuits and cakes, and sweet potato soup. Sha Tin Market Town was, in the 1950s, and even down to the early 1970s, a favourite place for youngsters from the City to come for an inexpensive evening or holiday out.

There were always shops in the town selling clothes, household items, and farming equipment for the villagers, and there were a few small industrial premises, mainly at the back of the town. The market town was thus never solely a suburban pleasure ground. Nonetheless, much of its prosperity came from its suburban functions.

Population Changes: Villas and Other Residences

In the 1911 Census (which was conducted before any significant changes to the population and society of Sha Tin had taken place), there were 3809 people resident in Sha Tin. This had risen to 4156 by the time of the 1921 Census, and to 4346 by the time of the 1931

Census, a 14% increase over these twenty years. Unfortunately, there are no Census figures for the next thirty years. It is known, however, that the 1930s saw a very large increase in population in Sha Tin. Very large numbers of new residential villas were being built then. By the time the Japanese came, the population of Sha Tin may well have been close to double that of 1911, although many of the new residents left as a result of the hardships of the Japanese Occupation.

The origins of this suburban development go back, in fact, to before the British takeover of the New Territories. Tsang Koon-man was born in 1808, the son of an impoverished Hakka stonecutter in Cheung Lok District a hundred miles to the northeast of Hong Kong. He and his brother moved to a village near Kowloon City in 1824, where they worked as stonecutters. In about 1840, Tsang Koon-man moved to Shaukeiwan, where he opened a quarry of his own, the Sam Li Quarry, and a shop. Initially, the stone he cut was shipped to Canton, but, after 1841 and the coming of the British to Hong Kong, he mostly supplied the building works in the new City. He became very wealthy as a result of this business. In 1848 he decided to look for land to build a permanent residence for his family. In Sha Tin he found a patch of marshy ground owned by the Tsang clan of Kak Tin, which shared the same surname as his. Rather to the disgust of the other indigenous clans, this family eventually agreed to sell this land to Tsang Koon-man, and he filled the land, and built a new village there for his descendants.[17] This village, Shan Ha Wai (more frequently called Tsang Tai Uk, "The Big House of the Tsangs") was begun in 1848, and was basically completed by 1865-1867, although a few features remained to be added as late as 1874. The development of Tsang Tai Uk was different from the later suburban developments in the area, since Tsang Koon-man was aiming at building a village for his descendants to live in. But, at the same time, Tsang Koon-man and his sons continued in practice to live in Shaukeiwan down to the 1914-1918 War, and used the new house only occasionally, and, in this, the development of Tsang Tai Uk has a good deal in common with the later suburban developments.

The earliest western-style villas in Sha Tin were undoubtedly those built in 1906 for the engineers overseeing the construction of the railway tunnel. These were bungalows, and were built along the Tai Po Road near the entrance to the upper Keng Hau Road, which was constructed at the same time. There was a ropeway running from the bungalows down to the northern entrance to the tunnel, to make access to and from the works easier for the engineers. It is unlikely that these bungalows survived after the completion of the tunnel works in 1910.

Of the weekend villas built in Sha Tin in the early years after the coming of the railway, the most prominent was that built by Ho Sai-wing (Ho Wing) the nephew and adopted son of Sir Robert Hotung, and called Hotung Lau. Just north of Lok Lo Ha village there was a rocky peninsula running out into the waters of Sha Tin Harbour for about a hundred yards. This had previously been used to shelter the ferry boats which plied from Lok Lo Ha. Ho Wing bought most of this peninsula at a date somewhen after the opening of the railway, probably about 1914, and built a house and garden there. In 1917 he bought a further strip to the seaward of the garden, and, in 1923 acquired the rest of the peninsula (it is probable that it was these purchases, which rendered the peninsula unusable by ferry boats, that led to the construction of the Government pier a little further down the coast in 1917). The site today lies near the northern end of the Kowloon and Canton Railway Corporation depot. Lady Hotung felt herself sufficiently a Sha Tin resident to contribute generously to the construction of the Tai Chung Kiu Bridge in 1914, and this is the likely date of Ho Wing's purchase and construction of the house. Hotung Lau was commandeered by the Japanese during the War, and used as an Army Storehouse: after the War it was not much used by Ho Wing's family: from 1962 it was rented out to various commercial users, until it was resumed in 1980.

Around Hotung Lau there grew up, in the early 1920s, a small group of weekend villas owned by important members of the Eurasian community and others. Hugh Anderson bought land for a villa here in 1920, and another large plot for a garden in the same year. The building site was adjacent to Ho Wing's lot on the Lok Lo Ha peninsula, and the garden was a hundred yards away, on the other side of the railway. Ho Wing acquired the building lot, probably in 1923, after which the Andersons probably used the garden as a summer resort, with a small house nearby. Irene Anderson continued to own the garden lot until 1952. Miss S. Anderson, who was probably a relative of Hugh Anderson, also had a house in Sha Tin. She bought a plot of Crown Land near the station, in Tin Liu, in 1950 to build a house and garden there, and, at that date, gave her address as "The Retreat, Sha Tin", which was probably the Lok Lo Ha house. It seems likely that the Lok Lo Ha property was sold once Miss Anderson's house at Tin Liu was built.

C.H. Lyson bought a plot of land south of Lok Lo Ha village, and a few hundred yards from Ho Wing's house, in 1921. The site included a garden, but a further strip of Crown Land was bought in 1922 to extend it. Much of this lot was reclaimed from the foreshore. On this lot a very large square house was built, larger than the Hotung Lau house. The house was sold shortly after the War.

About a hundred yards from the Lyson house, Abdul el Arculli, a merchant from the Muslim community, with an Arab background, bought Crown Land in Lok Lo Ha for a house and garden in 1923-1924: the garden was further extended in 1936. The Arculli house lay on the further side of the railway from the Lyson house. The Arculli family sold this house in 1953.

Another important weekend villa residence in Sha Tin was that built at the top of Tao Fung Shan for the Anglican Bishop of Victoria in 1934 (the premises were greatly extended in 1937). This was built by Bishop Hall. The villa continued to be used by the Bishop after the War (he reported a tiger in the garden there in 1947), but it was eventually sold. Few other Europeans bought land for building in Sha Tin before the War, although D. Wilson, of the "Hunter's Arms" at Fanling bought two Crown Land lots for houses with gardens at Wu Kai Sha in 1934, and R.B. Keen, of the Government's Road Office, bought a house and garden lot on the Tai Po Road in 1940 - this was the first of what was to become a major trend in the years after the War.

At the foot of Tung Lo Wan Shan, facing Tai Wai across the Shing Mun River, a great deal of Crown Land was bought, especially in the years 1938 - 1941, by Wong Yiu-tung and his son Parkin Wong, who were major property developers, especially in the Sham Shui Po area, at this date and earlier (Wong Yiu-tung is commemorated by Yiu Tung Street in Shamshuipo to the present day). Wong Yiu-tung had bought a building lot nearby in 1917. In addition to this lot, the family bought, in all, two building lots, an orchard lot, two garden lots, and seven agricultural lots between 1938 and 1941. The whole hillslope thus came into the hands of the Wong family. This area was designed by the Wong family to provide a site for a tomb for

Wong Yiu-tung, which was eventually, indeed, placed there. In the meantime, the family used the two buildings as weekend resorts, and planted all the agricultural land thickly with trees. Another developer active in Shamshuipo at the same time as Wong Yiu-tung, Li Ping, also bought Crown Land in this same general area, and at the same period (1940), as Wong Yiu-tung. Li Ping bought three building lots, including adjacent garden land. In this case, too, the aim was to provide for a tomb site. Li Ping's lots were a little to the east of Wong Yiu-tung's, near the foot of Tao Fung Shan, and his grave was eventually placed there too. It must be assumed that these two friends decided on this development together.

In the years 1917-1941 (the records of New Grants of Crown Land are not available for the period before 1917) there were 385 New Grants of Crown Land in Sha Tin for new buildings. Half at least of these were in the area near the station, that is, near the villages of Pai Tai, Sheung Wo Che, and Ha Wo Che, and in the area immediately west of the station called Tin Liu, and a little further west still, around the village of Tung Lo Wan. All this area was within a half-mile or less of the station (see Map 4, and Plate 7). The handful of New Grants at Lok Lo Ha, around Ho Wing's house, were the only significant group of New Grants further away from the station, although they were still within a mile of it. The villages in the area near the station (which had formed the Tung Lo Wan Yeuk of the Nine Yeuk of Sha Tin) were all very tiny. In 1902, when the surveyors for the Block Crown Lease mapped the area, there were less than fifty houses in the area: forty years later there were more than 350. The crowding of these New Grants immediately around the station makes it clear that what was developing here was a suburban, commuter, community, entirely dependent on the ease of access to the City provided by the railway. This was a pre-motor suburb: hardly any of these new houses were road accessible. Except in the Tao Fung Shan area, the new houses were accessed only by narrow footpaths from the station. Some of the houses were weekend retreats and holiday villas, but the bulk were the houses of people who lived in Sha Tin, but worked in the City.

After the War, suburban development continued in this area. A further 305 New Grants of Crown Land for building purposes were sold in Sha Tin between 1947 and 1959. Again, half were in the area close to the station, between Tung Lo Wan and Ha Wo Che. However, from 1949, there was also a growth of new buildings along the Tai

Po Road, especially along the upper Keng Hau Road, and along Sha Tin Heights Road, which was laid out at this time. J.F. Howarth, one of the partners of Leigh and Orange, bought a building-and-garden lot here in 1949 (and another in 1951), and F.D. Gardner followed suit in 1950 (again, a second lot followed in 1952, and Mrs Gardner bought yet another in 1955). A Mrs Gordon, for whom F.D. Gardner was the agent, bought another building-and-garden lot in that area in 1953. S.H. Louey, of Kowloon Motor Bus, also bought here, in 1956 (he bought another house-and-garden lot nearby in 1961). A large number of lots were sold here in 1959, along the upper Keng Hau Road, to various Chinese businessmen. These developments were the harbingers of a new type of suburb, because the locations of these houses were such that they clearly demanded that the owner had a car. Two of these developments were for small blocks of flats, the first such developments in Sha Tin.

Among the developments along the Tai Po Road in these years was the Sha Tin Heights Hotel. The "Hotel Edinburgh Company Ltd" bought a house-and-garden lot, and an "agricultural" (garden) lot here in 1952, and other house-and-garden lots "near Tin Sam" in 1954 (2 lots) and 1957. The hotel opened for business in 1955. It was used almost exclusively in early years by parties from the City looking for "a day in the country", and should be seen as further evidence of the suburban nature of Sha Tin development in this period.

Annual grants of Crown Land for building purposes are shown on the graph attached.[18] It will be seen that there was a steady increase in interest in taking out grants of Crown Land in Sha Tin between 1917 and 1959, interrupted only by the War, and the occasional downturn (see attached graph). The effects of the District Officer's ban on sales of land for Chai Tong in 1921, which is discussed further below, can be seen in the figures for 1922. The local depression caused by the General Strike can be seen from the figures for 1928 - 1931, and the problems of the Great Depression in those for 1936 -1937. The downturn between 1953 and 1956 may be ascribed to the new Sha Tin Market Town, since this must have soaked up most of the available capital for new houses here (the new market town was on private land, and hence does not appear on the Registers of Sales of Crown Land, except for the market itself, which was surrendered to Government, and then granted to the Rural Committee, in 1951).

After 1959, the developments which had marked Sha Tin since the early years continued, with every year seeing more sales of lots in the area near the station. However, these years saw the start of a new form of development as well. Around Tai Wai village an area for "exchanges" was laid out, where villagers surrendering agricultural land for development could get developable land in lieu. The roads to allow this development were built around the village in 1961-1962. A significant number of six storey blocks of flats were built here as a result, especially in the years 1961-1972. These new six-storey buildings all had shops on their ground floors. By the mid 1960s, therefore, Tai Wai was rivalling the 1951 market town as a commercial centre in Sha Tin. By that time, in fact, a second market for fresh food was developing at Tai Wai as well.

After the War, the population in Sha Tin rose very fast. In 1947 the District Officer classed Sha Tin as one of his district's "populous centres", along with Tai Po, Sha Tau Kok, and Shek Wu Hui. The increase in population in the New Territories generally was noted in 1949, and, in 1951, the District Commissioner noted the "high public demand" for Crown Land at Sha Tin to build residences on. The growth in the non-indigenous population at Sha Tin (much of it fuelled by developments paid for by capital from the City) was again commented on in 1952. In 1953 the District Commissioner again commented on the growth of the "town" of Sha Tin, and noted the "rapid development of country houses and villas" there. He noted that the area was taking on a "suburban character". In 1954, the development of "european style houses and a hotel" at Sha Tin Heights drew his attention. Between 1955 and 1956, the District Commissioner's attention was drawn to the increase in population in the New Territories in general, rather than to Sha Tin in particular. He noted, in the absence of any Census figures, that the number of births registered in the New Territories had risen from 4810 in 1950 to 11236 in 1956, a 233% increase. While a great deal of this increase was in the newly industrialising township at Tsuen Wan, a good part of it was from Sha Tin. There can be no doubt that the indigenous population of Sha Tin became a minority of the district's population in these early years after the War, if, indeed, they had not already dropped to that position in the last years just before the War. Certainly, by the time of the 1961 Census, the population of Sha Tin was well over 18,000, with more than 12,000 living in Tai Wai, and the area within a half-mile of the station. By 1961, the indigenous were no more than about a quarter of the resident population.

By 1971, the population of Sha Tin had risen to 30,000. As such, it formed a suburban township quite as big as any in Europe or America. The period of Sha Tin's history before the coming of the New Town in 1972 tends to be forgotten, but the ten-fold increase in population between 1911 and 1971, and the complete change in the character of the resident population and its facilities is in itself a most interesting development. Suburban Sha Tin is an interesting and vital development period.

Between 1917 and the start of New Town Development (1972), there were in total 1433 New Grants of Crown Land in Sha Tin. Of these, 472 lay between the Shing Mun and Fo Tan Rivers, in the zone of development close to the station. Another 371 lay near the Che Kung Temple, which was also easy of access to the station over the Tai Chung Kiu footbridge. 79 lay along the Tai Po Road or nearby. The remaining 511 were scattered all over the district, with the only other large concentrations being at Sha Tin Wai (105 grants), and Wu Kai Sha (96). These last two concentrations were both of grants following a re-arrangement by the villagers of their landholdings. About two-thirds of all these Grants were for buildings.

The New Grants between 1917 and 1959 were made to both villagers and outsiders. It was only in the early 1960s that it became difficult for outsiders to buy land freely in small houseand-garden lots from the Government. It was also from about this date that villagers were restricted to building a single "once-ina-lifetime" house. It is difficult to distinguish from the New Grant registers which purchasers were villagers and which outsiders, but two general points can be made: very few villagers were the purchasers of land in the zone near the station (probably the upset price for auctions in this very much sought-after area were too high for them), and very few villagers indeed were purchasers anywhere in the years 1947 to1956 (probably because of poverty following the War). Only after 1956 did villager purchases rise. About half the purchases in 1958 and 1959 were by villagers - one of the reasons for the ever-tightening policy on villager rights to houses in the 1960s was because numbers were getting out of control.

Three rather special types of new development in Sha Tin in

the pre-War period need particular mention, and one post-war: the foundation of Hin Tin Village, the coming of Buddhist monasteries and Chai Tong to Sha Tin, and the foundation of the Christian Mission to Buddhists in the mid 1930s, and the building of the first Christian churches in Sha Tin in 1957. In addition, squatter development and industrial development (both from the late 1950s) need discussion, but these are left for separate sections.

When the Government developed the Shing Mun Reservoir (begun 1923, and completed in 1937), the villages of Shing Mun (Lo Wai, Po Tau To, Shek Tau Kok, Kam Shan, Ho Pui, and Nam Fong To) were drowned below the waters, and their residents had to be relocated. Most chose to be resited to Kam Tin, but one group preferred Sha Tin. This group had lived by selling "mountain products" in the market at Tsuen Wan. They noted the abundant woods at the head of the valley in Sha Tin, and decided to settle there, so that they could continue to live by using the woods to make "mountain products", for sale in Sham Shui Po. This area also had some land which could be converted to rice-growing, but which was then unused. As part of their compensation, they received a large, premium-free, Forestry Lot in the adjacent woods. The new village of Hin Tin was built between 1929 and 1931, when the villagers moved in: the land was formally granted to the villagers in 1933. Unlike the development of Tsang Tai Uk, this new village was entirely a village: the villagers who moved there lived and worked there, and were quickly accepted as villagers of Sha Tin by the other indigenous residents. Indeed, many of the younger Sha Tin villagers tend to forget that the Hin Tin villagers have only had a couple of generations of residence in Sha Tin.

Between 1923, or even earlier, and 1926, the Government in Canton organised a series of "Anti-Superstition Campaigns". Their targets were not only the esoteric sects which had been the target of persecution for many years before the Revolution of 1911, but also the mainstream temples of the traditional folk religion, and particularly Buddhist and Taoist establishments. The great majority of the folk religion temples in Canton were closed and secularised at this period, with only a few of the bigger and more prestigious temples left.[19]

These Anti-Superstition Campaigns led to a flood of refugee monks and nuns fleeing to the sanctuary of Hong Kong. Most of Hong Kong's Buddhist establishments were founded in the 1920s or 1930s by these refugee monks and nuns or their disciples. Some of them went to remote areas (especially the Ngong Ping and Tei Tong Tsai plateaus on Lantau), where they built hermitages and small retreats, but others preferred sites near the City. Sites within the City were generally too expensive, and, in any case, Buddhist institutions generally prefer a quieter and more rural area. Buddhist institutions therefore appeared in a number of rural areas easy of access to the City, as for instance at Lo Wai above Tsuen Wan, at Fanling, near the station there, and at Tai Po, where three monasteries were founded in the hills about half a mile south of Kam Shan and the railway station. The largest collection of these new Buddhist establishments, however, was at Sha Tin, precisely because that was the site easiest of all for access from the City.

The District Officer noted with some alarm the great increase in Chai Tong (vegetarian retirement homes) in Sha Tin in 1920, and temporarily banned any sale of Crown Land for any further ones in Sha Tin in 1921 because of serious doubts as to their purpose (he believed they were attempts by urban groups to get access to good burial sites in the New Territories, or at least that they were aimed at diverting funds from believers to those running the Chai Tong). The District Officer noted in 1921 that the founders of these Chai Tong had been expelled from Canton. The records of sales of Crown Land in 1920 and 1921 do not show this large increase in Chai Tong clearly, since the purpose of the new building is rarely specified. In 1921 there were, however, five sales which were probably for Chai Tong purposes recorded, in Pai Tau and Tung Lo Wan, that is, the areas closest to the railway station. In that year there were a total of 20 sales of Crown Land for buildings, compared with a total of 27 for the.previous four years together. It is probable that some of the other 15 sales in 1921 were also for Chai Tong, in some instances probably by outsiders using villagers as agents..

The District Officer, however, was only able to slow down the flood of Chai Tong foundations by a year or so. Although the New Grant registers do not usually identify what building lots were expected to be used for, there are sales of Crown Land which were probably for Chai Tong in 1921, 1926, 1932, 1933, 1934, 1935, 1938, 1939, 1940, and 1941. Further certain or probable Chai Tong sales appear in 1947, 1949, 1950, 1951, 1955, 1958, and 1959. This plethora of retirement homes is, again, a reflection of Sha Tin's suburban situation.

Retirement homes here were cheaper than they would have been in the City, but were yet easily accessible from it.

Among the first refugees from the Anti-Superstition Campaigns in Canton were members of the Sin Tin To (先天道) sect. This sect had been persecuted intermittently from the early nineteenth century. It was present in Hong Kong from the late nineteenth century, but was greatly expanded in the 1920s because of these refugees from Canton. This sect usually operates Chai Tong: in the early 1970s they claimed to be running over seventy in Hong Kong. In Sha Tin they founded a monastery, the Po Ling Tung (普靈洞) with a number of Chai Tong supervised by it. The Po Ling Tung was probably founded in 1921, when four adjacent Crown Land building lots were bought by a group of men jointly near Tung Lo Wan village (it may well have been this sale which roused the District Officer's concern). It is probable that the founders were all refugees from Canton. Further Crown Land was bought by people giving the Po Ling Tung as their address in 1934, 1935 and 1939. The Sin Tin To established a more modern sort of Chai Tong at Ngau Tau Kok in 1943: this was moved to Sha Tin in 1946 (the "Sin Tin To Home for the Elderly" - the land sale was only finalised in 1950, however). This Home for the Elderly, and several of the sect's Chai Tong survive to this day, and still provide a valuable social service to the community.[20]

Taoists were also victims of the Anti Superstition Campaigns. One prominent Taoist, Leung Kei (梁基), established a Taoist monastery and Chai Tong in Sha Tin, the Sai Lam Monastery (西林). The first Crown Land building lot bought by Leung Kei was registered in 1931, although it is likely that Leung Kei was active in the area a year or so earlier. Further sales took place in 1932, 1933, and especially 1938. The monastery was certainly functioning fully by 1933.

There were three major Buddhist establishments founded in Sha Tin before the War. all by refugees from Canton: the Po Ye (般若) Monastery at Pai Tau Hang, the Ten Thousand Buddha (萬佛) Monastery, also at Pai Tau Hang, and the Chee Hong Monastery (慈航) near the Che Kung Temple. The Chee Hung Monastery was founded in 1923. A small group of nuns and novices fled from their monastery in Canton, to Sha Tin. At first they rented a small village house at San Tin. A few years later, their Master, Sik Chee-lam (釋智林) was also forced to flee from Canton, and joined them. He gathered funds, and was able to buy Crown Land near San Tin in 1934. On this land he erected a fine set of buildings. The buildings were basically complete by 1937, but the dedication ceremony was not held until 1941: it was being held, in fact, when the news of the Japanese invasion reached Sha Tin. Sik Chee-lam extended the land of the monastery by further purchases of Crown Land in 1941 and 1954, and a further purchase was made in 1956.

The Po Ye Monastery has a similar history to Chee Hong. Purchases of Crown Land building lots to buyers with Buddhist religious names (Yue Kui-chi, 余居之, Ching Fat, 澄法, and Sik Ching-shin, 釋淨善), in 1926, 1938, and 1952 may all be connected with this monastery: a purchase by Sik Chi-chi in 1954 certainly is. The nuns at Chee Hong believe Po Ye to be a little older than their house. There may have been a period when the religious of this house lived in rented accommodation, as at Chee Hong.,

The Ten Thousand Buddha Monastery may be connected with purchases of Crown Land made in the vicinity by Silent Yen (a wellknown Buddhist lay leader of the period) in 1931, and by Sik Kwoh-shing (釋果成) in 1940, but the main site of the monastery was sold in 1935.

Thus, between 1920 and 1935 at the latest, the AntiSuperstition Campaigns had sent refugee religious to Sha Tin who founded monasteries and Chai Tong there related to all three of the major Chinese religious groups, Buddhism, Taoism, and Sin Tin To. In 1920 the only religious buildings in the district were the two ancient villager-founded temples of the traditional folk religion: twenty years later there were at least several dozen new foundations. This development was a major social change for the community in Sha Tin.

The Rev. Karl Reichelt was a Lutheran missionary of Norwegian origin. He came to believe he had a special vocation to bring the Gospel to Buddhist religious. To do this, he felt, he must offer them a place to stay which was as Buddhist in "feel" and outlook as was possible, and he himself must study Buddhism deeply, and understand it, so that he could speak to Buddhist monks from the same standpoint. He looked for a site easy of access to the City, but quiet and surrounded by trees. He found what he was looking for at Tao Fung Shan, the hill immediately above the station at Sha Tin.

He bought the hilltop there in phases, in 1930, 1931, 1932, 1933, 1934, and 1937. After his death his institution, the Christian Mission to Buddhists, bought further land in 1955 and 1959. During the 1960s, continuing doubts about the wisdom of Reichelt's approach eventually led to the closure of the Christian Mission to Buddhists, and the conversion of its buildings into the present-day Tao Fung Shan Christian Institute, but, during the 1930s and after the War, the Mission to Buddhists played an important role in bringing Christian and Buddhist intellectuals in Hong Kong closer together. The free accommodation provided to any Buddhist religious at Tao Fung Shan also helped many Buddhist religious refugees in flight from political problems in China to settle in Hong Kong. Reichelt built the Tao Fung Shan Road (this allowed the Bishop to build his country house on Tao Fung Shan in 1934) in 1930: his Mission depended on access by car to make it viable (one of the two first buildings he built was a garage). The Christian Mission to Buddhists was an entirely urban institute, built in a suburban setting to get advantage of the beautiful views and the deep woods which surrounded it, but having very little to do with Sha Tin. Reichelt did not attempt any missionary work among the local villagers, for instance.

Reichelt's Mission seems to have been the first specifically Christian institution in Sha Tin, but its eclectic character, and its lack of interest in the local residents, made it less of an influence in Sha Tin than might have been expected. No other missionary body seems to have established any permanent presence in the district before 1957. This is perhaps surprising, since Sha Tin was so close to the City. Missionaries are known to have travelled through the district on a regular basis from the 1840s onwards, and there were some converts living there in the pre-War period. Missionaries, however, all seem to have passed through Sha Tin to settle in the market town at Tai Po.

In 1957 two churches opened, the Catholic church at Tai Chung Kiu and the Lutheran church at Tung Lo Wan. The land sales for the Crown Land sites of both were finalised in 1959. 1959 also saw the Crown Land sites for two further churches finalised: a Catholic Social Service Centre and Chapel at Ma On Shan (this predominantly served the miners there), and a Pentecostal Church and centre at Sha Tin Tau. These last two are believed to have been established later than the first two, in 1958 or 1959. Two Protestant Seminaries were established in Sha Tin in this period, the Ecclesia Bible Institute at

Tai Chung Kiu (this was essentially Pentecostal, and was established in the 1960s), and the Hong Kong Lutheran Seminary, which was established, probably in 1957, on the northern side of the Shing Mun River, set back from the river, on the slopes of the hill, and accessible only by a path running up from the river bank. The two Catholic churches moved to new, larger sites at a later date: the Tai Chung Kiu church in 1974, and the Ma On Shan church as part of the New Town development, in the early 1980s: the Lutheran church remains as a vivid reminder of early post-War Sha Tin.

Squatters

It is difficult to be very exact about the history of squatting in Sha Tin. The records of the various squatter surveys have not survived to give, for instance, any easy way of finding out the numbers of squatter structures at given dates. It is, however, possible to make some general comments.

There were five main types of squatter structure found in Sha Tin: illegal extensions to legal structures; residential and farming structures used by tenant farmers; residential squatter structures, squatter factories, and squatter shops. The first group (consisting of kitchen sheds, garden sheds, awnings, and peripheral structures of all sorts) comprised a large percentage of all surveyed squatter structures, but do not need further comment here. Such structures were attached to legal structures of all kinds, and in all areas of Sha Tin.

Farmers who rented the old rice-lands of the indigenous villages in the 1960s were not permitted, as noted above, to live within the old villages. They had to build homes and sheds for themselves in the midst of the fields they rented. There were no such farms in Sha Tin in 1960, or only a very few. Such squatter structures, mostly surrounded by small gardens, and separated from the next farm by a few hundred yards, were not clustered in any particular area, but were to be found wherever fields were being rented. By the early 1970s, they were present everywhere where there were fields within reach of a motorable road (ie, within about half-a-mile of such a road), where market gardening was feasible. These structures were illegal, and, as such, objectionable to the Government. Because of their scattered location, they could usually not be connected to the sewers and waterpipes which Government started to introduce into Sha Tin at the very end of the 1960s. Nonetheless, many of these structures were, by 1970, after up to a decade in existence, rather attractive, with their flower bedecked verandahs and neat vegetable fields around them. Many were built of tin-sheet and timber, but a significant number rebuilt during the late 1960s and 1970s in brick, tile, and stone. Since the flat rice-lands they occupied were Government's first target for the land resumptions required for the New Town, none of these tenant-farmer squatter farms now survive in Sha Tin, or only a very few, although plenty of very similar structures are still to be seen in places in Tai Po District and elsewhere in the New Territories. In 1970 there were several hundred such farms in Sha Tin.

Residential squatters in Sha Tin were a reflex of the development of residential squatter areas in the urban area from 1949 onwards. Refugees fleeing from the hardships of the Communist Revolution fled into Hong Kong in vast numbers in the years 1949-1952, and again at the time of the Great Leap Forward (1956-1957). At first the refugees sought space to put up their huts as close to the City as possible, since that was where they hoped to get work. Vast squatter areas sprang up along the periphery of the developed urban area, along the northern fringe of Kowloon from Kwun Tong to Cheung Sha Wan, in and around the New Territories township of Tsuen Wan, and along the eastern fringe of Hong Kong Island, from Causeway Bay to Chai Wan. All these areas were occupied by squatter development during the 1949-1952 period (Tsuen Wan a year or so later than the urban areas). At this early date, there were no squatters in Sha Tin.

A well-informed villager told me that the first squatter hut in Sha Tin was built in 1953, and that it was built against the exterior wall of the Lea Tai Textiles Company Factory, by the factory's night-watchman, as a residence. Other villagers also point to 1953-1954 as the date of the first squatter structures in Sha Tin. The Lea Tai Textiles factory was in the Tai Chung Kiu area, south of the market town, near the Shing Mun River. While this claim may or may not be strictly true, it is certainly true that the mid 1950s is the period when the first squatters settled in Sha Tin in any number. Unlike in the urban areas, where most squatters were simply illegal occupants of Crown Land, in the New Territories (Tsuen Wan being an exception), the majority of New Territories squatters had Crown Land Permits for the land they occupied. This was certainly true at Sha Tin. In

Sha Tin, the authorities were able to ensure that squatter huts did not crowd too closely together, and that the worst features of the urban squatter areas were avoided (populations far in excess of water supply; dense developments of huts on dangerous slopes; lack of access for emergency services; cheek-by-jowl development leading to serious fire risks; constant risks of disease from grossly inadequate refuse and sewage services and water supplies, etc). Most of the Sha Tin residential squatter areas were dispersed. Most huts had small gardens or vegetable plots, and water stand-pipes and concrete paths were provided throughout the areas where squatters were permitted. Squatter development was able to be restricted to one or two areas where such development was unlikely to be too offensive. This is not to say that the authorities in Sha Tin were at all times in full control of the squatter problem there: the Squatter Permit holders tended to extend their premises over adjacent ground when the attention of the Government was diverted (as, for instance, during the 1966-1967 Riots), and so to close up, to some extent, the originally dispersed pattern of settlement, and there were a couple of areas where development proceeded without permit and where some of the more offensive elements of the urban squatter areas did appear.

Residential squatting in Sha Tin existed, to a large extent, in four areas: Pak Tin, Sha Tin Tau, Ha Wo Che, and Tai Chung Kiu. A glance at Map 5 shows that all four areas were on the periphery of the area which had been legally developed by way of New Grants of Crown Land between 1917 and 1959 (these squatter areas can also be seen on Plate 8, the aerial photograph of central Sha Tin of 1963). As such, the squatter settlements, as well as the legal development areas, centred on the railway station, although the squatter settlements were a little further away from the station - between about half a mile and three-quarters of a mile from the station.

The squatters living in the Pak Tin and Sha Tin Tau areas were mostly permit holders. These areas were generally not too densely settled (the lower end of Sha Tin Tau was more densely settled than the upper part). Pak Tin consisted of the valley of the Shing Mun River north and west of Tai Wai. The squatter permit areas were mostly arranged on the southern bank of the valley, in irregular rows, one above the other, but with a good deal of space between them. On the northern bank there were fewer, but there were some, many being partly agricultural in character. At Sha Tin Tau, the squatter area was formed along the old path to Kowloon City. Sha Tin Tau village backs onto a hill. The other side of this hill is a narrow valley. Beyond that valley a second hill faces into the main valley of Sha Tin. The Che Kung Temple backs onto this second hill. The path to Kowloon City, and so the squatter area, filled the valley between the two hills. This valley was too narrow to be of much use agriculturally, and had been mostly vacant when the squatters began to look to Sha Tin in the mid 1950s.

The Pak Tin squatter area was cleared in part in 1965-1966, when the Shing Mun River was the subject of a flood- prevention channelisation. A road was built along the banks of the newly re-trained river. This involved clearance of many of the squatters living in the flat lands near the river: Most of the rest of the squatter area was cleared in the late 1970s as part of the New Town development programme, for the construction of Mei Lam Housing Estate. The upper part of the squatter area, furthest from Tai Wai and the station, which was always the least settled part, was cleared rather later, and used for the Mui Lee Temporary Housing Area. A few squatter residences still survive on the northern side of the river, in the Kuk Liu and Heung Fan Liu areas, from the river back as far as the road to the Shing Mun Road Tunnel.

The Sha Tin Tin Tau squatter area was cleared in part in 1966-1967 for the construction of the Lion Rock Tunnel Road. The part of the squatter area lying below the road was cleared in the early 1980s as part of the New Town development programme for the construction of the Chun Shek and Sun Tin Wai Housing Estates, and, a little later, for the Fung Shing Court Home Ownership Scheme Estate. However, the squatter area above the Lion Rock Tunnel Road survives uncleared. Squatter structures here go up almost as high as the Water Catchment, at close to 450 feet above sea-level. This part of the squatter area, the furthest from the flat lands and the roads and railway, was always the least densely settled, and this area is rather attractive today, with its cottages scattered among gardens and stands of well-established trees.

At Ha Wo Che, the squatters settled predominantly in the gaps left after the development of the legal small houses built there on New Grant lots. In this area Crown Land Permits were not usually granted, and squatters here were mostly illegal occupiers of Crown

Land or private land. Most huts here were built one by one wherever a gap allowed, but, at the northern end of Ha Wo Che, furthest from the railway station, a more densely settled squatter area grew up, around the Tung Lo Wan Yeuk Higher Earthgod Shrine. This squatter village spread up the valley of the nullah here, almost as high as the Shui Wo Court Home Ownership Estate. This squatter village survives uncleared except for the area cleared for the construction of the pedestrian flyover from the area to Wo Che Estate in the late 1970s. This squatter settlement is not very large, but presents the best surviving example of a densely built squatter settlement in Sha Tin. There are a few gardens in the upper part of the site, but the lower part has its huts quite closely packed together.

The earliest residential squatter area in Sha Tin was Tai Chung Kiu. This is where the Lea Tai Textiles Factory was, and where village opinion places the first squatter structure, in 1953. The Shing Mun, Keng Hau, and Kak Tin streams join opposite the Che Kung Temple, to form a joint channel to the sea.The area around these streams was reclaimed for agricultural purposes in the late nineteenth century, but the area was always at risk from flood, and the villages never settled there. Much of this area was used as the site of an airstrip by the Japanese, and later, down to the early 1960s, by the British military authorities. In 1914 the Tai Chung Kiu Bridge was built across the rivers just below the junction, along the line of a path from the railway station to Sha Tin Tau village. The market town was built in 1951-1955 at the railway station end of this path. The area near the junction of the streams was the only undeveloped land close to the railway station still unbuilt on in the mid 1950s, and a large number of squatters took advantage of this, building huts packed close together near the path and the junction of the streams, between the river and the airstrip. This area was built without any Crown Land Permit controls (in part because it was the first significant squatter settlement to be built in Sha Tin). It suffered all the problems of the older urban area squatter areas, and was a notorious centre for drugs and other forms of crime.

This squatter area was divided into two settlements: Tai Chung Kiu Village (大涌橋村), mostly along the path which ran along the bunds here near the western end of the Ta Chung Kiu Bridge, and Pak Hok Ting Village (白鶴墩村) , on the flat agricultural land behind the bunds, together with a further area north of the Shing Mun River, opposite Tai Wai. Much of this land was owned by the then Chairman of the Sha Tin Rural Committee, Ng Chung-chi, who leased it to the squatters. There was a further early squatter area on the other side of the river, between the mouths of the Shing Mun River and the Kak Tin stream, opposite the Che Kung Temple.

In 1962, this squatter area suffered a terrible natural disaster. Typhoon Wanda sent a tidal surge straight down the Tola Channel. The tide rose nearly twenty feet above the normal levels, in the middle of the night, and the nineteenth century sea-bunds were over-topped. Two hundred people were drowned. The Tai Po Road had been washed out in the same typhoon, and the rail track was also washed out north of Sha Tin, leaving a train stranded at Sha Tin Station. Rather gruesomely, to get the huge numbers of bodies back to the morgue in the City, they were placed on the seats in the train, and so taken through the railway tunnel to the City. The remaining part of the squatter area was cleared in the late 1970s and the very early 1980s, at the same time as the market town was cleared. The area was then raised. Part of the Sha Tin Town Centre and Park occupy the site today. This disaster struck the consciences of the older residents of Sha Tin strongly. The following year they got together to celebrate the Yu Lan festival for the first time, to appease the spirits of those who died, and have continued to do so every year to the present.

Since the Sha Tin squatter areas were all built on the edges of earlier development areas, there were very few squatter shops in Sha Tin. The squatter area residents shopped in the shops in the market town, and at Tai Wai, like everyone else. A man who lived in the Sha Tin Tau squatter area from the mid 1950s told me that there were no shops or workshops there, except for three people who dealt in the tin sheeting and timber needed by newly arrived squatters to build their huts with. The only significant shops were those which were built on the periphery of the market town between 1955 and 1959, which have been mentioned already. These shops were more part of the history of the market town than of the history of the squatters themselves, and their trade was entirely assimilated with the trade of the market town. Commercial squatting was, therefore, never a very significant part of the squatting scene in Sha Tin.

Up to about 1970 there were no squatter factories in Sha Tin, either. Squatter factories were only viable where there was road access to the factory, and, well before 1955, there were no remaining areas road accessible in Sha Tin available for squatter factory development(or, more precisely, there were so few that the authorities were able to police them effectively so that squatter settlement along them was impossible). This changed when the Keng Hau Road was resurfaced and a concrete bridge built over the Tin Sam River in 1969. This road connected with the Tai Po Road at its eastern end, at Tai Wai, and with the 1906 Upper Keng Hau Road at its western end. The development of the Sha Tin Water Treatment Works (1962-1963), which was built between the end of the Upper Keng Hau Road and the railway tunnel had made a through road from Tai Wai an urgent necessity, but it was only in 1964 that a temporary bridge was built, and not until 1969 that a bridge and an all-weather road were provided. From the new road spurs ran to Hin Tin and Keng Hau villages, and to near the Che Kung Temple.

In 1970, a number of factories cleared from squatter factory areas in Kowloon, were given Crown Land Permits to occupy land along this new road, in the general area of Keng Hau. A variety of industries were established there, mostly in the timber and light metalwork trades. This was a completely new departure for Sha Tin. These squatter factories, however, had a relatively short life, since they were all cleared in about 1980 for the New Town development programme, for the construction of the Hin Keng Housing Estate.

In 1970 there were probably two or three thousand squatter structures in Sha Tin, ignoring the squatter extensions to legal structures. Perhaps a sixth of the population of the district was living then in such structures. Now there are almost certainly fewer than two or three hundred, the vast majority being in the uncleared upper part of the Sha Tin Tau squatter area and at Ha Wo Che. As the small houses built legally on Crown Land New Grant sites between 1917 and 1959 or thereabouts have aged, and as the squatter huts have consolidated themselves, and been improved in the sixty years since they were first erected, it is, in parts of Sha Tin, difficult now to distinguish the legal from the illegal or semi-legal structure, since they now tend to look very similar. Very few squatter structures in Sha Tin display the crude sheet-metal finish and the rubbish-strewn surrounds of the "classic" squatter area. Almost all of those still surviving look like small, but well-established cottages. The growth, and then the wiping out, of squatting in Sha Tin - a development which began and finished within a bare twenty-five years (1955-1980) is one of the major social changes in Sha Tin this century. The almost complete removal of squatters from the district, however, must not blind enquirers from the realisation that, for one generation, they were of immense importance to Sha Tin society.

Industrial Developments

Four placenames in Sha Tin testify to traditional industries practised there before the coming of the British to the New Territories: Heung Fan Liu (香粉寮, "Incense Powder Sheds"), Min Fong (麵房, "The Flour Factory", or "The Noodle Factory"), Fui Yiu Ha (灰? 下, "At the Limekilns"), and Fo Tan (火炭, "Charcoal Village"). Presumably, all these trades were at one time or another conducted at the villages which bear these names. Certainly, incense pounding at Heung Fan Liu, and limeburning, very probably at Fui Yiµ Ha, were still being conducted in Sha Tin at the end of the nineteenth century. Charcoal-burning was a common traditional craft throughout the New Territories, and there is no reason to doubt that Sha Tin villages were engaged in it.

The products from these traditional industries would have been sold in the market towns at Tai Po and Kowloon City. These villages were the industrial equivalent of the specialist market garden villages in the Kowloon Peak area. These industries were all handicrafts: operating from relatively small-scale workshops, with little in the way of mechanisation. The incense-pounding industry used waterwheels to power the heavy stone hammers used to pound the incense wood to dust (see Plate 9, which shows an incense-powder mill, possibly one og those at Heung Fan Liu). The limekilns and charcoal-burning died out in Sha Tin soon after the coming of the British, but the incense industry continued down at least to the 1930s. Incense dust was in considerable demand by the makers of joss-sticks in the City, and the traditional New Territories workshops which pounded the wood to dust (in Tai Po, and especially Tsuen Wan, as well as Sha Tin) all seem to have survived until the 1930s, when the industry started to fail in the face of mechanized incense-dust factories outside Hong Kong. Between 1900 and the 1930s, these incense factories developed as typical suburban trades. They supplied a vital raw material to urban factories, but were obliged to operate from rural sites far from habitation because of the intensely anti-social nature of the trade, with its clouds of choking incense dust spreading around the workshop. In Sha Tin, the incense factories probably stopped operation after 1937 at the latest, when the Shing Mun River, after the completion of the Dam, almost certainly would not have had enough water to operate the waterwheels on which they depended. The 1957 Ordnance Map of Hong Kong still marks "sandalwood mills" at Heung Fan Liu, but this was probably in error, a reference to a past, not a current situation, as was noted in the Government Gazetteer of 1960.[21]

Another important early traditional industry in Sha Tin was the manufacture of bean-curd. Before the War, this was centred in the Shing Mun River valley, near Heung Fan Liu, and the beancurd was mostly carried on shoulder poles for sale in Kowloon City. After the War, the industry expanded considerably, with workshops being established near Tin Sam, Keng Hau, and Siu Lek Yuen, as well as in the Shing Mun valley. After the War the bean-curd was mostly carried to the City by lorry, but a great deal was also sold within Sha Tin, since the restaurants there developed a name for the quality of their bean-curd products. The last bean-curd workshops closed down at the very end of the 1970s, by when, indeed, the quality of the available water was no longer of the high standard it had been thirty and more years before.

The first modern industrial development in Sha Tin was the Ma On Shan Iron Mine, which has already been mentioned above. This mine was certainly in operation from before 1936, and resumed business after the War in 1948. In 1950 there were 2,000 workers there, "hundreds" in 1951, and 1,700 in 1953. In 1954 the mine was updated with a new ore-crushing plant. This mine was run entirely on modern lines. It was by far the largest employer in Sha Tin until its closure in 1976. The influence of the mine on Sha Tin, however, was very restricted. The company refused to employ local Sha Tin people, and insisted on employing refugee labour from the interior of China, believing that there would be greater opportunities of controlling the work-force if they had no relatives nearby to fall back on. Nonetheless, there was a major industrial dispute at the mine in 1956. The output of the mine ran at between 150,000 tons and 170,000 tons a year.

Modern industrial development, apart from the Ma On Shan Mine, started in Sha Tin in the 1930s. The Tsangs of Tsang Tai Uk operated a spinning factory in empty units of that village at a date which is probably in the middle 1930s. Not much is known of this venture, which did not last more than a few years, but several village girls were employed there.

In 1940 Crown Land was sold at Pai Tau for a garage. This was probably a motor-repair workshop (it was not a petrol-filling station, as the only such station in the Eastern New Territories at this date was at Tai Po). More importantly, there is a reference to the "Po Tak Powder Factory", owned by Cheung Mo-san, which bought Crown Land in Pak Tin in that same year. Nothing more is known of this venture, but the title of the concern suggests a modern industrial operation. It may have been in the incense business, since the site is near Heung Fan Liu. It did not survive the War. Evidence is thus very thin for pre-War industrial development in Sha Tin. There was some, but most of it was slight in scale and ephemeral.

The villagers of Tai Wai claim that there was an industrial development across the river from Tai Wai immediately before the War, on the site which was later used by the Lea Tai Textile Factory, although they believe that it was not a textile factory before the War. Unfortunately, there are no Annual Reports surviving for the last two years before the coming of the Japanese, so that it is difficult to confirm this. However, this was a period when very large numbers of factories were being established all over Hong Kong, mostly by refugees from the Japanese, and establishment of a factory here (at the place best positioned to use both the road and the railway) would not be at all unlikely. There is no mention of any new development in this area after the War, and the District Officer was trying to restrict large-scale industrial development to Tsuen Wan in the years before the middle 1950s, so it is indeed likely that Lea Tai was established in Sha Tin immediately after the War on a lot which had been used before the War for industrial purposes. At all events, Lea Tai was wellestablished by 1953, when, as noted above, its night-watchman is believed to have built a squatter hut against its walls, and even more so by 1956, when work there was brought to a stop by a major industrial dispute. The company bought three Crown Land New Grant Building Lots in 1959, at Lai Chi Yuen, probably as residences for senior staff. Lea Tai continued to be the largest industrial concern in Sha Tin (apart from the Ma On Shan Mine) until the area was cleared in the late 1970s as part of the New Town development programme, for the Sha Tin Town Centre Development, of which it forms the southernmost part.

After the War, apart from the Ma On Shan Mine and the Lea Tai Textile Factory, there were a number of industrial initiatives in Sha Tin. In 1948, Crown Land was sold for a Paper Mill at Tai Shui Hang. Nothing, however, seems to have come of this. More significantly, Jardine Matheson bought land in the mouth of the Fo Tan valley in 1958, and established Jardine Dyeing there. This was extended by further purchases in 1959. Next door to Jardine Dyeing the Blood Protection Company (a manufacturer of mosquito coils) established a factory in 1961, after the Fo Tan Road (built in 1961) made the area more road accessible. The Railway Depot at Hotung Lau opened in 1966 (reclamation for this project was undertaken from 1965): this was also a significant employer.

Thus, after the War, Sha Tin had a considerable amount of industrial development, for a suburban town of 20-30,000 people. As well as a major mine, there were three large-scale modern industrial works, and, especially from 1970, a number of smaller concerns. Although the New Town development was to bring in many more factories, the period before the New Town development also saw a significant development in this field; had the New Town never eventuated it is likely that the industrial component of the area would, nonetheless, have slowly increased.

Services

Government Institutions and Works

In 1899, when the Colonial Secretary, Stewart Lockhart, made his detailed tour of inspection of the "New Territory", he recommended that there should be an urgent programme of improvements undertaken by the Government there. These should include a programme of building Police Stations, linked by telephone, to improve public security; new roads to improve communications; and action to improve medical and educational services. We have already seen how the Government telephone service was extended to the New Territories within weeks of the Government taking up the administration of the New Territories (on 16th April 1899), and we have also already discussed the building of the Tai Po Road. All the other of Stewart Lockhart's recommendations were taken up by Government, although, in some cases, probably far more slowly than he would have wished.

There was nothing slow, however, in the programme of provision of Police Stations. Three opened on the first day of British administration, and ten more within the following six months, with two more in the next following few months, together with a few smaller police posts. These fifteen Police Stations proved enough for the security of the New Territories for the next seventy years, except for the New Kowloon area. Sha Tin was one of the three Police Stations opened on the first day of British administration. A police post was also opened within this first year, at the top of Sha Tin Gap, where the paths crossed over to Kowloon City.

At first, the Police in Sha Tin used the old Ch'ing military fort at the foot of the ferry pier at Yuen Chau Kok. Although the strength of the Police at Sha Tin was not large (7 or 8 in the first decade of British administration, comprising European, Indian, and Chinese police constables under a Sergeant, with three more at Sha Tin Gap), this old fort was far too small. Matsheds were put up in the courtyard as overflow offices, but they were very exposed to typhoons (they were damaged by a typhoon in 1909, destroyed in the typhoon of 1913, and seriously damaged on several other occasions, including 1915, and again very seriously damaged in 1922). Also, the Police Station at Yuen Chau Kok was found to be very susceptible to malaria. The Police Post at Sha Tin Gap also used an old Ch'ing installation, and this, too, was found to be seriously lacking.

For these reasons, a new Blockhouse was opened at Sha Tin Gap in 1920, and a new Police Station in Sha Tin in 1924 (the old Police Station at Yuen Chau Kok was demolished in 1929). The new Police Station was built on top of the hill between the river and Sha Tin Tau village. It was hoped that the hill-top site would be breezy and healthy, but the new station was found to be just as susceptible to malaria as the first, until mosquito netting was fitted (1926). The hilltop site, however, was inconvenient (among other problems, it had no road access - vehicles could only get to Tai Wai, a full half mile away. After the War, when it was found that the building was seriously delapidated and needed major repair, it was decided to abandon it, and to move to a better located site, above Tung Lo Wan village (the Japanese had used this latter site for their Militia Post, although the Japanese premises needed a complete rebuild before the site could be re-used). This site was accessible off the Tung Lo Wan Hill Road, which was built at this time to serve the New Grant sites in this area. The new Police Station at Tung Lo Wan was opened in 1950: before that the Police operated from the old premises, which were patched up here and there to make them usable. After the Police moved to the new station, the old one was handed over to the Mennonite Central Relief Committee for use as a hostel for tuberculous children. It has ever since been used as a social welfare centre for children, and is still used for this purpose today.

The 1950 Police Station sufficed Sha Tin until the modern Police Station at Wo Che was opened as part of the New Town development process in 1979. After the move to Wo Che, the 1950 Police Station was used for many years to house various police units, but it has recently been used mostly as a youth centre, and has recently been demolished for redevelopment.

The development of medical services in the Eastern New Territories went very slowly, after a promising early beginning. Two Dispensaries were opened in Tai Po in 1900 - a Government Dispensary, which looked after the health of the Police and other Government servants posted to the New Territories (the staff of this Dispensary were responsible, for instance, for dealing with the malaria at the Sha Tin Police Station), and the Tai Po Village Dispensary, which served the villagers. In the first year, the Village Dispensary treated 616 patients. The Dispensaries were under the control of a Chinese doctor, and then, after 1912, were staffed only by a Chinese "dresser" (male nurse), under the intermittent supervision of a Medical Officer from Kowloon. In 1910 the Village Dispensary was called the "Cottage Hospital". The two Dispensaries were merged in 1917, in which year a hand-pulled ambulance was provided to help get people to the clinic.

The Dispensary seems to have been well-received by the residents of the Tai Po Market, at least for the treatment of some medical problems. Mostly, in the early years, residents approached the Dispensary to have wounds disinfected and bandaged, and for treatment of skin and eye diseases (which were not very effectively treated by Chinese herbal medicine), and to get quinine for malaria. The records of cases treated shows a generally steady increase year by year between 1900 and 1941, with almost 16,000 patients being treated in 1935. Every Summer the Dispensary was the centre of a vaccination campaign run by the Tung Wah Group of Hospitals - in the early years a couple of hundred vaccinations were conducted there each year, and this also rose steadily between 1900 and 1941. By 1935, more than 2,000 vaccinations a year were being conducted there. Theoretically, the dresser-in-charge was supposed to visit the villages as well as dealing with cases arising from the market, but, clearly, he was too busy to do so, except for his duty visits to Police Stations. The Tai Po Dispensary must have had a significant effect on the health of that market town in the years between 1900 and 1941, but it must have had almost no effect on the health of the surrounding villages.

That there was a need to improve medical services there can be no doubt. The Annual Reports refer to serious malaria outbreaks in the New Territories in 1912, 1914, 1915, 1922, and 1924 (various tests on children in the.New Territories at various pre-War dates found evidence of previous malaria infection in up to 79% of children tested - the best series of tests, in 1934, showed the malaria spleen rate in Sha Tin to be 11.2%, which was one of the lowest rates recorded for the New Territories). The Annual Reports also speak of serious outbreaks of plague in 1914 and 1922; of smallpox in 1902, 1903, 1914, 1917, 1923, 1933, 1938, and 1939 (the Government doctors in 1937 believed that nearly 47% of smallpox sufferers with access only to Chinese herbs died); of cholera in 1903, 1919, 1932, 1937, 1938, and 1939; of dysentery in 1939; of influenza in 1918; and of meningitis in 1918 also. Only epidemics specifically recorded in the Annual Reports as affecting the New Territories are listed here - there were others which affected the urban area, but where there is no specific reference to the epidemic affecting the New Territories, although many of them must have. Animals did not escape, either: serious rinderpest outbreaks are recorded in 1913, 1921, and 1923. Tuberculosis was rife, with a death rate in the New Territories of 23%. Many visitors to the New Territories in the pre-War period mentioned as well the high rates of skin infections and eye diseases. Other outbreaks of one epidemic disease or other probably occurred more or less every year (the apparent reduction in problems during the 1920s is due to the Annual Reports not being as specific as in previous years, and almost certainly not to any general improvement). At the time of the 1911 Census, the average age of death in the New Territories was only a little.above 20, with at least a quarter of live-born children dying in their first few years, and half dying before the age of marriage.[22] In 1936 the average age of death in Sha Tin for all registered births was only just over 40, and, since very large numbers of births (especially of children who died soon after birth) were not registered, the position was, almost certainly, very much worse than that, and probably little better than it had been in 1911.

That there was a serious health problem relating to childbirth, and the care of the newly born was evident from as soon as the British came into the New Territories. Little, however, was done about it until 1914, when a Government Midwife was appointed for Yuen Long. Another followed for Tai Po in 1915, for Tsuen Wan in 1916, and Cheung Chau in 1917. The Pok Oi Hospital opened in its new premises at Yuen Long in 1920. This provided only Chinese herbal treatment (a vigorous attempt by the Government to introduce western medicine there in 1932 failed). Probably spurred on by the example of the Yuen Long elders in establishing the Pok Oi Hospital, the Government opened a Dispensary at Yuen Long in 1925, with a dresser, along the lines of the Tai Po Dispensary. In 1928, the New Territories were made a Medical District, with a Medical Officer in charge, but initially this appointment was held in commendam with the Kowloon Medical District. In 1931, however, a full-time Government doctor was at last posted to the New Territories. That year also saw the introduction of a Government Motor Dispensary, which travelled around the New Territories Circular Road on a regular timetable. Sha Tin was visited by this travelling dispensary three times a week from 1931.

Thus, by 1931, after thirty years of British administration, modern medicine had only been introduced to the market towns, and, at that, only in Tai Po and Yuen Long was there both a dresser and a midwife. By the 1920s, the state of medical services in the New Territories was becoming something of a public scandal, with considerable pressure being brought on the Government to do something more effective about it. Very little was done, however, and, in 1931, two voluntary agencies, the St John's Ambulance and a body called the New

Territories Medical Benevolent Association (this body amalgamated with the St John's Ambulance in 1933) decided to step in. Between them, these two associations opened clinics at Kam Tin, Fanling, Tsuen Wan, and Cheung Chau in 1931, and added to this a Motor Dispensary in 1932 which stopped regularly at various major villages along the New Territories roads. A St John's doctor also started to visit Tai O, Sai Kung, and Cheung Chau. In addition, in 1932, St John's Ambulance clinics were set up at Sha Tin, Yuen Long, San Tin, Fanling, Sha Tau Kok and Tai Po. All of these were staffed with a nurse-midwife. In 1933 the New Territories Medical Benevolent Association added a small maternity ward to the facilities at the Sha Tin Clinic. The St John's Ambulance posted a doctor full-time to supervise its New Territories clinics in 1932.

All this spurred the Government into a somewhat belated response. A Government doctor started to visit the outlying islands (by 1932). The mainland New Territories medical district was divided into two, and two Government doctors were posted full-time to supervise the new districts from the Tai Po and Yuen Long Dispensaries (1933), in addition to the St John's doctor. An attempt by the Director of Medical and Health in 1933 to claim that the New Territories was "generally healthy" (and, by implication, did not require heavy expenditure to improve it) was not well received, and was, in fact, generally ignored. Between 1932 and 1934 there was an undignified scramble between the two agencies, with the St John's Ambulance clinics at Tai Po and Yuen Long trying to divert patients from the Government Dispensaries, and the Government Motor Dispensary stopping at the same places as the St John's clinics and travelling dispensary and attempting to divert patients to the Government service. In 1934 there was a meeting between Government and St John's, when it was agreed not to duplicate services. St John's closed its Tai Po clinic, and the Government Motor Dispensary agreed only to stop at places not already served by St John's facilities. At the same time, a Motor Ambulance was provided at Tai Po to bring patients in to the clinic there as needed (unfortunately, this vehicle was completely destroyed when the 1937 typhoon destroyed the Police Garage at Tai Po).

Government, after 1935, made a major effort to improve its New Territories medical services. By 1935 there were nine Government midwives in the New Territories compared with the four of 1931, and, by 1936 the Government midwives at Sai Kung, Tai O, Ko Tong (near Kam Tsin), and Sham Tseng, as well as at Tai Po and Yuen Long, had been trained as dressers as well as midwives, and so could offer a full range of services. In 1939, the Government produced plans for a large and fully equipped modern Health Centre (this would have been in fact a small hospital) which it proposed to build at Tai Po "as soon as funds permit" (in the event, this project was deferred until after the War - it was built in 1955). Thus, whereas in 1930, modern medical services had reached only the market towns (and not all of them), and were only intermittently supervised by a doctor, five years later almost every part of the New Territories was well served with both accident and maternity services, there were three full-time doctors supervising the system, and there were plans in hand for a modern small hospital at the centre.

What did the coming of the Motor Dispensary in 1931, and the St John's accident and maternity clinic in 1932-1933 mean to Sha Tin? According to village elders, the impact of the midwifedresser was immediate and spectacular. There was a five-bed maternity ward at the clinic, which was available free-of-charge to anyone who wished to use it, and she also attended for free all home births to which she was called. She also conducted free follow-up services for a week after the birth. She taught village women at every birth the basic facts about infection, and on the value of cleanliness at childbirth. She also gave free vaccination, bandaged and disinfected wounds, and distributed basic medicines. The villagers say that, "before 1933" half of all children died, "after 1933" only very few did. The spectacular nature of her successes were so great that, very soon, she attended every childbirth in Sha Tin that she could reach. The elders were all very quickly convinced of the value of her services. The first midwife posted to Sha Tin in 1933 remained there until well into the 1960s. Throughout the Japanese period, although she was not paid, she struggled to continue to provide her services. After she retired she continued to live in Sha Tin until recently, revered and respected by the entire community.

The village elders also state that one of the staff of the clinic visited every village on a once-a-month schedule to disinfect the village wells. This was a duty accepted by the Government in 1939, when.. Government started work to improve the village water supplies, with particular attention being paid to the quality of well-water.

After the War, the Government took over the St John's clinics in the New Territories in 1950. At Sha Tin they left the St John's maternity clinic to the care of the midwife, but instituted a new medical clinic, under a doctor, initially using a room at the newly opened Sha Tin Rural Committee Office. This grew into the Sha Tin Government Clinic which remained, until the coming of the New Town, the sole medical facility available in the main part of Sha Tin (the Ma On Shan Mine also had a clinic for its staff). It was rebuilt in 1965.

As well as action on medical care, in the years just before the War the Government became increasingly concerned about the state of public health in the New Territories. In District Office, South, experiments in hiring coolies for street-sweeping and other basic sanitation purposes began in 1931. This proved a success, and after discussion as to the best way forward over the previous year, three Sanitary Inspectors were appointed for the New Territories in 1939, one each for Tai Po, Yuen Long, and South, under the supervision of a full-time Chinese Health Inspector. A start was made on building refuse incinerators in the market towns. Legislation to control the sale of food, and the hygiene of food premises was drawn up. It is probably in the context of this development that the disinfection of village wells was begun.

This initiative was resumed immediately after the War. In 1947 Sanitary Committees were set up in each of the three New Territories Districts to assist the Sanitary Inspectors, and new, improved public health legislation was introduced. New slaughterhouses, with Health Inspectors inspecting all meat, were introduced at Tai Po and Yuen Long in 1954. Additional Health Inspectors, with responsibilities for scavenging and general public health work, were appointed in 1956. By 1961, the Government accepted responsibility within the New Territories for public cleansing, markets and hawker control, public latrines and bathhouses, cemeteries, burials, parks and playgrounds (although there were none in Sha Tin before the Tai Wai Playground and the Tung Lo Wan village playground were completed in 1962 and 1961), beaches, and the licensing of premises for the processing and sale of food. Throughout the 1960s New Territories public health legislation was subject to steady improvement: by 1970, the situation in the New Territories was broadly similar to that in the urban area. In 1972, in a reform of the Urban Services Department, each district was given its own Urban Services Officer, responsible for all public health work in that district. A Sha Tin Urban Services Officer was appointed as part of this reform. Thus, between 1939 and 1972, public health work in the New Territories in general, and Sha Tin in particular, was brought from nothing to a fully modern system.

It should be noted that this process was completed before the start of the New Town development.

When the British occupied the New Territories there were large numbers of village schools in being. From the 1911 Census and other School Censuses of about the same date, it is clear that over half the men of the mainland New Territories were literate, and that well over half the men had had some schooling. Very few women, however, were literate (only about 1%).[23] Government officials were, however, dismissive as to the quality of the traditional village education. Stewart Lockhart urged in 1899 that Government schools be set up, to teach an advanced, more modern, curriculum, in the hope that this would act as an example to raise the standard of village schools generally. This proposal was supported by the Brewin Committee of 1902, and Government schools were accordingly established at Tai Po (1906), and Yuen Long (1904), and, a little later, at Cheung Chau. They taught the same curriculum as the Government Vernacular Schools in the City, and, in particular, taught some English. They were not at first very successful. In 1911 they only had a hundred pupils between them. Even as late as 1920-1921 the Tai Po Government School had only between 70 and 80 pupils (even so, it was by far the largest of the three Government schools at that date).

By 1911 it was clear that the three Government Schools were not acting as the spur to change that the Government had hoped. Between 1912 and 1926 a number of new policies were implemented to try to improve matters. In 1912, a system of free scholarships, to be awarded after success in competitive open examinations, was considered. Graduates of the village schools could take these exams, and, if successful, go on to the Yuen Long or Tai Po Government School, or, if the pass-mark was high enough, even to King's College in the City. The system was introduced in 1915. There were, initially, to be six scholarships a year, three each to the Yuen Long and Tai Po Schools, which would allow the successful candidates to study the final three years of the Government Primary School curriculum free of charge. In the first year, there were five successful candidates, and the scholarship system was well received. The Government did not consider the Government Schools to be Secondary Schools, but Senior Primary Schools. The candidates for the scholarships had usually completed five years of education at a village school, and this was considered equivalent to the first three years at the Government. Schools. The scholarship system was, as noted above, well-received by villagers. The ShaTin villagers, in fact, because of the difficulties and expense their scholarship children were facing getting to and from Tai Po each day, asked in 1920 if a Government English School could also be established in Sha Tin. This request was rejected, but the Government extended the scholarship scheme, so that scholarships could also be taken up at the Yaumatei Government Senior Primary School in the City, and increased the total number of scholarships to 26, ten of which were to be at Yaumatei, specifically for Sha Tin boys. We do not have year-byyear records of how many Sha Tin boys were successful in these scholarship examinations, but we know that there were six successful in 1923, seven in 1925, three in 1928, three again in 1929, two in 1930, and one in 1931. In 1935 and 1936 all the available scholarships were taken up, and, in 1936, one boy was able to take up a scholarship at King's College. The scholarship system was reintroduced after the War, for a few years, and several Sha Tin elders have spoken of going to school in Yaumatei immediately after the War, when the Yaumatei School was utterly without furniture, and each boy had to bring a desk and chair with him when he first joined the school.

This scholarship system was extended further in 1926, when a Government Vernacular Normal School was established in Tai Po. This school trained youngsters to become teachers in rural schools. It took in between about 10 to 16 boys a year. Most were graduates of the Government Schools, or the dozen or so better quality village schools. The Normal School had high standards, and only about half of those who studied at the school eventually passed the final exams. The curriculum was originally a two-year course, but was extended to three years in 1928. It seems likely that a large percentage of the boys studied here on scholarships. The curriculum was "modern", and included training in art and handicrafts, physical education, and gardening. In 1935 it was noted that even boys who failed the final examinations at the Normal School were still out-performing other village schoolteachers who had not been trained at Tai Po. In 1935,

27 of the 32 successful graduates of the Normal School from the then seven or eight graduations, and 12 of the 37 failed graduates were teaching in New Territories schools, to the complete satisfaction of the Director of Education. The school moved to better premises in 1932, and, in 1939, to custom-built premises. In 1939 it was agreed that all teacher training in Hong Kong was to be centred in the new Teacher Training College, but so successful had the Tai Po Normal School been that an exception was made for this school: rural teachers would still be trained there separately from the Teacher Training College. However, the Normal School closed with the coming of the Japanese, and, after the War was not re-opened. It is usually stated that the first Secondary School in the New Territories was the Yuen Long Middle School (1937), but the Tai Po Normal School should also be seen as essentially a Secondary School, since it took in graduates from the Senior Primary Schools.

The effect of the scholarship system on Sha Tin was profound. Most of the Sha Tin boys who became schoolmasters in the area in the period immediately before and after the War had studied at Yaumatei and at the Tai Po Normal School on scholarships. The system had led to the marked improvement in educational standards that the Government had been searching for ever since 1899, although the main benefits of the system really only began to be seen from the late 1930s.

The other major reform of the New Territories educational system, introduced following the Sung Report of 1913, was a grant system, by which grants were made to those village schoolmasters who could teach to a certain minimum standard. Since the grants were quite generous (up to $120 a year, at a time when a village schoolmaster would normally earn less than half that), it was hoped that the village schoolmasters would struggle to meet the minimum standard set. Schoolmasters accepting a grant would be subject to frequent inspection. In the years after 1913, the grant system was made more generous, with a wider range of grants (from $30 to $120, and even more in special cases), and a larger number of grants. In 1920 all village schools, whether they applied for a grant or not, were to be inspected. In 1926 they were to abide by a Government curriculum if they wished to get the grant (this required "modern" subjects, including world geography, mathematics, hygiene, and modern Chinese - generally called "the new books" - although it still allowed up to 50% of the time to be used for the teaching of the Classics).

"Acceptable" schools were classified into four classes. Class "A" were those entirely satisfactory schools, which received the full grant of $120 or above. Class "B" were acceptable schools, who received a lower grant: this was divided into an upper band (usually receiving $60 a year), and a lower band ($30). Class "C" schools were acceptable, but received no grant, and Class "D" were, while they were still seen as acceptable, were felt to be only just so. Other schools failed to reach even this Category "D" level. We have lists of the schools receiving grants from 1920 to 1926, and lists also of the schools in Classes "C" and "D" from 1923-1925. This system, like the scholarship system (and closely related to it, since a very high proportion of the scholarship boys came, in the event, from Class "A" schools) had a pronounced beneficial effect on the teaching in the village schools, although, like the scholarship system, the effects only really became noticeable from the 1930s.

From the lists of schools from 1920-1926 it is clear that the Government had not succeeded in getting all the village schools into its net. There was also a class of school which the Government considered unacceptable. In Sha Tin it is clear that the Tai Wai school was by far the best. This was the school from which the great majority of Sha Tin scholarship boys came. It was graded Class "A" in every year except 1921, when it slipped to the upper band of Class "B" ($60 grant). The Kak Tin school started in 1920 as a Class "B" school, at the bottom end of the grant range (it received $30). In 1921 it had improved, and, while still a Class "B" school, was now at the upper end of the grant range ($60). In 1922 and 1923 it improved further, and was accepted as a Class "A" school, with a grant of $120. In 1924, however, disaster struck (probably, a new teacher was employed, who was not up to the standards demanded), and the school sank to Class "C", where it stayed until 1926. Tsang Tai Uk was graded in the upper band of Class "B" in 1920, in the lower band of Class "B" in 1921, and dropped to Class "C" thereafter, again probably because of changes of teacher. The Sha Tin Wai School was graded Class "C" throughout. No other Sha Tin school, however, is included on a regular basis in the seven years for which we have records, and it is clear that the Government Inspectors of Schools considered a considerable number of schools in Sha Tin to be unacceptable.

The most obvious omission is the Tin Sam school. This school had a good reputation, and a solidly built schoolhouse outside the walled village. It is not mentioned even once in these years. Similarly, the Keng Hau school, which served Upper and Lower Keng Hau, and which was, again, a school with a good reputation in the district, is mentioned only once, in 1925, when it was graded Class "D". The very important school at Siu Lek Yuen is only mentioned in the years 1923-1925 (Class "A" in 1923, and thereafter upper Class "B"). The Fo Tan school, which served all the villages in the Fo Tan valley, again appears only between 1924 and 1926 (upper Class "B"). The Kau To school (another very important and highly respected school) again appears only twice, in 1921 and 1922 (upper Class"B"). A school in the Tung Lo Wan Yeuk appears between 1920 and 1923 (it was in Ha Wo Che as an upper Class "B" school in 1920; in Tung Lo Wan as an upper Class "B" school in 1921 and 1922; and in Pai Tau (as a lower Class "B" school later struck off and regraded Class "C"). Of other schools known to have existed during this period, no mention is made of the school at Kwun Yam Shan which served the Kowloon Peak villages, and only stray references are made to the schools known to have existed in the mountain villages above Fo Tan (Wong Chuk Yeung and Shan Mei), and to those at Sha Tin Tau, and To Shek (which is recorded as having been struck off the register, but which does not appear on the lists.

It is likely that there were, at all dates during the 1920s and 1930s, some sixteen or more schools operating in Sha Tin. The largest number listed by the Government Inspector as acceptable was nine, in 1925. Probably, the system was worked more effectively during the 1930s, when, unfortunately, we do not have lists of schools inspected. Nonetheless, the system did have an effect. The singling out of the Tai Wai school as the district's only Class "A" school accelerated a process which had been in hand even earlier, whereby the brighter boys from the other villages went to Tai Wai to school if they could. This in turn brought in more fees to the teacher there, as the Tai Wai school became much bigger than the others in the area, and that again led to steadily improving standards. The low standard of so many of the other schools is, in part, doubtless due to the Tai Wai school syphoning off the cream of the crop. Those schools which escaped the Government net in these years may well have been generally of a very low quality, although villagers do not consider this to be the case, especially in the case of the Tin Sam and Keng Hau schools.

The establishment of the Tai Wai school as a "centre of excellence" is probably the reason for the drop in the number of successful scholarship candidates from Sha Tin to Yaumatei after 1928: the Tai Wai school was of a sufficiently high standard by then that its brighter boys could go straight into the Tai Po Normal School without passing through the Government School first. In other words, by 1928, the Tai Wai school was probably already operating to Senior Primary School standards.

All this demonstrates that the improvement of educational standards in Sha Tin during the pre-War period was slow, but very real, with marked effects, especially in the later 1930s. One thing stands out, however, during this period. While the population of Sha Tin was changing markedly during these years, with ever more newcomers settling in the district, the indigenous kept complete control over education throughout the period. No schools other than village schools were operating in Sha Tin when the Japanese arrived.

After the War, the number of scholarships taken up by Sha Tin boys at Yaumatei rose up to 1952, because the option of the Normal School was no longer available. The numbers dropped away to nothing after 1952, when a Senior Primary School again became available in Sha Tin itself. The Yaumatei Government School, indeed, was to close in the early 1960s, and the scholarship scheme came to an end before then, at some date during the 1950s.

In 1950, the Government introduced a scheme by which it would assist rural communities to build new schools on a dollarfor-dollar basis, plus assistance with sites. This scheme was enthusiastically taken up throughout the New Territories, and Sha Tin was no exception. New schools were built under the scheme during the 1950s in, for instance, Tai Wai, Keng Hau, Tin Sam, Kak Tin, Tsang Tai Uk, Siu Lek Yuen, and many other places. Few of the prewar schools were still in use in Sha Tin after about 1955. This scheme led to a huge improvement in facilities and standards. Most, if not all, of the new schools, for instance, had playgrounds and ball-courts for the physical education of the youngsters there, whereas this had been almost unheard of before the War.

The most important of these new schools was the "Sha Tin Public

School", built on the top of a small hill just outside Tai Wai. It was run by the "Sha Tin School Committee", which consisted of the core members of the Rural Committee. The Crown Land for the school was sold in 1952. This school was much larger (by three or four times) than any other of the schools built in Sha Tin in this period, and was designed, from the first, to be an elite school. It aimed at taking over from the pre-War Tai Wai School the role of providing a full primary education (many of the other schools only provided three or four years of primary education). This school was of a high quality, and was able to bring its students up to Secondary School Entrance level without problem. The Sha Tin Public School remained the best and most respected school in Sha Tin until the New Town development programme started building newer, and bigger, primary schools in the new estates. The villagers and others who had previously sent their children to the village schools deserted them for these new schools very quickly. None of the village schools in villages accessible by road remained in operation after about 1975, except the Sha Tin Public School, and even that was forced to close in about 1980 (it was re-established in a new school building in Mei Lam Estate, and the School Committee converted the old premises into a much needed Special School), and the Chee Hong Primary School run by the Chee Hong Buddhist nunnery near the Che Kung Temple.

The village schools, in the 1970s, became by-words for inefficient education. Their small size (few had as many as six classrooms), and lack of sophisticated facilities damned them as soon as large, and well-appointed schools were available. But, in the 1950s, they represented a huge step forward, and a major advance in the quality of available education in Sha Tin.

The late 1950s saw two major developments in education in Sha Tin. The first was the advent of schools run by groups other than the indigenous. Both the Lutheran and the Catholic churches established in Sha Tin in 1957 had attached primary schools (both were little more advanced, however, at that date, than the village schools nearby). The Catholic school moved with the church to a new, and much bigger site in 1974, and remains there to the present. The Lutheran school was established near the market town. When the market town was to be cleared it was proposed not to reprovision this school but there was a great deal of opposition to this, and eventually it was re-provided in Wo Che Estate.

The other major new development of the late 1950s was the easier availability of secondary schools to Sha Tin youngsters. The Yuen Long Middle School had reopened in 1948, and it was soon clear that there was a desperate need for more secondary schools in the New Territories. A new Government Primary School was built at Tai Po in 1952, to replace the pre-War school. The Tai Po Government School was re-arranged, to provide both primary and secondary education in separate buildings, in the late 1960s. Similarly, at Sha Tin, a Government Secondary School was opened in 1972 (it had been under planning since 1966). Thus, from 1952, Sha Tin had a Senior Primary School, and, from the late 1960s had access to Secondary Schools in either Sha Tin or Tai Po district. Although the post-war development of education in rural areas such as Sha Tin was not fast, nonetheless, by 1972, a modern system of education was available in Sha Tin. The New Town development programme swept much of that system away, to replace it with a similar system, but in better planned facilities, but it should not be forgotten that the basic provision was in place before.

A special educational development in Sha Tin was the foundation there of the Chinese University. With the coming of the Communist Revolution many academics from China fled to Hong Kong. A group of these, from Protestant universities in China, came together to found a new tertiary college in Hong Kong. This they called Chung Chi College, and it was founded on private land the founders had bought from the Ma Liu Shui villagers (1956). In 1961, the College was allowed to buy out the remaining private land, and was sold Crown Land to build the remaining buildings required (including the chapel). This coincided with the re-establishment of the College as a constituent College of a new University, the Chinese University of Hong Kong. Two other Colleges (New Asia College and United College) had also been founded by this date, and were operating in temporary premises in the City. In 1970 a huge site was granted at nil premium to the Chinese University immediately above Chung Chi College to allow the other colleges to move there, and for the administrative buildings of the University to be built. Here again, as with so much else, critically important developments for Sha Tin came just before the decision to proceed with the New Town, but should really be seen as part of the suburban phase of Sha Tin's history.

Another Government service which came to Sha Tin surprisingly early was a Post Office. A Branch Post Office was established in Sha Tin in 1912. There were five such Branch Post Offices in the New Territories before 1935, at Tai Po, Yuen Long, Tsuen Wan and Cheung Chau, as well as at Sha Tin. These Branch Post Offices were run by the Police. Anyone with a letter to post would take it to the Police Station, where stamps could be bought and any other postal business done. The Police would then put the letter in a post-bag. Once every so often the bag would be taken to the Post Office in the City and handed over, when letters for Sha Tin would be handed over in return. These would then be held in the Police Station until the Village Headman came to collect them. It was the Headman's job to carry them back to the village and deliver them.

This arrangement was always awkward (and must have been entirely so in the market-towns, which needed a daily delivery and collection service). In 1935 the New Territories postal services were (at last) taken over by the Post Office. Full Branch Post Offices were established in 1935 at Tai Po, Yuen Long, and Cheung Chau, with post boxes, and postmen who delivered letters daily (at least to the market towns, and major lowland villages) by bicycle. It is unclear what happened at Sha Tin, but it is probable that a Sub-Branch Post Office was established, with at least basic delivery and collection services, and a post-box. The remoter mountain villages, however, still had to come in to pick up their mail. A new full Branch Post Office was established in Sha Tin in 1955: it was required because of the increase in business arising from the new market town.

There were no modern social welfare institutions in Sha Tin before the War, just the dozen or so Chai Tong which had been founded in the area near the station in the 1920s and 1930s. As we have seen, the Government's view of these Chai Tong was, at best, doubtful. Just outside Sha Tin, the New Territories Orphanage (now known as St Stephen's) was completed in 1937, and was the first modern social welfare institution in the wider Sha Tin area. It was unreservedly welcomed by the Government. Immediately after the War, as noted above, two modern social welfare institutions opened in Sha Tin, the Sin Tin To Home for the Elderly at Sheung Wo Che (1946), and the Mennonite Children's Home at Sha Tin Tau (1950). The Sin Tin To Home was a very much larger, and more modern type of institution than the Chai Tong the sect had previously run in Sha Tin, and the view of Government towards it was very different - the Governor, in fact, visited it in 1957. At Wu Kai Sha, a children's camp was established in 1955 by the Christian Children's Fund: the site of this camp was extended in 1957 and 1958. The Gilman's Scout Camp, high in the Kowloon peak area, near Mau Tso Ngarn Village, was established in 1959. Also in 1959, the Catholic Church established a Social Welfare Centre in Ma On Shan, aimed predominantly at the miners and their families. In 1961, the Hong Kong Society for the Blind opened a Centre in Sha Tin as well. During the 1960s a number of other social welfare institutions were opened there as well: prominent among them were a number of Kindergartens, mostly managed by religious groups.

The Social Welfare Department opened offices in the New Territories districts (apart from Tsuen Wan, which had one much earlier) in the mid 1960s. Before that, Public Assistance and Relief were handled by the District Officers on behalf of the Director of Social Welfare. However, well before the start of New Town development, Sha Tin had progressed to the point where it required the full provision for social welfare as enjoyed in the urban areas.

Other Government agencies operating in Sha Tin before 1972 should be mentioned briefly. The Vegetable Marketing Scheme formed co-operatives in Sha Tin in the early 1950s, as everywhere else in the New Territories, and the great bulk of the vegetables grown in Sha Tin during the 1950s and 1960s were marketed through them. As well as these co-operatives, the Agriculture and Fisheries Department advisory service to farmers provided a very valuable service as well.

The growth in television and radio broadcasting in Hong Kong led to a number of broadcasting stations being established on the hills around Sha Tin during the 1960s. Television Broadcasting Ltd bought Crown Land for a station in 1969, for instance.

The Rural Committee paid for the construction of a Fire Station in Sha Tin in 1956. Before that date there had been no fire-fighting facility in the district.

More important for Sha Tin was the Integrated Water Scheme. This was introduced in 1961-1962, to coincide with the coming on stream of the Tai Lam water scheme, and in advance of the High Island and Plover Cove schemes, then under active planning. It involved building tunnels under the mountains so that all the water supplies could be handled as a single co-ordinated system. Central to the scheme was the Water Treatment Plant at Sha Tin, and tunnels constructed through the mountains to Sha Tin, especially from Tai Po, and, a little later, from Sai Kung. The treated water was eventually taken through the mountains to Kowloon through the Lion Rock Tunnel.[24] This scheme involved a number of stretches of new roads being built in Sha Tin (especially the Fo Tan Road, but also the roads to Mui Tsz Lam and Wong Chuk Yeung). It also, for the first time, allowed Government treated water to be piped to developments in Sha Tin (the older Sha Tin water system had merely provided untreated stream water from Fo Tan to the market town and Tai Wai). Water was made available by stages during the later 1960s to all the lowland areas of Sha Tin. Thus, the Integrated Water Scheme brought modern water supplies to Sha Tin. Modern sewerage systems, however, had to wait for the New Town development.

There was an airfield in Sha Tin for a couple of decades. Private agricultural land had been bought, probably in 1940, by a group of Japanese businessmen, who used it as a golf-course for the Japanese community. Under the Japanese military administration this golf-course was resumed, and converted to a military airstrip. The context may be the closure of KaiTak airfield while it was being extended. After the War, the airstrip was used by the British military (specifically, by the Army Air Corps, who had some spotter planes here, and, for a time by the Royal Air Force, which had some fighter planes here). During the period 1951-1956, when Hong Kong was heavily defended against possible attack, this airstrip was quite busy, and significant numbers of military personnel were posted here. These soldiers and airmen helped with their custom the establishment of the bars and restaurants in the new market-town on their doorstep. After the mid 1950s, the military establishment in Hong Kong was scaled down, and the airstrip became progressively less important. It was finally abandoned in the early 1960s, probably in the aftermath of Typhoon Wanda (1962). The airstrip lies under the southernmost section of today's Sha Tin Centre Street. This airstrip affected the post-War development of the area. The Lee Tai Textile Factory occupied the area west of the airstrip. The squatter settlement which developed after 1953 was thus forced into the lowest-lying ground, between the airstrip and the river, with disastrous consequences in 1962.

Government public works in Sha Tin fall in two phases before the coming of New Town development. Between 1900 and 1924 there was a good deal of work undertaken. The building of the Tai Po Road, and then the Railway (especially the tunnel), then the rebuilding of the road to fully motorable standard, and the construction of the new Police Station of 1924, meant that there was active public works in progress throughout the period. Thereafter there was a lull. Very little public works took place in Sha Tin during the twenty-five years after 1924. There were, of course, the regular repairs carried out to the road following typhoon or heavy rain damage, but very little that was new. The railway, too, merely did small-scale repairs and station improvements during these years.

After the War, again, there was, initially, not much done. The market town was built by private developers, all Government did was advise and support morally. In these early postwar years, Local Public Works under the District Office did a certain amount of good work repairing bunds, paths, and bridges damaged under the Japanese. New roads were built in 1949 in Tai Po (the Fan Kam and Lam Kam Roads), but not in Sha Tin, where all that was done was to build the new Police Station (1949-1950), and rebuild on a better alignment, and to a better, and wider, design the important bridge which took the Tai Po Road over the Shing Mun River at Tai Wai (1953). A new railway station was added at Ma Liu Shui in 1956, to serve Chung Chi College.

The second major phase of public works began in 1961, with the Integrated Water Scheme. This was, as noted above, a huge development project, involving, in Sha Tin, the Water Treatment Works, and tunnels to Tai Po and Sai Kung, with access roads. Contemporaneously with it came the re-training and channeling of the Shing Mun and Tin Sam Rivers, and the building of a road alongside the latter (completed 1961). This was the first phase of a major flood-prevention campaign, and was completed when the area immediately north of the Lion Rock Tunnel Road bridge was retrained in 1968. Also undertaken at the same time were the roads required for the planned development around Tai Wai (1961). Also built during the period of the Integrated Water Scheme was the first Lion Rock Tunnel, and the Lion Rock Tunnel Road in 1967 (this was originally only a two-way single-carriageway system, the second tunnel, and the dualling of the road was part of the New Town development process, and done in 1978). The Lion Rock Tunnel Road was a major development improvement to Sha Tin, since it provided a second motorable bridge over the Shing Mun River, and opened access to the villages south of the railway and river. Previously, Sha Tin had only had the Tai Po Road bridge at Tai Wai. The opening of the Lion Rock Tunnel provided a major relief for the Tai Po Road south of Tai Wai, through the hills, which had, by 1967, become rather congested.

After the completion of the Lion Rock Tunnel and Integrated Water Schemes there was a pause: when public works of substance began again, in 1972, with the reclamation for the Lek Yuen Estate, they were part of the New Town development.

Entertainment

One of the most widespread community uses of suburban areas is for entertainment, and Sha Tin was no exception to this, particularly in the period between about 1930 and about 1975. Much of Hong Kong's countryside was formed into Country Parks from 1976 onwards. The formation of Country Parks involved improving access into Hong Kong's wealth of unspoiled hills and forests from the urban and suburban areas. Before 1976, however, access into these areas was more difficult. Urban residents wanting access to areas of natural beauty had to content themselves with areas which would nowadays be considered merely on the edges of the unspoiled. Only a very few people in those days ventured to hike into the mountains. There were plenty of paths, but, by 1975, with the majority of the mountainside villages abandoned, they were becoming faint and overgrown, and dangerous to use except by people who knew what they were about.

From about 1950 to 1967, by far the most heavily used area of natural beauty in Sha Tin was Hung Mui Kuk (紅梅谷, "Red PlumValley") in Sha Tin. There can be very few people in Hong Kong of between seventy and eighty-five years of age who passed their teenage years in Hong Kong who did not go there for a picnic at least once. Hung Mui Kuk was an area behind and above Kak Tin village. During the 1930s a landslide sent a huge mass of silt down the hill and into a small and deep valley there, called Tong To ("The Pit"). The silt blocked the valley completely, and formed a level, sandy, plain. During the period of the Japanese Occupation this area was not much used, and this plain became deeply covered with grass and flowers, and surrounded by trees. Well-used paths ran from here up to the Amah Rock, and on to Kowloon City. A conventional day out grew up: the practice began about 1950, or perhaps a little earlier, as part of the cult of physical exercise and fresh air, which began to be considered important by teachers and the bettereducated teenagers in this period. The picnickers would go out to Sha Tin by rail. They would walk out to Kak Tin, crossing the Tai Chung Kiu Bridge. The Che Kung Temple formed the half-way point of the walk, and the picnickers would stop there to worship, and spin the fortune-wheel (see Plate 10, showing the Che Kung Temple about 1970). Once at Hung Mui Kuk, the picnickers would walk up one of the paths for an hour or two, and then come back for their picnic. Afterwards, they would return, paying their respects to Che Kung a second time en route back to the station. After the market-town was founded, the day out usually ended with a meal in one of the market-town restaurants before return by an evening train. This picnic area, which is remembered with affection by almost everyone old enough to have been there, was destroyed in large part in 1967 as part of the construction of the Lion Rock Tunnel Road, which ran across the upper edge of the site.

Of course, there were always the more energetic and daring who went for hikes into the hills even before the Country Parks Authority improved and signposted the paths. Before the War, that meant planning a walk which could start and finish at a dependable public transport point, and public transport was by no means as widespread or as frequent in the New Territories then as now. Two frequently used walks were Tsuen Wan to Sha Tin and Tai Po to Sha Tin. The Tsuen Wan to Sha Tin walk started at Tsuen Wan (accessible from Hong Kong by ferry), and then went up to the Shing Mun Dam, and then down through the Shing Mun valley to the railway station at Sha Tin. The Tai Po to Sha Tin walk started at the railway station at Tai Po, crossed into Shing Mun via Leadmine Pass, and so to the station at Sha Tin through the Shing Mun valley. Half way down the ShingMun valley (approximately where the Shing Mun Road Tunnel crosses the valley today) there was a waterfall with a deep pool, and it was customary for walkers to refresh themselves with a dip in the pool before the last part of the walk. Sometimes, less hardy walkers would walk up and back to this pool from the station at Sha Tin. As a result, a whole generation of Tai Wai village youths had their erotic imagination stirred by the sight (or the report) of "naked maidens" bathing there! This idyllic practice doubtless stopped in 1937, after the Dam cut the water supply to the river.

After the War, families with small children (for whom the walk to Hung Mui Kuk would have been too much, let alone the trek over the hills), would often come out to Sha Tin to enjoy themselves with the rowing boats and bicycles which were available for hire there up until the area around the market town was cleared for the construction of Lek Yuen Estate in 1972. Such families, too, usually ended their day with a meal in one of the market town restaurants, which came to be very busy indeed, especially at weekends.

All these entertainment uses of Sha Tin were urban uses. The village youths (when not hopefully spying on the Shing Mun maidens) were too busy farming, and most of the outsiders resident in the new houses were no less busy. Before the War, it was essentially the urban jeunesse dor?e who had the leisure and inclination to go out into the country for a day out. After the War the practice was greatly extended, especially through School Picnics.

In the period immediately before the War, as noted above, there was a golf-course in the area near the station, run by a group of Japanese businessmen for the Japanese community in the City. This was another very clearly suburban land-use.

Another urban entertainment use for Sha Tin land was horse-riding. The Equine Sports Club (headed by Mr F.W. Grinter) bought a Crown Land New Grant lot near Tung Lo Wan for a club-house and riding ground in 1941. This venture came to an end with the coming of the Japanese, but was restarted after the War (at a date at present unclear) on a site near Tai Wai, off the Tai Po Road.

Horse-riding leads on inevitably to the Sha Tin Racecourse. The decision to build a Racecourse at Sha Tin was taken in 1971, and was the last major development decision made before the start of the New Town.[25] The Racecourse must, therefore, be seen, not as a New Town feature, but the last and greatest of the entertainment uses of Sha Tin by the urban masses while the district was still a suburban area, and before the New Town began to be developed. Its size and magnificence should be taken as a reflection of just how important the suburban phase of Sha Tin's history was.

Prehistory of a New Town:
New Town Proposals for Sha Tin, 1910-1965

A firm commitment to proceed with the current Sha Tin New Town development was made only in 1972, but there had been nugatory proposals made in every decade of the fifty years before that. These proposals, therefore, were part of the period of suburban development in Sha Tin: it should be remembered that all the unplanned suburban developments in the district were undertaken in the shadow of possible long-term planned developments.[26]

Garden Suburb Proposals: 1910-1954

Proposals for some form of planned development of the Sha Tin area area were made as soon as the Kowloon-Canton Railway was opened in 1910. When the Governor, Sir Henry May, opened it in 1910 he said: "The railway will enable some of us to take short holidays … Others will prefer to lead the simple life in the country, visiting Hong Kong for their business." Two years later, the District Officer, G.N. Orme, added in his Report on the New Territories: "The railway will bring European residents with their customs and institutions into the New Territory". Both the Governor and the District Officer probably had planned suburban garden-suburb type developments in Sha Tin in mind while making these comments, since Sha Tin was the most easily accessible rural area from the City, the first station beyond the mountains.

In the event, the substantial suburban developments which eventuated, as noted above, were unplanned. Individuals sought plots of Crown Land to buy to develop as small houses with gardens. The District Office sold land as requested, without any plan in mind. As noted above, the developments were scattered over the hillslopes near the station, connected by narrow footpaths, with the houses facing in whatever direction seemed most suitable to the new owner, taking into account the general lie of the land. The District Officer was unwilling to allow developments of this suburban character to invade the agricultural land, and the new houses were thus limited to the Crown Land hillslopes behind the railway, and to the similar Crown

Land areas near the Che Kung Temple. As noted above, by the late 1950s there was a zone full of this unplanned suburban development stretching for a mile from just north of Ha Wo Che village to Tung Lo Wan village to the south, plus the smaller pockets of a similar character at San Tin and Lei Uk, across the river from the station, and accessed over the Tai Chung Kiu footbridge.

However, in 1916, a planned garden-suburb was built in Fanling, at On Lok Tsuen. This consisted of several well-laid-out streets, with some hundred houses and gardens, a short walk from the Fanling Railway Station. This development was very successful.

In 1923 a similar project was proposed for Sha Tin. Immediately opposite the railway station was an area of marshy ground. It was proposed by a group of wealthy Chinese businessmen to raise this, and extend it by reclamation to the north, and to build a garden suburb there. If agreed, this development would have been two or three times as large as On Lok Tsuen, and would have housed several thousand people. Nothing came of this, as the Government was unsympathetic (even as early as this, the Government probably felt that this area was just too valuable for such low-density development). Part of this site was eventually used for the Sha Tin Market in 1951, and it lies today below the Sha Tin Town Centre development.

There was a second proposal for a garden-suburb type of development in Sha Tin, after the War. In 1954, following the successful establishment of the Sha Tin market, it was proposed to use the sea-bed and agricultural land to the north and south of the market for a planned, low-density, house-and-garden type of development, generally along the lines of the pre-War and post-War developments at Yau Yat Tsuen and Kowloon Tong. Plans survive of this proposal. However, the Government rejected the proposal out of hand, because they felt the area had to be reserved for a high-density New Town, which was, by then, already Government's preferred future for Sha Tin.

The Development of the New Town Plan
The 1939-1947 Proposals

Proposals for a high-density New Town in Sha Tin had, in fact, been made as early as 1939. In that year there were hundreds of thousands of refugees in Hong Kong, fleeing from the Japanese. The

Government was much exercised as to how to house these refugees, and how to find them work to support themselves. A Committee was set up which proposed New Towns at Sha Tin, Tai Po, and Tsuen Wan, together with substantial developments of new rural settlements wherever Crown Land or unused private land made this feasible. Unfortunately, nothing survives of the details of these proposals, although it is known that investigations of the various sites were made. It is probable that the Sha Tin New Town as proposed in 1939 would have been built on much the same site as the garden-suburb of 1926 had been proposed for. The occupation of Hong Kong by the Japanese put an end to these proposals before any action to implement them could be made.

Sir Patrick Abercrombie, the author of The Greater London Plan (1944, published 1945), which established the New Town Programme in early post-War Britain, visited Hong Kong in 1947 at the invitation of the Government to advise on the optimum reconstruction strategy for Hong Kong. He endorsed the 1939 New Town proposals, and recommended proceeding with planning for New Towns at Sha Tin, Tai Po, and Tsuen Wan. No actual planning work was done by Sir Patrick, but the proposals for New Town development at Sha Tin can be said to have been generally agreed within Government ever since 1939 as a result of his support for them in 1947. Certainly, ever since 1947 this New Town development was the Government's preferred long-term option for Sha Tin, although no actual proposals were made public until 1961. It was because Government was already committed to New Town development of the area that the 1954 garden-suburb proposals were rejected.

The 1954 Plan

In 1954, the Government produced a sketch-plan for an "Abercrombie" New Town at Sha Tin. It was a simple plan, proposing river-training and reclamation, to provide for a zone of high-density housing occupying the land opposite the station. Across the river, there was to be another zone of high-density housing near Lei Uk, and Open Space in front of Tsang Tai Uk. This Plan established the basic reclamation lines for the New Town of today: they were refined, but generally confirmed in the 1961 Plan, and subsequently were changed very little, if at all.

The Government, however, by 1954, was overwhelmed by the need to deal on an emergency basis with the million refugees who had fled to Hong Kong from the Communists in 1949-1952. The 1954 Sha Tin New Town Plan was, therefore, shelved for three years. Government remained broadly committed to New Town development in this period, but just did not have the money to undertake more than one New Town at a time. Kwun Tong was accordingly developed as a New Town in the late 1950s. It was felt then that this New Town was all that the Government could cope with, especially given the heavy quasi-New Town expenditure under way at the same time in the new Resettlement Areas of, especially, Wong Tai Sin.

The 1957-1961 Plan

In 1957 the 1954 Sha Tin New Town Plan was dusted off, and detailed new proposals were produced. The Government Annual Report 1957 stated: "New Towns are to be developed at Tai Po, Sha Tin, Kwai Chung, Tsuen Wan, Tuen Mun, and Junk Bay with all possible speed", but, in the event, lack of funds stopped most of this development in this period.

The 1957 Sha Tin New Town Plan as finally published in 1961 strongly supported the river-training proposals of the 1954 sketch plan, as the risk of flood in the area around the junction of the rivers was fully recognized. In 1966 the Public Works Department, in a briefing prepared for a visit by the then Secretary of State for the Colonies, put the problem of flooding at the top of the list of technical problems requiring solution at Sha Tin before New Town development could begin there: "Among the major engineering problems posed by the intensive development of Sha Tin [are] the possibility of flooding at times of high tides, strong easterly winds, and heavy rain …".

The original 1954 proposal to deal with this flooding problem was for the re-trained rivers to run within concreted channels, between high bunds, with the development proceeding behind the bunds, but in 1961 this was rejected as too risky, and the decision was made that the development areas would have to be raised to the height proposed for the bunds (5.5 metres above sea-level – the original ground level was about 2.5 metres above sea-level) to avoid any risk of floods over-topping the bunds.

The river-training and land-formation proposals were detached from the New Town proposals, and implemented in stages from 1959-1960. The raising of the land behind the bunds was of necessity deferred until the rivers had been re-trained. In 1962 Typhoon Wanda, which did overtop the bunds, proved how necessary the raising of the development land was. The Government Annual Report 1962 says of Typhoon Wanda:﹁At Sha Tin a tidal surge breached the sea-wall in two places, flooded the town, and swept away many huts﹂. This tidal surge reached as high as 7.4 metres above sea-level.

The river re-training works began in 1959-1960, in accordance with the lines suggested in the 1954 Plan, with the section of the Shing Mun River in front of Tai Wai, and the Tin Sam River from the head of the valley to the river's junction with the Shing Mun River near the Che Kung Temple. This phase of the work was completed in 1960-1961. The remaining work was under detailed planning in 1964-1965, and was implemented in phases between 1965 and 1969. By 1967 the re-training was completed up to the Lion Rock Tunnel Road Bridge: in 1968 the area immediately north of the bridge was re-trained, to ensure the safety of the bridge.

The Tin Sam River re-training was required so early because of the construction of the Sha Tin Water Treatment Works, which opened in 1963. The Upper Shing Mun River, above Tai Wai, became urgent once the Lower Shing Mun Dam was built (constructed 1963-1965), and the whole re-training programme had to be completed before the Lion Rock Tunnel Road Bridge could be built (1967).

As part of the re-training, the land behind the new river banks was reclaimed and raised to the new development level, and development began there straight away. A new Clinic and Maternity Home was built here in 1965 on the innermost and first formed land (although a proper access road was only provided in 1968). Quarters for railway staff were built here in 1969. The Government Secondary School (which had been in the Public Works Programme since 1965) was opened near the river bank in 1972, and the new Catholic Church was opened nearby in 1974.

From 1970 onwards the river re-training work continued to the north of the Lion Rock Tunnel Road Bridge, but only on the northern bank, behind the market.

The 1961 Plan took from the 1954 sketch-plan the proposal for a high-density residential development in the Tai Wai – Wo Che area, but added to it other residential areas, especially one where the Racecourse now stands, and in the Valley, and at the site of today's Sha Kok. Industrial areas were proposed for the Fo Tan Valley, and along the Siu Lek Yuen stream, where that stream would pass through the new reclamation.

Many of the basic parameters of the eventual 1972 New Town Plan were thus taken over from this 1961 Plan. As well as fixing the major industrial areas of the New Town, it was the 1961 Plan, for instance which determined the basic line of the Lion Rock Tunnel Road, and, more specifically, the site of the bridge which was to carry it over the river. The lines of the major distributor roads which are today's Che Kung Miu Road and Tai Chung Kiu Road were also fixed in this Plan. It was the 1961 Plan which proposed the additional Railway Stations at Tai Wai and Fo Tan which were eventually built.

The 1961 Plan also provided for the protection of the existing major landscape features of the area: this was in advance of its time, but the major landscape protection proposals of the 1961 Plan were eventually included in the New Town as it was built, after they had been revived and refined in the 1977 Master Landscape Plan. The boundaries of the reclamation of the 1972 New Town as actually implemented are those proposed in 1954 and refined in 1959-1961.

It is fair to say that the planning for the New Town at Sha Tin has been a process of continuous development ever since 1954: the present New Town is a development of these earlier proposals, but not radically different them.

The 1961 Plan, however, was for a relatively small town, of 275,000 initially, growing to 360,000 on final completion. It assumed that the New Town would take a very long time to build, as there was no prospect in 1961 of money being found for the reclamations, other than those immediately required as part of the ongoing programme of river re-training above the Lion Rock Tunnel Road Bridge.

In 1963 it was decided to shelve the 1961 Plan for a further three years. Engineering feasibility studies were conducted (completed in 1964) on the identified major engineering restraints (flooding, pollution from sewage, and inadequate public transport access between Sha Tin and the City). In 1966 most further work on Sha Tin New Town was again halted. A hydrological study of Tolo Harbour, and its capacity to absorb sewage was, however, conducted in 1967. In part these delays were because it was felt that nothing practical could be done in Sha Tin until the Lion Rock Tunnel Road and Bridge were opened.

The shelving of action on the Sha Tin Plan was not due to any lessening of commitment on Government's part to the New Towns: The Tsuen Wan New Town began construction in these years (1960-1961). Once again, Government was, at this date doubtful of its financial capacity to handle more than one New Town at a time, and Sha Tin was felt to be less advantageous than Tsuen Wan, because of the transport problems between Sha Tin and the City. Government was also concerned at the very high costs which would be required to treat the sewage of any New Town at Sha Tin to levels which Tolo Harbour could absorb.

The 1965-1967 Plan

In fact, however, the Sha Tin Plan was revived only two years later, in 1965. At that time there was a planning panic within Government, as the 1961 Census seemed to suggest that the eventual population of Hong Kong would be far higher than had previously been believed. It was felt that the New Towns had now become even more vital than previously believed, and Government accepted that it would have to find the funds to develop more than one at a time.

The major difference between the 1961 and 1965 Sha Tin New Town Plans was that Government raised the planned population for the New Town by three times (to 1,090,400 persons). It was again noted, however, that development could not go very far unless the sewage disposal problem was overcome.

There was relatively little difference between the 1961 and 1965 Plans as to the areas to be used as residential areas – they were just to be developed to far higher densities. The only major exception to this was that one major residential area was removed from the 1965 Plan. The northern residential area as identified in the 1961 Plan was removed from the 1965 Plan, because the Jockey Club was already seeking in 1965 to use that site as a second racecourse. The area was shown as undeveloped sea-bed in the 1965 Plan, so as not compromise the eventual decision as to whether or not it was to be given to the Jockey Club. The industrial areas as identified on the 1961 were left untouched (a third area was identified in the Valley), but the development densities were sharply increased. The areas identified as Open Space on the 1961 Plan were mostly converted to residential areas, and the advanced landscape protection features of the 1961 Plan were dropped.

It was at this stage that the line of the Lion Rock Tunnel Road was finalised. The 1965 Plan also assumed that additional road-tunnels would be built, to Laichikok and through Tate's Carin. The Tate's Cairn Tunnel was eventually built (1991), and the proposed tunnel to Laichikok was eventually superseded by one to Tsuen Wan (1990). It was also this 1965 Plan which identified the line for the Sha Tin By-pass on the southern side of the town, and which required that the Tai Po Road be made a dual-carriageway from the City to Tai Po.

The 1965 Plan was completely driven by the need to provide housing sites. Professional and public comments on this Plan, once it was published in 1967, were very negative, with criticism centring on these very high population and development densities, on the lack of any attempt to preserve the landscape, or to provide enough Open Space to make the New Town a pleasant placed to live in. Nonetheless, despite all these criticisms, the Government accepted the 1965 Plan (1967), and set up a Planning Co-ordination Committee to consider how to implement it.

In the event, however, very little was done. This was, to a large extent, because of serious doubts within Government as to the wisdom of the Plan, even though the Government had accepted it. Furthermore, 1967 saw the Riots, and Government believed that it was, once again, in financial difficulties. Tuen Mun was also being planned in this 1965-1967 period, and it was felt that whatever money there was ought to be spent there (Tuen Mun was seen as cheaper to build than Sha Tin, since it was felt that a New Town there would not need a sophisticated sewage treatment system – sewage there could be allowed to flow untreated out to sea). The first reclamations at Tuen Mun accordingly began in 1966, and the first Housing Estate was built there in 1967.

Action on implementing the 1967 Plan for Sha Tin did, however, begin in a very small way in 1970, when a small area of land was reclaimed behind the Market to provide a "by-pass" road, but this development had not got very far when action on it was halted, this time because of a complete reconsideration of the whole New Town Development Programme, in 1972, a reconsideration which led to the Plan for the New Town which was actually implemented. That plan dropped the excessively high population densities of the 1965 plan, ensured acceptable open space was included, and was generally welcomed.

Thus, genuine New Town proposals for Sha Tin were in being from 1939, but were constantly deferred. The 1939 proposals were deferred because of the Japanese, and those of 1946 because of the refugee influx. The 1954 Plan was given a lower priority than Kwun Tong, and shelved. Similarly, the 1961 Plan was shelved in favour of Tsuen Wan. Again, the 1967 Plan, while formally adopted by Government, was deferred in favour of Tuen Mun. These constant shelvings and deferrals gave Sha Tin a much longer life as a suburban district than would have seemed likely when the first decision to build a high-density New Town was made, in 1939, but, in fact, it was to be only thirty-three years later that action to build one was begun.

Footnotes

1　Factual statements in this paper are taken, in the main, from the oral accounts of village elders (interviewed at various dates between 1980 and 1998), and from the annual Administrative Reports (to 1939) and Annual Reports (after 1946) issued by the Government. The Registers of Sales of Crown Land have also been used, from 1917 to 1970. Specific references are not made here where the facts are taken from one of these three sources: it is usually quite clear from the context which is the source. The date of Kwun Yam Shan is confirmed by old land deeds in the possession of the villagers, dating from the later eighteenth century.

2　See P.H. Hase, with J.W. Hayes and K.C. Iu, "Traditional Tea Growing in the New Territories", *Journal of the Hong Kong Branch of the Royal Asiatic Society*, Vol. 24, 1984, pp. 264-281.

3　See P.H. Hase: "The Alliance of Nine: Traditional Sha Tin", *Village Studies: Settlement, Life, and Politics in Traditional New Territories Village Communities, forthcoming.*

4　See P.H. Hase: "The Alliance of Nine: Traditional Sha Tin", *Village Studies op.cit,* for Hui Wing-hing and his poetry.

5   For these rituals see P.H. Hase: "The Alliance of Nine: Traditional Sha Tin", *Village Studies* op.cit.

6   References to the District Officer in this paper are to the Annual Reports of the District Officer, North, to be found in *Administrative Reports, Hong Kong* for the pre-War period.

7   Wong Chuk Yeung learnt about the invasion by the Japanese when two villagers carried a pig to the station, where they found that there were no trains. The station-master told them that the Japanese had invaded. Abandoning their pig, they ran back to the village, but the Japanese were already crossing the pass behind the village by the time they got back

8   At the same time, most villagers rented the fields out at the old, rice-field rental rates, which were far below what the value of the fields as vegetable plots could have supported.

9   G. Aijmer, Economic *Man in Sha Tin: Vegetable Gardeners in a Hong Kong Valley*, (London, 1980), and *Atomistic Society in Sha Tin: Immigrants in a Hong Kong Valley*, (Gothenburg, 1986). Judith Strauch: "Middle Peasants and Market Gardeners: the Social Context of the 'Vegetable Revolution' in the New Territories, Hong Kong", in *From Village to City: Studies in the Traditional Roots of Hong Kong Society,* ed. D. Faure, J. Hayes, A. Birch (Hong Kong 1984) gives a valuable insight into the attitudes and life of vegetable farmers renting land fromn the indigenous, although concentrating on farmers in Tai Po rather than Sha Tin.

10   The exact site of Wang Au is unclear: it may have been just on the Tai Po side of the pass. For Ngau Au and Wang Au see P.H. Hase: "The Alliance of Nine: Traditional Sha Tin", *Village Studies* op.cit.

11   At Au Pui Wan and elsewhere, the abandonment was very final. When I visited the villages in 1981, the village houses all stood open, the remains of the last meal left on the tables, clothes abandoned in chests, bedding left onn the beds. The difficulties of carrying belongings down the hill had induced the villagers to just leave everything behind them.

12   For this speech, see *Kowloon-Canton Railway (British Section): A History,* Robert J. Phillips, Urban Council, Hong Kong, 1990, Appendix, pp. 171-172

13   "Report on the New Territories, 1899-1912", G.N. Orme, District Officer, in *Papers Laid Before the Legislative Council of Hongkong, 1912* (Sessional Papers), No. 11/1912 (9th June 1912).

14   See P.H. Hase: "The Alliance of Nine: Traditional Sha Tin", Village Studies, op.cit,. See also P.H. Hase, "Land Hunger and Emigration from the New Territories Area in the Late Nineteenth Century", in 香港的歷史與社會研究, *Studies in Hong Kong History and Society*, pp. 130-153, and "Traditional Life in the New Territories: The Evidence of the 1911 and 1921 Censuses", in *Journal of the Hong Kong Branch of the Royal Asiatic Society*, Vol. 36, 1996, pp. 1-92,

15   See Ng Lun Ngai-ha, "Village Education in Transition: the Case of Sheung Shui" in *Journal of the Hong Kong Branch of the Royal Asiatic Society,* Vol. 22, 1982, pp. 252-270.

16 Depending on the number of through-trains required, and a number of other factors, the actual number of local trains each day varied from 18 to 28, but the manager of the Railway claimed that 24/26 trains a day was 'normal', and this timetable does seem to have been in place for much of the 1930s period. See Robert J. Phillips, *Kowloon-Canton Railway (British Section): A History*, Hong Kong, Urban Council, 1990.

17 See Rosemary Lee, "Tsang Tai Uk" in *Beyond the Metropolis: Villages in Hong Kong*, ed. P.H. Hase, Elizabeth Sinn, Royal Asiatic Society, Hong Kong Branch, with Joint Publishing (Hong Kong) Ltd, pp. 159-164.

18 It should be noted that delays in the processing of grants usually meant that the formal date of the grant was some six to eighteen months behind the actual date when the land was handed over, and this factor should be taken into account when considering these figures.

19 See Poon Shuk-wah, *Negotiating Religion in Modern China: State and Common People in Guangzhou, 1900-1937*, Chinese University Press, Hong Kong, 2011, for this period in Kwangtung.

20 See Marjorie Topley, *Cantonese Society in Hong Kong and Singapore: Gender, Religion, Medicine and Money*, Royal Asiatic Society Hong Kong Branch, with Hong Kong University Press, 2011, pp. 203-240 (reprinted from *Bulletin of the School of Oriental and African Studies,* 1963), and pp. 405-422 (with James W. Hayes) reprinted from *Journal of the Hong Kong Branch Royal Asiatic Society*, Vol. 8, 1968, pp. 135-151.

21 *A Gazetteer of Place Names in Hong Kong, Kowloon, and the New Territories*, Government Printer, Hong Kong, 1960.

22 See P.H. Hase, "Traditional Life in the New Territories: The Evidence of the 1911 and 1921 Censuses", in *Journal of the Hong Kong Branch of the Royal Asiatic Society*, Vol. 36, 1996, pp. 1-92.

23 See P.H. Hase, "Traditional Life in the New Territories" op.cit.

24 The Lion Rock Tunnel opened for traffic in 1967, but the waterpipes were opened through the tunnel in 1964, while the road tunnel was still under construction.

25 The New Town, however, had been agreed before the work on the racecourse had progressed beyond the initial reclamation stage, and the facility was planned into the New Town from the beginning.

26 A full discussion of these early proposals can be found in R. Bristow, *Hong Kong's New Towns: A Selective Review*, Oxford University Press, Hong Kong, 1989, especially ch. 5.

Plate 1: The Valley in 1930

Plate 2: The Valley in 1970

Plate 3: A Vegetable farmer in Sha Tin

Plate 4: The First Tai Po Road and the Valley in 1910

Plate 5: The Railway Station and Market 1955

Plate 6: The Railway Station and Market 1960

Plate 7: The Market 1955

Plate 8: Central Shatin 1963

Plate 9:An incense powder mill
about 1930

Plate 10: The Che Kung Temple 1970

Map 1　　The Kowloon Peak Villages

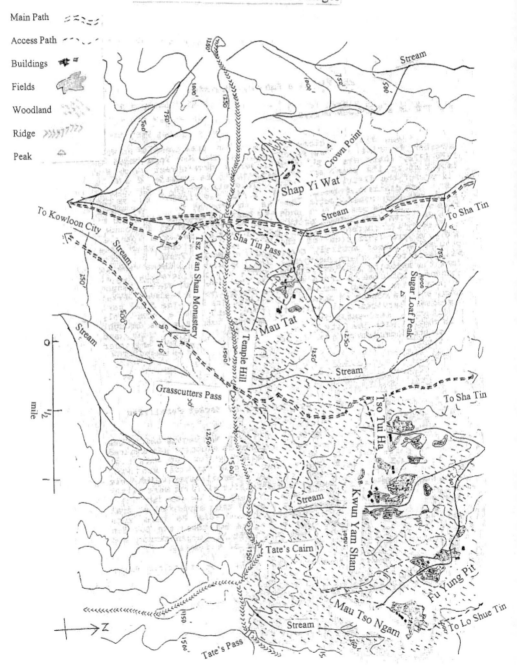

Map 2   Villages Abandoned in Sha Tin

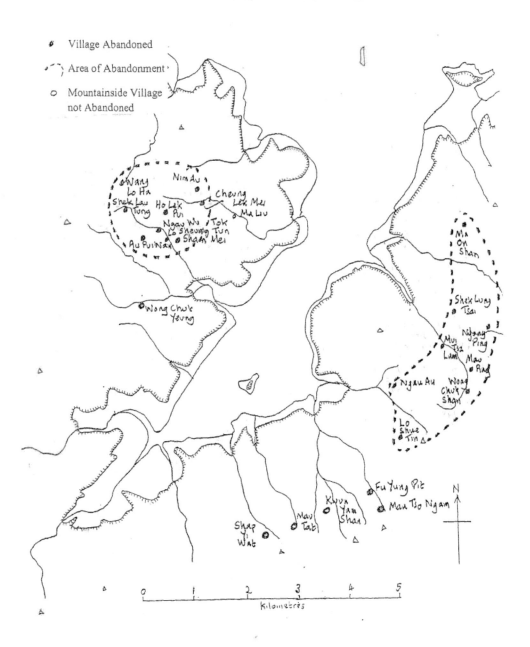

Map 3. Sha Tin Market

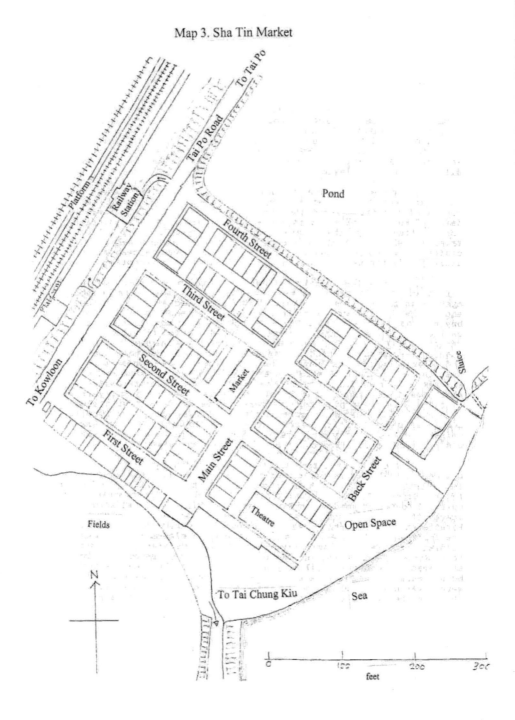

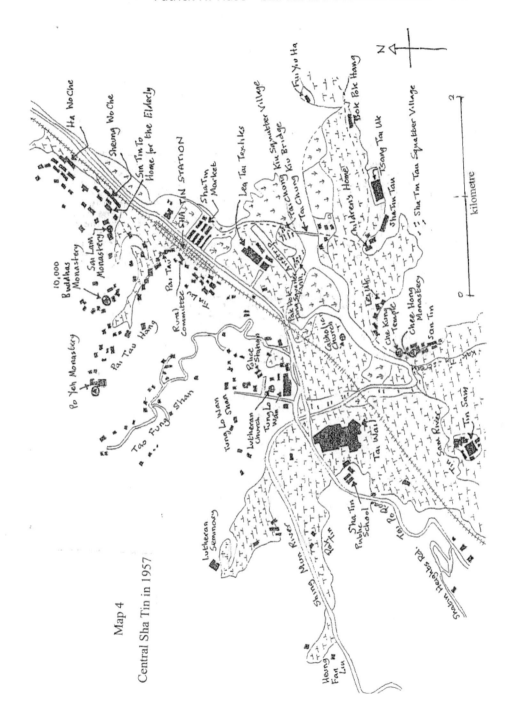

Map 4

Central Sha Tin in 1957

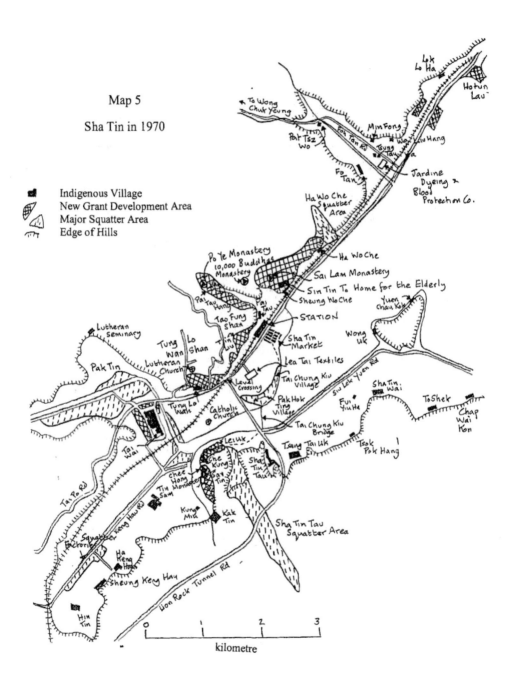

Map 5

Sha Tin in 1970

Indigenous Village
New Grant Development Area
Major Squatter Area
Edge of Hills

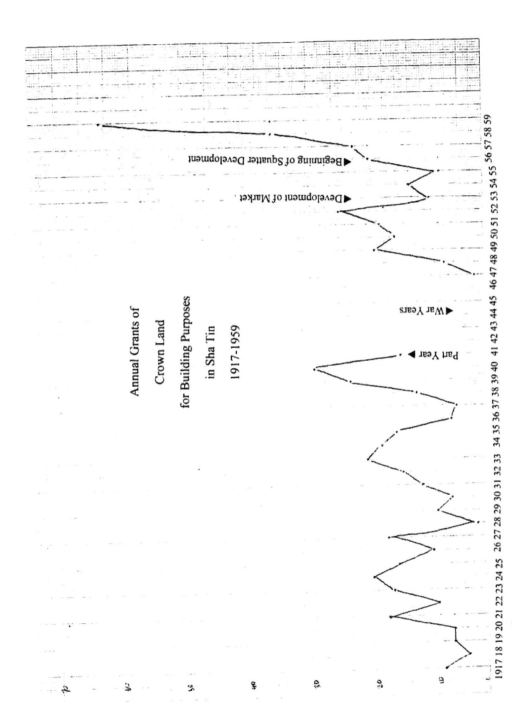

Annual Grants of

Crown Land

for Building Purposes

in Sha Tin

1917-1959

見步行步：
殖民地時期鯉魚門地區的防禦工事

鄺智文

香港浸會大學　歷史系

一、前　言

　　位於香港島東區的鯉魚門海峽是維多利亞港的東端出入口，其水道頗為狹窄，容易控制和監察，但亦容易被敵軍堵塞，是防衛海港與香港島的重要戰略據點。鯉魚門北岸有魔鬼山、海灣山，南岸則有西灣山等高地可以據守，這些山嶺均可以俯瞰鯉魚門海峽和藍塘海峽（Tathong　Channel，舊稱南堂海峽）。在英治時期（1841-1997），港島和九龍中間的海域成為亞洲其中一個最繁忙的港口——維多利亞港，加上鯉魚門是港島東的門戶，因此鯉魚門海峽的戰略地位極為重要。早於1880年代英軍在鯉魚門建立永久防禦工事以前，英軍、殖民地當局，以至在港英商已在討論如何在此地佈防。本文即以鯉魚門為案例，討論十九世紀末期至二十世紀中期香港防務的變遷及其各種背景與考量、不同參與者在政策制定與防衛布局討論中的角色，以及軍隊、文人政府與商人之間的合作與衝突，從中進一步認識英國與香港在殖民地時期的關係。本文認為，英軍處理防務問題時要應對不斷轉變的內外因素，其防禦設施的設計在實施時亦會不斷發現問題，

因此只能採取靈活的態度處理，不時進行改動以堵塞漏洞，
迹近「見步行步」之狀。

　　1841年英軍佔領香港島後，卑路乍海軍上校（Capt.
Edward Belcher）製作了一幅香港海圖，並在上面註明「鯉
魚門海峽」（Lye-moon Pass）的位置。兩年後，哥連臣海軍
上校（Capt. Richard Collinson）到香港島測量，他測量了
鯉魚門地區各山頭，並把海峽以西的一端以哥連臣角（Cape
Collinson）命名。[1]英軍在鯉魚門的首次駐軍並不成功。1840
年代初期，英軍曾派出20人到鯉魚門駐紮，但五周後已有五
人病死、六人需要留院。[2]戴偉思（Stephen Davies）研究西灣
砲台時，發現1845年的鯉魚門測量圖（繪制者為哥連臣工兵
中尉，哥連臣海軍上校的弟弟Lt. Thomas Collinson）曾標示
出「紫色位置預定興建堡壘地點（Proposed site for The Keep
coloured purple）」，認為該地可能曾有一個防禦工事，其
後更成為現存西環碉堡的一部分。[3]可是，在《1889年防衛
報告》（1889 Defence Scheme）中，西環並無可用的防禦工
事，預定在緊急時期才由皇家工兵負責興建。[4]因此，至1880
年代，鯉魚門並無英軍的永久防禦工事，此說應可成立。

　　自克里米亞戰爭（1854年至1856年）結束以來，香
港的防務均無多大變化。當時，香港的陸上駐軍只有約
千人，海軍兵力則通常只有一艘鐵甲艦、四艘蒸汽巡防
艦（Frigate）、四艘蒸汽護衛艦（Corvette）、一艘砲艇
（Sloop）、13艘小型砲艇（Gun Vessels），以及一艘通報

1　Stephen Davies, "Charting the China Coast 1841-1930,"Hong Kong
　　Maritime Museum.

2　Kwong Chi Man, Tsoi Yiu Lun, *Eastern Fortress: A Military History of
　　Hong Kong* (Hong Kong: Hong Kong University Press, 2014), p. 11.

3　Stephen Davies, et. al., "Saiwan Redoubt Part I: A Unique, Intriguing but
　　Neglected and Abused Example of Hong Kong's Military Heritage,"in
　　Surveying & Built Environment, Vol. 25, No. 1, 2016, p. 14.

4　"Report of Local Committee, with Letter of General Officer Command-
　　ing, and Appendices,"1889, CAB 11/57, p. 3.

艦（Despatch Vessel）。[5]以上所見艦艇雖多，但它們需要防護的範圍不只是香港，而是整個中國海岸以及東南亞水域，因此兵力實際上足襟見肘。與此同時，火砲與造船技術的躍進，使克里米亞戰爭或以前配置在香港的海防火砲大多已經落伍，不能面對新型的鐵甲軍艦。加上當時俄、法兩國在第二次鴉片戰爭（1856年至1860年）以後逐漸在亞洲拓展其勢力，英國國內遂出現加強殖民地防衛能力的聲音。早於1859年，香港政府已把白沙灣土地交給軍部興建砲台，但軍方未有實際行動。[6]1863年，時任助理要塞總監兼陸軍部防務委員會秘書賈維士上校（Col. William Jervois）提議加強香港的防務。其後，當時廣受關注的英國海軍思想家哥林白（John Colomb）亦提出香港在英國亞洲貿易與戰略的重要性。他寫道：「如香港或星加坡失陷，[英]帝國各地與中國或印度的貿易將受打擊⋯⋯如我們的海軍因兩地設防不足而被迫處於守勢而不能主動出擊，則貿易仍受傷害，結果將如上同。」[7]

可是，由於1860年代英國面對的實際外患並不嚴重，因此即使賈維士提出多個關於在香港建立新砲台的建議，歷屆政府均沒有實行。在這些建議中，他曾提出在維港東西兩端的出入口建立砲台；這是首次有英國軍官提出在維港東端建立永久防禦工事。[8]直至1877年，由於英國政府與俄國因近東問題再次交惡，英國政府才組成了殖民地防務委員會（Colonial Defence Committee）再次研究殖民地港口的防務安排，並在翌年4月由米憐海軍上將（Adm. Alexander Mline）擔任主席的委員會提交報告，把香港列為第二個最

5　*The NavyList* (London: John Murray, 1876), pp. 131, 136-137, 142-143, 147, 155, 158-160, 164, 177-179, 182-183.

6　Philip Bruce, *Lyemun Barracks: 140 Years of Military History* (Hong Kong: Self-Published, 1993), p. 8.

7　John Colomb, *The Defence of Great and Greater Britain: Sketches of its Naval, Military, and Political Aspects* (1880), (London: Eilbron, 2005), p. 106.

8　Kwong Chi Man, Tsoi Yiu Lun, *Eastern Fortress*, p. 21.

優先要加強防禦能力的港口。[9]

二、1870年代在鯉魚門海峽佈防的想法

正如米憐委員會提交的報告指出，當時香港「沒有防務可言」，僅有的美利（Murray）與威靈頓（Wellington）砲台均被其後興建的建築物包圍，因此全無作用。當委員會要港督軒尼斯（John Pope Hennessy）與在港英軍首腦討論防禦問題時，他在1877年7月與時任駐港陸軍司令柯布連陸軍少將（Maj. Gen. Francis Colborne）見面，後者提到如果英國與其他國家在歐洲開戰，香港的守軍人數將大為減少，因此有必要預先加強香港的工事。其後，軒尼斯與以香港為司令部的中國艦隊（China Station）兩任司令賴德海軍中將（Vice-Adm. Alfred Ryder）與曉義海軍雅中將（Vice-Adm. CharlesHillyar）分別再次討論如何有效保護香港的方法。以上三人均認為應該以砲台與魚雷封鎖維多利亞港東西兩端的入口，以保護市中心以及港內船隻。可是，當時駐港英軍代任司令巴山路陸軍上校（Col. Bassano）卻拒絕在維港兩端安裝砲台，只是在市區建立了臨時砲台。[10]

在最後報告中，委員會的意見與賈維士以及柯布連、賴德、曉義雅等人一樣，認為香港最重要的防衛問題是維港兩端的出入口，因此有必要在兩地建立砲台。報告特別提出鯉魚門的戰略重要性：「港島東端的鯉魚門需要以防禦設施封鎖，以免敵艦得以進入……要達成這個目的，則需要一定數量安裝在永久砲台中的火砲，以及大量水雷」。[11]可是，報

9　Kwong Chi Man, Tsoi yiu Lun, *Eastern Fortress*, pp. 21-22.

10　"GovernorHennessy to Hicks Beach," 11/5/1878, The National Archives UK, (TNA), CAB 7/1, p. 88.

11　"Report of a Colonial Defence Committee on the Temporary Defences of the Cape of Good Hope, Mauritius, Ceylon, Singapore, and Hong Kong,"TNA, CAB 7/1, p.

告亦指出當時並不應該立刻在鯉魚門設立砲台：[12]

> 如要在鯉魚門建立有效的防禦，則必需在可以俯瞰海峽的地方興建兩個砲台，使它們可以射擊嘗試穿過狹窄海峽的船艦。可是，這個海峽不能以障礙物完全封鎖，加上該地水流湍急，因此不可以只依靠鯉魚門的砲台，而是需要有第二道防線。因此，北角與九龍船塢均需要配備火砲，以阻止敵艦穿過海峽砲擊市區、設施，以及港內船隻。

> 鯉魚門附近有些可以俯瞰它的山頭，更在其步槍射程範圍內，而附近又有一些可以登陸的地點，加上有數千名異族（alien）居民住在鄰近地區（指筲箕灣一帶）；另一方面，此地距離駐軍集中地市中心有七哩之遙；因此，在此地配置重砲並建築防禦工事保護它們並不可行，因為此舉將牽制[守軍]大量兵力。故此，本委員會放棄在此地建立砲台的想法。

可見，當時英軍認為雖然鯉魚門對防衛維多利亞港以及市區頗為重要，但由於上述原因，英軍放棄了建築砲台的想法，而從下文可見，後來建築鯉魚門要塞時，亦可見以上考慮主導了要塞以及其設施的設計以及兵力配置。

三、興建鯉魚門要塞，1878-1886

殖民地委員會提交臨時防禦設施的報告後，內閣成立另一個委員會研究各殖民地的長遠防禦辦法。1881年，皇家工兵上校哥士文（Col. William Crossman, RE）被派到香港協助計畫永久防務。他和由港督以及海陸軍司令組成的「本

---

12 Ibid., p. 14.

土防務委員會」（Local Defence Committee）在香港島和九龍進行實地視察，並提交了完整的計畫。與1878年的計畫一樣，哥士文的計畫以及香港防務委員會的修訂計劃均未有打算把砲台設置在鯉魚門，而是將之設置在鰂魚涌（英文稱為石場角，Quarry Point，即今日太古船塢的位置），並於對開海面佈置水雷，以保護正在計劃興建的新船塢。[13]當時，政府已有計劃在石場角附近興建新船塢；哥士文提交其報告到內閣委員會時，附上的地圖已清楚指出此事。[14]其後，英國政府撥出37,500鎊購買新砲予香港安裝，並開始計劃興建新砲台。[15]1884年，駐港英軍在鯉魚門試驗佈雷，並以中英文在憲報刊登此事，要求所有船隻「倘經過鯉魚門之時須駛向中國地界而去，切勿駛近香港之界，防遇水雷之險。」[16]其後，陸軍部研究在香港島一側的鯉魚門岸上以1,000英鎊興建一個小砲台，以保護雷區，計劃配置在這個砲台的火砲是1860年代已投入服務的40磅後裝砲（40-pounder breech loader）。[17]

可是，在鯉魚門興建輔助砲台這一安排，竟引來香港本地商人頗大反彈。自1880年代英國研究香港長期防務開始，香港的輿論已不時提出在鯉魚門興建砲台的問題。[18]得知鯉魚門的砲台將會裝備40磅砲後，時任定例局非官守議員的匯

13　"Third and Final Report of the Royal Commissioners Appointed to Enquire into the Defence of British Possessions and Commerce Aboard,"1882, TNA, CAB7/4, unpaginated map; "Colonel Crossman to the Inspector General of Fortifications,"24/10/1881, TNA, CAB 7/4, pp. 315-325.

14　"Third and Final Report of the Royal Commissioners Appointed to Enquire into the Defence of British Possessions and Commerce Aboard," unpaginated map.

15　"Governor Sir Bowen to the Secretary of State," 31/1/1885, Sessional Papers 1885, p. 151.

16　《香港轅門報》，1884年2月9日。

17　"GovernorSir Bowen to the Secretary of State," 31/1/1885, p. 149.

18　Philip Bruce, *Lyemun Barracks*, p. 8.

豐銀行總經理昃臣（Sir Thomas Jackson）就此事質詢港督，直言這些火砲過於老舊，「比沒有任何防禦工事更壞」。他又再次指出應擴建香港的工事，使海軍無需擔心香港防務，使之可以離港攻擊敵國艦隊並保護香港的對外貿易，使香港這個「東方的瑰寶可以成為船隻的避難所」。[19]昃臣的質詢使定例局決定由香港出資55,625鎊用作增強香港海防工事之用，但條件是英國必需提供「最佳和最新型的後裝火砲，而且是可以抵抗最重型的現代鐵甲艦的款式」。[20]有見在港商人決意要港府出鉅資在鯉魚門興建要塞，倫敦承諾給予香港80,000鎊的火砲，並增加砲兵數量。由於香港與倫敦方面均大幅增加撥款，因此軍方重新規劃海岸砲的佈局。本來，軍方只打算興建三個大型砲台（昂船洲、卑路乍角、石場角），以及鯉魚門的小砲台。新計畫則有八個砲台，其中鯉魚門砲台最為昂貴，造價25,000鎊（不計算火砲）。[21]這個安排明顯是為了安撫在倫敦擁有一定勢力的英商群體。

四、鯉魚門要塞的設計與功能

至1889年6月，新建成的鯉魚門砲台第一次進行演習，砲台不久即啟用。[22]在《防衛計畫》（Defence Scheme）中，鯉魚門砲台的主要任務就是要保護海峽以及要塞對開海面的鯉魚門雷區（Lyemun minefield）。其時，守軍已撤回石場角外海的雷區，使維港東端的防禦重心西移至鯉魚門海峽。當時，守軍即已發現要塞的武裝極不理想，其武裝以及實際射

19　"Governor Sir Bowen to the Secretary of State," 31/1/1885, p. 150.

20　"Governor Sir Bowen to the Secretary of State," 31/1/1885, p. 151.

21　"Extract from letter from the War Office to Colonial Office," 19/9/1885, Sessional Paper 1886, p. 126.

22　"Government Notification No. 26," The Hongkong Government Gazette, 22/6/1889, p. 522.

界如下：[23]

1.　　兩門9吋12噸前裝來福線重砲（1887年安裝於西砲台）：其中一門只能覆蓋港內雷區，不能指向海峽；另一門雖然指向海峽，但由於位置太高，因此只能覆蓋四分之一的海峽水面。[24]

2.　　兩門6.3吋64磅前裝來福線重砲（1887年安裝中央砲台）：只能向對岸射擊，並不能向水面發砲。

3.　　兩門6吋IV型（6-inch BL Mark IV）後裝隱沒式來福線砲（鯉魚門碉堡）：射程最遠，可以覆蓋內港與海峽以外的水面，但位置仍然太高，因此船隻可以在死角下面經過。

4.　　三門9吋12噸前裝來福線重砲（1887年安裝於反向砲台）：由於射界太窄，它們射擊通過海峽的船隻時只能各發射一砲，但它們又不能保護雷區，因為其砲火覆蓋範圍會威脅到防禦雷區的警備艇。

　　當時，要塞分為西、中央、反向（West, Central, Reverse）三個主要砲台，以及鯉魚門碉堡（Lyemun Redoubt）本身。可是，英國政府和軍方明顯沒有兌現在港英商的要求，即為鯉魚門要塞提供「最佳和最新型的後裝火砲，而且是可以抵抗最重型的現代鐵甲艦的款式」。上述火砲幾乎全是前裝來福線砲，只有兩門6吋IV型後裝來福線砲可被稱為新式火砲，但它們的位置亦嫌太高，不能全面控制海峽。從要塞以及保護砲台的防禦工事規模可以看出，守軍仍然認為鯉魚門比較孤立，因此需要加強其工事以防被敵軍登陸佔領，並

23　Alan Harfield, *British and Indian Armies on the China Coast, 1785-1965* (London: A and J Partnership, 1990), p. 211;"Report on the Defence of Hong Kong,"30/7/1886, CAB 11/57, Part II, p. 4.

24　Philip Bruce 指英軍在香港使用的9吋砲可能可以大仰角射擊；如根據以上《防禦計劃》的描述，則它們很可能只是普通仰角的火砲。Philip Bruce, Lyemun Barracks, p. 9.

以工事彌補士兵數量，以免守軍需要分割出大量步兵防守要塞。1889年《防衛計畫》中，負責守備要塞的兵力包括200名步兵、26名皇家砲兵、110名印度砲手、22名皇家工兵（其中12人負責雷區）。當時香港守軍人數一共3,061人，即鯉魚門要塞一地的守軍已佔全體守軍百分之十。[25]

　　從上述可見，要塞各砲台未能有效阻止船隻突破鯉魚門海峽，而且這些火砲根本不能應付快速通過海峽的敵艦。其後，要塞不斷新增設施，尤其是增加可以有效阻止敵艦接近海峽雷區的火砲。1892年，英軍考慮安裝兩門6磅哈乞開斯（Hotchkiss）速射砲於西砲台附近近岸位置，以抵禦可能出現的魚雷艇攻擊。[26]其後，軍方決定安裝6磅速射砲（即今日之渡口砲台）並在鯉魚門碉堡以西的海岸安裝兩門12磅速射砲。[27]布倫南魚雷（Brennan Torpedo）站亦於1894年啟用。[28]布倫南魚雷由愛爾蘭工程師布倫南發明，早於1879年已曾進行試射。經十多年研發後，英國陸軍部終於在1891年決定在英帝國15個港口建立魚雷站。由於香港可能受俄法兩國鐵甲艦的威脅，因此陸軍部亦建議在香港建立魚雷站，而由於魚雷射程只有約2,000米，因此最適合使用的地點自然是鯉魚門海峽。[29]另外，砲台附近的西灣亦增設榴彈砲位，它們以高仰角射擊，其砲彈可以打在其他火砲不能覆蓋的水面上。至1895年，要塞附近開始興建軍營，造價為8,850鎊。[30]英軍亦於軍營後方的西灣山興建一個碉堡，於1895年完成，但規模

25　"Report of Local Committee," 7/1889, CAB 11/57, Part II, pp. 15, 22.

26　Alan Harfield, p. 211.

27　"Report of Local Joint Naval and Military Committee of April 1894," CAB 11/57, Part I, pp. 17.

28　"Remarks by the Colonial Defence Committee," 23/7/1894, CAB 11/57, Part I, p. 13.

29　Kwong Chi Man, Tsoi Yiu Lun, *Eastern Fortress*, pp. 42-43.

30　"Estimate for Barrack Works for Accommodating Increased garrison, and for some Other Urgent Services," Sessional Papers 1895, p. 468.

較小，只大約容納一個步兵班。[31]同年，駐港英軍建議在鯉魚門要塞增設三個探射燈，其後亦陸續安裝。[32]

五、鯉魚門要塞的軍事生涯，1886-1945

鯉魚門要塞投入使用時，正是軍艦設計再次出現巨大變化之時。當時，英國剛於1889年通過《海軍法案》（1889 Naval Act），建造一批新型的軍艦，其中包括懷特（William White）設計的新型戰列艦（皇權級，Royal Sovereign Class）以及擁有裝甲甲板的防護巡洋艦（protected cruisers）。它們的出現，隨即引起英國的潛在對手法、俄等國設計出一批新型軍艦。它們的火力、防禦力，以及速度均比以往的軍艦大增，鯉魚門的前裝來福線砲顯然不能面對新的威脅。與此同時，後裝來福線砲亦解決了以往砲尾不夠可靠的問題，並成為制式武器，安裝在新型軍艦和海岸砲台上。由於火砲、造艦技術的改進，駐港英軍以及部分政府和商界人士均提出向清政府租借新界，以增強香港的防衛。1899年英國佔穩新界後，鯉魚門的砲位再有不少改動。1901年，英軍開始在鯉魚門碉堡的西端興建白沙灣砲台（Pak Sha Wan Battery，1903年啟用），並於對岸的魔鬼山興建砵甸乍（Pottinger Battery）和歌賦砲台（Gough Battery）。它們全部備有新型的後裝來福線砲，其射界均可以覆蓋藍塘海峽，意味著敵艦早於接近維港時即會被截擊。[33]此舉亦使鯉魚門要塞的武裝基本上已

31 Stephen Davies, et. al., "Saiwan Redoubt Part I: A Unique, Intriguing but Neglected and Abused Example of Hong Kong's Military Heritage,"in *Surveying & Built Environment*, Vol. 25, No. 1, 2016, p. 19.

32 "Electric Lights as Proposed by the Local Joint Naval and Military Committee in their Report dated July 1895," CAB 11/57, Part I, p. 28.

33 Tse Tak-San, "Pak Sha Wan Battery: A Case Study of a Hong Kong Military Heritage Site," Hong Kong University Unpublished MS Thesis, p. 17.

無多大作用，包括花費鉅大的布倫南魚雷發射站。日俄戰爭
（1904-1905）後，英國軍方派出陸軍上將奧雲（Gen. John
Owen）率領委員會研究減少並更新香港的海防砲台，該委
員會決定把鯉魚門要塞的所有火砲拆下，剩下白沙灣砲台（
改為三門6吋砲）以及對岸的砵甸乍和歌賦砲台。[34]至1912
年，鯉魚門要塞只剩下這些裝備：[35]

1.　西砲台：兩門4.7吋後裝速射砲、兩門6磅速射砲
2.　鯉魚門碉堡以西海岸：兩門12磅速射砲
3.　四個探射燈

　　第一次世界大戰（1914-1918）後，鯉魚門要塞的固定
砲台已不在《防衛計畫》的固定武器名單之中，但何時拆去
則屬疑問。由於飛機的出現，鯉魚門要塞這種巨大的建築群

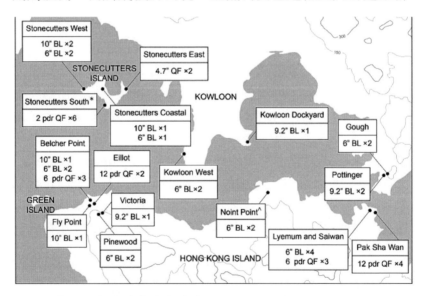

圖一：約1905年的香港海岸砲台（資料來源：Kwong Chi Man, Tsoi Yiu
　　　Lun, *Eastern Fortress: A Military History of Hong Kong* (Hong Kong:
　　　Hong Kong University Press, 2014), p. 44.）

34　"Revision of Fixed Defences," 7/3/1907, CAB 11/57, Part II, pp.
　　4-5.
35　Alan Harfield, p. 210.

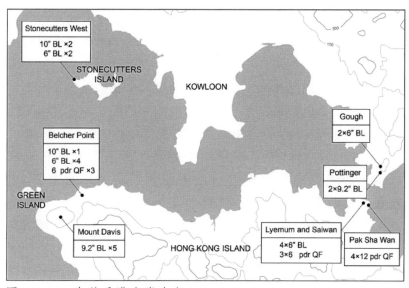

圖二：1912年的香港海岸砲台（資料來源：Kwong Chi Man, Tsoi Yiu Lun, *Eastern Fortress*, p. 45..）

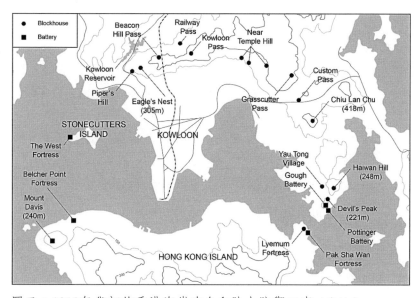

圖三：1910年代初的香港海岸砲台和陸上防禦工事（資料來源：Kwong Chi Man, Tsoi Yiu Lun, *Eastern Fortress*, p. 60.）

太易被發現並集中攻擊，因此英軍沒有在此地配置火砲，而只有在附近興建了有掩蔽的彈藥庫。[36]1930年代末期，英軍在鯉魚門地區的主要固定防禦設施，包括擁有四門3吋高射砲的西灣砲台（Sai Wan Battery）、擁有三門6吋火砲的白沙灣砲台，成為彈藥庫的要塞，以及海岸的探射燈和機槍堡。可是，西灣山雖然是港島東其中一個最重要的制高點，並於1890年代建成碉堡，但在1930年代竟未有被計劃者留意並加強其防務。

　　1941年12月8日日軍進攻香港時，鯉魚門要塞已沒有火砲，鄰近的白沙灣砲台（由香港義勇防衛軍砲兵第4連負責）和西灣的高射砲台（由香港義勇防衛軍砲兵第5連負責）仍有岸砲與高射炮，要塞和軍營用作彈藥庫以及儲藏物資之地，守軍有加拿大皇家來福槍營A連的兩個排。此外，附近亦有皇家香港星加坡砲兵團的陣地。[37]可是，不明就裡的日軍卻以為要塞仍有砲台，因此在英軍撤出九龍後不斷砲轟要塞，使之彈痕累累。[38]根據日軍資料，日軍曾利用其重砲轟擊鯉魚門要塞，詳細情況如下：[39]

1. 白沙灣砲台
   攻擊日期：12月13至17日（所有時間為東京時間，即GMT+9；當時香港使用星加坡時間，即GMT +7.5）
   負責部隊：獨立重砲兵第三大隊
   所用彈藥：八九式150毫米加農砲穿甲彈165發、榴彈226發
   結果：觀測所被毀、英軍放棄砲台陣地

2. 鯉魚門要塞西砲台附近營房

36　Philip Bruce, *Lyemun Barracks*, p. 32.

37　Ibid., 33.

38　鄺智文、蔡耀倫，《孤獨前哨：太平洋戰爭中的香港戰役》（香港：天地，2013），頁215-217。

39　北島騏子雄，《香港要塞ノ研究》，1942年1月，東京靖國神社遊就館藏

攻擊日期：12月14日下午3時40分至4時40分
負責部隊：獨立重砲兵第三大隊
所用彈藥：八九式150毫米加農砲榴彈18發
結果：9彈命中，營房被破壞
備註：當時日軍誤認此兵房為英軍6吋砲砲台

3. 鯉魚門要塞
攻擊日期：12月14日下午12時40分至2時05分
負責部隊：獨立重砲兵第三大隊
所用彈藥：八九式150毫米加農砲榴彈125發
結果：要塞表面受損

4. 鯉魚門軍營
攻擊日期：12月15日下午6時06分至6時23分
負責部隊：獨立重砲兵第三大隊
所用彈藥：八九式150毫米加農砲榴彈20發
結果：9彈命中，營房損毀

5. 鯉魚門探射燈台
攻擊日期：12月18日下午20時35分至9時45分
負責部隊：獨立重砲兵第三大隊
所用彈藥：八九式150毫米加農砲榴彈7發
結果：1彈命中，探射燈被毀

　　日軍登陸時，要塞的探射燈曾協助照射登陸的日軍，引導守軍向其開火，但日軍上岸後，第229聯隊很快便佔領了鯉魚門要塞；日軍更在附近的西灣砲台屠殺了部分英印軍以及本地官兵和醫務人員。[40]日軍快速佔領西灣，使使之得以控制港島東，並逼使英軍向赤柱方向撤退。在日據時期，日本在港駐軍不多，而且多集中在港島西面，沒有使用鯉魚

---

40 同上註，頁236、388-392；Philip Bruce, *Lyemun Barracks*, pp. 34-35.

門要塞的紀錄，只有西灣砲台曾繼續被使用為高射砲台。戰後，由於鯉魚門要塞太容易從空中被發現，而且接近市區，加上大多設備均在戰爭中損毀，駐港英軍重新使用鯉魚門要塞及其設施為倉庫而非軍事基地；1946年3月21日，英軍清理該地軍火時曾發生爆炸，導致一名英軍死亡，鄰近村落亦有一名老婦死亡，多人受傷，海上的艇戶亦遭波及。為表揚該英兵休士（Joseph Hughes）在爆炸前嘗試救火並提醒他人走避，他榮獲喬治十字勳章（George Cross）。[41]

　　1957年，英軍撤去所有香港的海防砲台，鯉魚門要塞和白沙灣砲台均被棄用。該地只剩下鯉魚門軍營以及鄰近的西灣高射砲台（擁有四門Mark 2C 型3.7吋高射砲，有雷達協助射擊）尚在服務。鯉魚門要塞本身雖然繼續是軍事範圍，但英軍已不再使用該地。1973年，該地發現一門不知何時從要塞拆下來的6吋火砲。1965年開始，要塞南面的鯉魚門軍營成為華籍陸軍部隊「香港陸軍服務團」（Hong Kong Military Service Corps）的營房。據曾經服務於鯉魚門軍營的華籍英兵回憶，他們只會於野外訓練時才會到舊要塞，該地已無現役的軍事設施。至1980年代初，香港陸軍服務團的基地轉移至剛完成改建的昂船洲軍營，鯉魚門軍營則由第7愛丁堡公爵喊喀步槍團第2營（2nd Bn., 7th Duke of Edinburgh's Own Gurkha Rifles）接手使用，直至1986年。翌年3月，所有英軍從鯉魚門撤出。

六、結　語

　　綜觀殖民地時期鯉魚門軍事設施的發展歷史，可見英國在應對不斷變化的軍事技術、國際環境，以及國內情況時，在有限的資源下加強香港的防務，直至1950年代英國不再是亞洲軍事上的要角為止。由於皇家海軍在英國佔領香港初期

41　Philip Bruce, *Lyemun Barracks*, pp. 38-39.

對東亞水域有幾乎絕對的控制，除了在克里米亞戰爭時的緊
急狀態之外，香港無須興建大規模的海防設施。至1870年代
末期，有見法、俄威脅增加，加上後裝砲和鐵甲軍艦出現，
遂有在鯉魚門興建新型砲台之議，但香港和倫敦政府，以至
軍民雙方卻對如何實行有不同看法，其中殖民地商業精英亦
極力施加其影響力。可是，1880年代初開始興建，1886年完
成的鯉魚門要塞可謂大而無當，未能實際提供足夠的保護。
這是因為砲台設計本身的缺陷，而且未能應對科技急速的轉
變。其後，英軍即嘗試利用速射砲和魚雷加強防備，最終於
1900年代在鯉魚門北岸的魔鬼山興建兩個備有後裝重砲的砲
台，以覆蓋藍塘海峽，並以鯉魚門要塞以西的白沙灣砲台提
供近距離支援，才暫時解決了鯉魚門的防衛問題，直至第一
次世界大戰結束為止。其後，由於日本空軍日漸強大，加上
香港防衛計劃改變使英軍決定將所有海防火砲設於港島，鯉
魚門要塞和北岸兩個砲台遂不再使用，只剩下白沙灣砲台和
西灣的高射砲台。至日軍於1941年入侵香港時，該地砲台亦
曾使用，但成效有限。第二次世界大戰後，鯉魚門地區的砲
台已無軍事價值，但在該地的軍營則繼續被英軍使用，直至
1990年代。從本文可見，研究香港軍事歷史時，必須將之置
於國際與軍事技術/科技發展背景之下，並瞭解殖民地和帝國
整體防務之間的張力、殖民地社會（主要指其精英）對英國
國防政策的影響，以及軍事變革的複雜性與侷限。

附錄：鯉魚門防禦工事曾使用的火砲

前裝砲

- ### 6.3、9吋前裝來福線砲（6.3, 9-inch Rifled Muzzled Loader, RML）

火器特別委員會建議暫時停用後裝砲後，英國海陸軍推出了一系列中型與重型前裝來福線砲，用以裝備軍艦與海岸砲台。它們在1860年代開始出現，直至英軍1879年英軍再次決定使用後裝砲後才被逐漸替換，至1900年代從香港的第一線退役。這些火砲的設計基本相同，全都擁有數層熟鐵加強的砲身，其後膛部分比前膛更厚，以抵住引爆推進藥時的壓力，有來福線的一層砲管被多層砲身套上，有三條坑紋（grooves）。此砲的砲彈彈上有圓釘（stud），使砲彈發射時可順著來福線射出。1878年，香港第一次配備這種前裝來福線砲，其口徑為7吋，來自皇家海軍中國基地的艦隻。使用這些火砲，是因為倫敦方面在1877年命令香港緊急增加海防砲台，因此只能就地取材。鯉魚門的防禦工事曾使用以下前裝砲：[42]

·6.3吋64磅前裝來福線砲（RML 64-Pounder）

口徑6.3吋（160毫米），砲膛長97.5吋（2.477米），倍徑為15.48，砲重約3,300公斤，砲彈為64磅（29公斤），最大射程約4,000碼（3,657.6米）

·9吋12噸前裝來福線砲（12 Ton 9-inch RML）

42　Royal Gun Factory, Treatise on the Construction and Manufacture of Ordnance in the British Service (London: HMSO, 1877), plates V, X, XI, XII; Ordnance College, Textbook of Gunnery (London: HMSO, 1902), table XII, p. 338.

口徑9吋（228.6毫米），砲膛長125吋（3.6米），倍徑為13.88，砲重約12,192.6公斤，砲彈為250 至256磅（113.4至116.1公斤），最大射程約6,000碼（5,486.4米）

後裝砲類

．6吋後裝來福線砲IV、V型（6-inch BL Mark IV, Mark V）

1879年英國陸軍決定重新使用後裝砲後，艾斯域公司（Elswick，台譯艾斯維克，中同）於翌年提出新設計，其重點是新型的隔螺式後膛（interrupted screw）。新系統在後膛和尾栓均刻有斷續的螺旋紋，尾栓關上後，砲手要旋轉尾栓使兩者的螺旋緊扣。此舉使砲尾鎖死，阻止高壓空氣從後膛溢出。新系統不但更為安全，更允許火砲裝上更多推進藥，把砲彈射得更遠，因此砲管亦隨之得以增長，使其射程可達約8,000米，遠超所有前裝來福線砲。1880年，英國海陸軍開始使用此砲，在香港使用者為該砲的IV、V型，安裝在1880至1890年代建成的砲台，包括鯉魚門要塞的隱沒式砲台。其主要參數如下：[43]

．　IV型

口徑為6吋（152毫米），砲管長156吋（3.962米），倍徑為26，砲重約4,100公斤，砲彈為100磅（45.3公斤），最大射程約8,000米（15度射角）。

．　V型

口徑為6吋（152毫米），砲管長183.48吋（4.66米），倍徑為30.58，砲彈為100磅（45.3公斤），最大射程約7,300米。

．6吋後裝來福線砲VII型（6-inch BL Mark VII）

此砲由維克斯公司（Vickers）研發，1899年開始使

43　Ibid, table XII, p. 336.

用。1910年代奧雲委員會提出更新香港砲台的建議後開始使用，直至第二次世界大戰結束為止，是除了早期的滑膛砲以外，香港服役最長的海岸砲之一。它使用絲絨袋包裝的推進藥，和砲彈分開裝填。其口徑為6吋（152毫米），砲重6,350公斤，砲管長269.68吋（6.85米），倍徑44.9，砲彈為100磅（45.3公斤），最大射程約12,000碼（10,972.8米）。鯉魚門要塞附近的白沙灣砲台裝備了此種火砲。[44]

速射砲類

·4.7吋後裝速射砲（4.7-inch QF）

　　1880年代英軍轉用後裝砲後，艾斯域兵工廠設計了「速射砲」（Quick-firing Gun, QF），它使用砲彈與推進藥合為一體的彈藥。與以往彈藥分離不同，速射砲砲彈利用合金彈殼把砲彈與推進藥包裹在一起，使砲手毋須分開裝填，加上後裝設計，砲彈的裝填時間大減，改良後的砲架亦有效吸收火砲射擊時的後座力，使火砲能快速回到本來位置與角度，增加了射擊的速度。如操作得宜，一門4.7吋速射砲每分鐘可以發射大約十砲，是舊式火砲的數倍。甲午戰爭期間，裝備有大量速射砲的日本艦隊對清帝國的北洋艦隊造成重大損毀，但由於速射砲口徑通常不大於6吋，因此破壞力有限，未能把北洋艦隊的鐵甲艦「定遠」和「鎮遠」擊沈。在此期間，英軍的速射砲大多安裝在戰列艦與巡洋艦上，成為它們的副砲，其主要功能並非攻擊鐵甲軍艦，而是擊退體型小而速度快的魚雷艇。英軍在香港使用的4.7吋速射砲口徑為4.72吋（120毫米），砲身長189吋（480.06厘米），倍徑為40，砲身重4,592磅（2,082.89公斤），彈重45磅（20.41公斤）射程8,500碼（7,772.4米）。[45]可見，雖然此砲名為「速射砲」，但砲彈重逾20公斤，要在射擊時不斷迅速裝填，實非易事。在香港，只有鯉魚門西砲台和1930年代興建的春坎角砲

44　Ibid, table XII, p. 336.

45　Ibid, table XII, p. 337.

台曾安裝此種火砲。

・12磅後裝速射砲（12-Pounder QF）

此砲主要安裝在各級軍艦上用以驅逐敵軍水雷艇，或成為驅逐艦和水雷艇等小型軍艦的主砲。它的口徑為3吋（76.2毫米），砲身長84吋（213.36厘米），倍徑為28，砲身重896磅（406.42公斤），彈重12.5磅（5.67公斤），射程5,100碼（4,663.44米）。[46]鯉魚門要塞的西砲台（現稱渡口砲台）曾於1891年安裝此砲，但1941年前已經拆除。

・6磅後裝速射砲（哈乞開斯Hotchkiss型）
（6-Pounder QF Hotchkiss）

此砲用途與上述12磅砲相類，其口徑為2.24吋（57毫米），砲身長89.76吋（228厘米），倍徑為40，砲身重821磅（372公斤），彈重6磅（2.7公斤），有效距離約4,000碼（3,700米）。鯉魚門碉堡以西的海岸砲台曾安裝此砲，但1941年前已經拆除。

46　Ibid, table XII, p. 337.

香港科學工藝教育的源頭:
以李陞格致工藝學堂和
香港實業專科學院為例

馬冠堯

香港大學房地產及建設系

　　中國於1905年廢科舉,作出歷史重大改變,士人出路有根本的轉變,西方的科學工藝教育傳入遠東,無論是放洋或在本土學習科學工藝,都大有機會進身士途。在這過渡期間,香港科學工藝教育又是怎樣,筆者選取了李陞格致工藝學堂和香港實業專科學院,簡單介紹香港科學工藝教育的源頭。

一、科學工藝教育(Technical Education)

　　甚麼是科學工藝教育?東西方工藝一般是指以手做成的工藝品(Hand Made)。西方工業革命帶來了機器和電源,工藝品亦從手做轉變為機造,及後蒸汽機亦發展至電動機。機器和電動機的發明來自科學的應用,而科學就有一大堆理論,如物理、化學和生物等。將科學理論運用到改善日常生活,粗略地講就是科學工藝,例如以蒸汽機推動輪船和火車取代人力車,又例如運用力學去建造房屋,又或運用電學製造電話等,都是科學工藝技術。在西方,科學工藝(technical)一詞是包含科學(science)和藝術(art)，亦帶有專門行業(professional trade)之意。[1]將科學理論應用到改善人類生活必先要掌握科學基本知識。西方大學早期只講授和研發科學理論，甚少應用，但工人必須擁有基本科學知識，才可製造出有效能的機器或電器，更重要是生產過程時的安全。工人因此也分技術和非技術性。要培訓技術工人，那就要從教育入手，因而衍生了科學工藝教育。

二、中國科學工藝教育

中國的四大發明開啓了人類的資訊、軍事和導航的新方向。當中造紙和印刷術更是文明傳承的重要工具，開闢學術領域。雖然指南針最早是用於占卜和堪輿，但其後的發展至定位，三維空間，甚至包括時間的四維空間，至今天的衛星導航，亦無法完全取代。磁力學後更發展至電磁學，徹底改變了人類的生活習慣。火藥的發明常給人一個負面感覺－戰爭的禍害。其實它有其主要功能如開墾土地、開鑿隧道和捕魚等。那時沒有甚麼科技教育，似乎先賢全都是自學成功。一個有趣的問題就是這些新科技是如何承傳呢？通常新科技會被視為秘密，不容易向別人透露。故此，父子相傳是最可靠，又或是通過師徒關係傳承。宗師通常不易授徒，我們常在小說或戲中看到一代宗師在挑選徒弟時抱嚴謹態度，往往以最高道德標準和天份為依歸，而拜師儀式莊嚴。香港在廿世紀五六十年代，常見到中醫或跌打醫生的廣告：「某某授男或某某授徒」，又常聞武術界有「家傳祕笈」。這些見聞雖然很難找到歷史實証，但社會無專利法規，道德是法律審判的唯一標準，其亦有可信的一面。鄺華汰於十九世紀末在美國的成人教育運動刊物發表廣州和美國的華人工會文章時

1　Merrian Webster dictionary and Cambridge Dictionary

提及中國的學徒制，他以奴隸形容學徒三年的辛酸。[2]到西方
科技文化入侵中國，掀起一場自強運動。1860 年代的福州船
政學堂見到法國導師教授科目包括法文、幾何、數學、微積
分、物理、機械等。[3]學堂的航海課由英國導師教授，科目包
括英文、數學、幾何、天文、地理、航海和航海天文學等。[4]
而射擊、兵操、中文經史則為必修科。1880年代的天津電報
學堂由丹麥、法國和英國老師教授數學、製圖、英文、電磁
學、電測試、材料學、基礎電信、儀器規章、電報實習、國
際電報公約等課程。[5]然而中國新科技背後的認知究竟如何
承傳，此問題李約瑟先生窮一世的精力亦未能找到完美的答
案，倒不如看看西方科技教育的發展。

三、英國科學工藝教育

　　由於香港曾經被英國管治，她的科學工藝教育發展容
易受其影響，因此就選了英國的科學工藝教育一談。事實
上，英國的科學工藝教育亦受其他歐洲國家影響。英國結構
工程師學會主席爾昌斯(Ernest Fiande Etchells, 1876-1927)於
1923年的主席就職演説以工程師學會的演化 (The Evolution
of Engineering Institution)為題講述英國工程師學會的歷史。[6]
他追溯到埃及時代的建築行業公會一般被視為祕密組織，以
自己的符號和語言溝通，內容深不可測。到希臘年代，天文

2　Walter N. Fong, Labor Unions in China; Chinese Labor Unions in America,
　　in Flood, Theodore L., *The Chautauquan A Monthly Magazine April 1896
　　to September 189 Volume XXIII, New Series Volume XIV* (Meadville : The
　　T.L. Flood Publishing House, 2015)p.320-334; 399-402

3　高時良、黃仁賢：《中國近代教育史資料滙編──洋務運動時期
　　教育》(上海：上海教育出版社2007)，頁370-373

4　同上，頁373

5　同上，頁566

6　Ernest Fiande Etchells, Presidential Address, *The Evolution of
　　Engineering Institutions, Part I to Part IV*, Institution of Structural
　　Engineers, 1923

學和幾何學都只屬於這些祕密組織，最有名是Dionysian Ar-
tificers，壟斷建築業，但仍有規定建築師收費不可收取高於
建築物造價百份之25。[7]到羅馬年代，有建築學院，享有特
別權益，Vitruvius 強調建築師除必須懂行業知識外，還要掌
握歷史、哲學、音樂、醫學等知識，非等閒人可擔當。[8]到中
世紀，出現石匠公會(Guild Mason)，倫敦石匠公會可追溯到
1220年。這些行業公會(Livery Companies)主要是提供技術工
人和保持工人手工藝的水準。公會會員分三級，管理、自由
師傅 (Journeymen)和學徒 (Apprentice)階層。管理層包括僱主
(Masters)、院長(Wardens)和董事助理(Assistants of Court)，
其組成通常有一位僱主、三位院長和十位董事助理，主要工
作是管理工人工資。自由師傅是滿師後的技術工人，學徒完
成訓練後會將其手工藝品呈上董事，再由管理層決定可否進
身師傅行列。[9]不同年代有不同的行業公會，在商討成立倫敦
市及行業公會科學工藝學院(City and Guilds London Institute
for the Advancement of Technical Education)時，就有八十行業
公會。這師徒制影響英國培訓專業人才深遠，今天的工程師
和律師同樣要跟師傅，當然今天已制度化，與當年的有很大
分別，但在觀念上，年輕人要成為認可的專業人士，必先通
過實踐，從經驗中學習行業精髓，這必須靠前輩指點，在書
本上是絕對沒有的。

1. 打破大學傳統

　　英國學者堅尼 (Thomas Kelly)認為工業革命做就了一批

7　Martin S. Briggs, *The Architect in History,* (Oxford: Clarendon Press, 1927) page 19

8　Vitruvius, translated by Morris Hicky Morgan, *Ten Books on Architecture* (New York: Dover Publication,1960) p. 13-19

9　Dick Evans,*History of Technical Education: A short Introduction*(Cambridge: T Magazine Limited)Chapter 1; https://technicaleducationmatters. org/2009/05/13/chapter-3-the-guilds-and-apprenticeships/ 3 November 2017 閱

有學識的工人，而慈
善機構帶著愛心和關
懷發展兒童免費和星
期日學校的同時，促
使成人教育的出現，
一個有系統地教授工
人日常工作背後的科
學理論由此而生。在
英國叫「機械學院運
動」(The Mechanics
Institute Movement)。[10]
早於1712年，德薩古
利耶斯(John Theophi-
lus Desaguliers, 1683-
1744)開始教授如何運
用理論至實驗給非學
術界人士，他將機械
和實驗哲學教材寫成
名著而獲後世稱為示

圖1　蘇格蘭格拉斯哥大學約翰安德
　　　遜教授像

範實驗先驅。[11]1717年，史必度菲數學會 (Spitalfield Mathematical Society)成立，會員人數是八平方，即64人。會長
米道頓 (John Middleton)是海洋工程師，教授數學和實驗給
工人，聽眾有紡織、釀酒、造鐵、藥劑和造儀器等工人，
到1846年，被納入皇家天文學會。[12]將實驗哲學再應用到生

10 Thomas Kelly, The Origins of Mechanics Institute Movement in *British
　Journal of Educational Studies* Volume 1, No. 1, November 1952, page
　17

11 Nicholas Hans, *New Trends in Education in the Eighteenth Century*
　(London: Routledge & Kegan Paul Ltd., 1951), p.136-160

12 JWS Cassels, The Spitalfield Mathematical Society, in *Bulletin of the
　London Mathematical Society* Volume 1, Issue 3, October 1979, p.241-
　258

活上，而傳授給工人大眾的實用科學教育，格拉斯哥大學(Glasgow University)自然哲學教授約翰安德遜 (John Anderson, 1726 – 1796, 圖1)窮一生之力，不但獨自打破大學傳統，受同袍誹議推動實用科學教育，死後更捐出身家，為自己夢想造出最後一件事。

2. 約翰安德遜的實用科學理想

為何一位自然哲學教授走上實用科學之路？原來當時大學由數學主導，衍生物理和化學，純屬理論，歸自然哲學領域，學生數學成績優異才可進身物理和化學科目。而實驗化學只剛起步，實驗物理學仍在摸索中。安教授認為科學除了從數學入手，亦可以從實驗入門，因此他修改了課程，每週一、三、五和六上理論科學，週二和四上實驗科學。他打破傳統，讓平民百姓旁聽，上課時學生無需穿袍[13](gown)，工人亦無需更衣，惹來同事評擊。[14]他的名著《物理研究所》(Institutes of Physics)將物理分成14部：人體工學 (Somatology)、物料學、植物學、動物學、電力學、磁力學、萬有引力、力學、靜力水學、水流力學、氣動力學、金光學、天文學、宇宙學等。[15]當中力學、光學、電力學和磁力學仍然是主流物理基本課程。他死後，原本屬意助手Thomas Mellquham或Meikleham當自然哲學教授，可惜未能如願。一名愛丁堡大學畢業的利勿浦醫生嘉力(Thomas Garnett, 1766-1802)原欲移民美國教授自然哲學和化學，在等待船期中授課。聲名傳至格拉斯哥，1796年5月受聘為新學院的教授，新學院命名為安德遜學院(Anderson Institution)。嘉力享有很大自由度，不受大學條款約束，開了三課程，物理和化學在早上上課、實驗哲學在晚上上課(不同抽象理論)。地點在佐治街文法學校

13　筆者70年代在英時仍有學生和教授上課時穿袍

14　A. Humboldt Sexton, *The First Technical College* (London: Chapman and Hall Ltd., 1894) p.8-10

15　Ibid, page 15

(Grammar School George Street)。課程非常受歡迎，結果要借用行業禮堂(Trade Hall)上課。1797年學生達972人，當時全市只有七萬人口。學生亦開放至女生，可見其創意。嘉力聲譽遠播，但喪妻後，1799年離開蘇格蘭往倫敦，投身新成立的皇家學院 (Royal Institution)。[16]接手的貝百(George Birkbeck, 1776-1841)，比嘉力更有聲名，他最受歡迎的課程是機械能源的原理和能量。起初是免費，後收五先令。他只做了五年，工人學生達五百人，由於收入未能維持生計，跟上手一樣往倫敦去。[17]貝百其後於1824年創立倫敦機械學院 (London Mechanics Institute)，即後來的貝百學院 (Birckbeck College)。堅尼認為貝百在「機械學院運動」中是重要一員，從格拉斯哥、倫敦和愛丁堡三間最早機械學院，兩間與他有關。貝百走後，柯安尊(Andrew Ure, 1778-1857)接任安德遜學院，嘉力和貝百都以教學出名，柯先生是化學家，以大膽研究負名。其實安德遜亦有不少發明如合金槍、子彈和保險線(俗稱錶示)等軍事用品。[18]有一說稱柯先生對機械班學生態度不太好，做成機械班另起爐灶，成立格拉斯哥機械學院。[19]但根據後來一位當場者屈臣(Sir James Watson)在56年後的憶述，學院與機械班的爭執是圖書館擁有權，結果在大會上雙方同意分家。因此成立格拉斯哥機械學院，並邀得貝百為榮譽會長(Honorary Patron)。1923年11月8日開幕，比成立倫敦機械學院的會議只早了三日。[20]柯安尊亦與他的前任

16　Ibid, p.21-23

17　Thomas Kelly, The Origins of Mechanics Institute Movement in *British Journal of Educational Studies* Volume 1, No. 1, November 1952, page 27

18　James Muir, *John Anderson: Pioneer of Technical Education and the College he founded* (Glasgow:John Smith and Son, 1950) page 40

19　http://www.theglasgowstory.com/image/?inum=TGSS00019　Read　7 November 2017

20　A. Humboldt Sexton, *The First Technical College* (London: Chapman and Hall Ltd., 1894) p.70-71

一樣於1830年請辭後往倫敦，不過繼續他的化學專業，而非機械教育。1881年，格拉斯哥機械學院改名科學及藝術學院 (College of Science and Arts)。1886年，安德遜學院、科學及藝術學院、阿倫堅學校(Allan Glen's School)和阿堅信學院 (Atkinson Institution)合組一學院，名格拉斯哥及蘇格蘭西部工業學院 (Glasgow and West Scotland Technical College)。但安德遜學院的醫科班就脫離安德遜學院，自組安德遜醫學院 (Anderson Medical School)。1912年改名格拉斯哥皇家工業學院(Royal Technical College Glasgow)。1956年轉入皇家科學及技術學院 (Royal College of Science and Technology)。1964年升格斯克來德大學 (University of Strathclyde)，即Strath of the River Clyde，是克來德河的大山谷。克來德河最著名是海洋工程和造船工程。香港兩大船塢的工程人才，多來自此地。前香港立法局工程界議員黃秉愧就是皇家科學及技術學院畢業生。

3. 1851年萬國工業博覽會 (Great Exhibition of the Works of Industry of all Nations)的影響

上文提及中國偉大發明家是無師自通，西方又如何？發明電話的衛斯 (Johann Philipp Reis 1834-1874)是老師 、貝爾 (Alexander Graham Bell 1847-1922)是聾人老師、聾的愛迪生 (Thomas Alva Edison 1847-1931)是自學小販、史高格(Almon Brown Strowger,1839-1902)是承辦殯儀業。[21]郭享利(Henry Cort,1740-1800)把生鐵提煉成熟鐵，打鐵工人廖高文(Thomas Newcomen,1664-1729)發明蒸汽機[22]，原本讀法律的史勿頓

21　Lewis Coe, *The telephone and its several inventors* (North Carolina: McFarland & Co, 1995), page 47.

22　Jim Andrew, Thomas Newcomen and the first recorded steam engine in *Proceedings of the Institution of Civil Engineers, Transport, Volume 168, Issue TR6*, 2015, p570-578

(John Smeaton, 1724-1792)變成偉大工程師[23]，他們都是自學成功。繼後的布林利(James Brindley, 1716-1772)[24]、杜福(Thomas Telford, 1757-1834)和赤高 (Thomas Tredgold, 1788-1829)等雖然接受過英國的學徒制而踏上成功之路，[25]但沒有証據顯示他們的成功與學徒制有直接關係。西方學徒制源自教堂，四世紀已教授木工、紡織、裁縫和建築。七世紀傳入英國，最早學徒制記錄發現於12世紀。1261年的學徒制是七年。1563年的工藝條例是將學徒制伸延全國，並強制12至60歲失業男士當農業，而12至40歲失業女士當家務。至18世紀，學徒制仍然是兒童學習工藝最便宜和方便的做法。[26]上文的「機械學院運動」被視為未能推動成人教育，學者多引用克信 (James Hudson)於1850年的評論和實証。[27]獲加更認為機械學院運動的課程含高程度科學內容，未有顧及成人情況。

　　1851年5月1日，維多利亞女皇在倫敦主持萬國工業博覽會(下簡稱萬博)開幕，見圖2。短短五個月，入場人數超過六百萬，入場費收入每天要動用兩輛馬車運送英倫銀行。不少學者認為萬博除經濟收益外，其對工人的影響深遠。工人的產品得到支持，其地位亦受確認。參加者體會到新機械時代的來臨。法國獲得無數獎項，對英國政府正是迎頭棒喝，

---

23 Huge Ferguson, Mike Chrimes, *The Civil Engineers: the Story of the Institution of Civil Engineers and the People who made it* (Institution of Civil Engineers: Thomas Telford Limited 2011) page 17

24 Samuel Smiles, *Lives of the Engineers: Early Engineering* (London: Murray Albemarle Street, 1904) p.158-161

25 Huge Ferguson, Mike Chrimes, p13-14

26 W.H.G. Armytage, Sources for the History of Technical Education in England in British Journal of Educational Studies, Volume 5, No. 1 (Nov. 1956), pp. 73-76

27 Martyn Walker, The impact of the Great Exhibition of 1851 on the development of technical education during the second half of the nineteenth century in *Journal Research in Post Compulsory Education Volume 20, 2015 Issue 2*, p. 193.

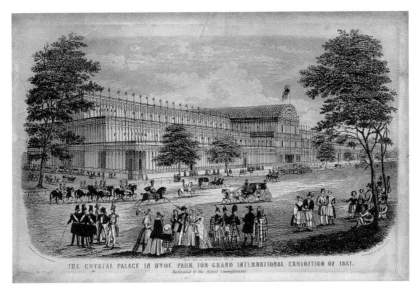

圖2　1851年萬國工業博覽會

其科技正被歐洲趕上。[28]當時列斯(Leeds)機械學院的何占士(James Hole)提出教育非年輕人之事，是每個人生在世上之事，即今天流行的「終身學習」觀念。[29]何先生不但提出新思維，更倡議從合適老師、媒體、展覽、會議、讀書室、儲蓄銀行等領域入手，改善科技教育。他的建議於1856年初見成效，政府成立藝術協會考試局 (Society of Arts Examination Board)，主辦科技和商業科目考試。1859年更成立藝術和科學處 (The Science and Arts Department)，支助科學老師。1861年舉辦公開考試。政府陸續公開報告：1855年的 Report of the Commissioners appointed to inquire into the State of Popular Education in England of 1858-1861; 1864年的 Report of Her Majesty's Commissioners appointed to inquire into the Revenues and Management of certain Colleges and Schools, and the studies

---

28　Ibid, pp.9-10

29　Hole, J. 1853, *An Essay on the History and Management of Literary, Scientific and Mechanics Institutions*, London, 1853, p.44 quoted in Ibid, p.11

pursued and instruction given therein；1867年的 On the best means of Promoting Scientific Education in Schools: A Report presented to the General Committee of the British Association for the Advancement of Science; 1872年的 Report of the Royal Commission on Scientific Instruction and the Advancement of Science; 1884年的 Report of the Royal Commission on Technical Instruction。1870年立了教育法，開張明義說明工業繁榮有賴加快基礎教育。1884生年的報告就衍生出1889的科技指引法和1890稅務法，以加稅改善科技教育。

4. 倫敦市及行業公會學院

　　1829年法國巴黎中央理工學院 (Ecole Centrale des Arts et Manufactures of Paris)誕生，1862年頒發工藝製造文憑 (Ingenieurs des arts et manufactures)。Ingenieurs 一詞是工程師，特與科學家識別。瑞士蘇黎世聯邦理工學院(Ecole Polytechnique Federale of Zurich)亦於1855年成立，做就不少諾貝爾獎得主。美國麻省理工學院於1861年成立。英國的安德遜學院雖然最早創立，但其發展限於蘇格蘭。倫敦的行業公會與倫敦市一起成長，勢力強大，籌組科學工藝學院必須咨詢各行業公會。1876年7月3日，各行業公會代表召開代表大會，通過決議不單推廣倫敦的科學工藝教育，更伸延全國，培訓各行業年輕技術工人。[30]

　　臨時籌備委員會邀請各界專家和學者制定報告，報告建議成立一中央學院推廣英國的科學工藝教育；籌組科學工藝科目考試；鼓勵地方成立科學工藝學校培訓技術工人和工人；各科學工藝學校需與地區市政府緊密合作。倫敦市及行業公會科學工藝學院於1880年成立，以董事會 (Board of Gov-

---

30　City and Guilds of London Institute, *A Short History of the City and Guilds of London Institute for the advancement of Technical Education* (London: The Institute?,1899) page 1

ernors)、評議會 (Council)和執委會 (Executive Committee)管
理學院，並邀得威爾斯皇子為主席，主持奠基儀式及1884年
開幕。學院設三年制課程，包括土木、機械和電機工程及化
學，畢業頒發倫敦市及行業公會科學工藝文憑(Associate   of
City and Guilds Institute)，簡稱ACGI，是英國著名科學工藝
文憑。負責油麻地避風塘和大潭篤水塘工程的謝斐(Daniel
Jaffee,1875-1921)就是持有此著名文憑。入讀學生八成擁有大
學入學試資格(matriculated)，畢業生一般被視為相等於大學
畢業。[31]學院最重要工作是舉辦科學工藝科目公開考試，每
年四至五月舉行。合格考生頒發證書，優異考生頒發獎狀。
公開考試除在本土外，澳洲、紐西蘭、印度、西印度群島等
地均有舉行，1899年，試場達397個，考生34,176人。20世紀
50至60年代，香港學生參加此試，獲獎無數。[32]這些科學工
藝科目公開考試最困難是聘請合適主考官，原因是要測試考
生不但要掌握科學理論，還要擁有工場內的手工藝。主考官
需具備理論和實際經驗，人才難求。學院因此創雙主考官制
(co-examiner)，理論和實際經驗考官各一。[33]學院不但統一
了英國科學工藝水平，其影響遠至全世界英聯邦地方。1907
年，皇家科學院(Royal College of Science)、大英帝國研究院
(the Imperial Institute)、皇家礦業學院(Royal College of Mines)
和倫敦市及行業公會學院合併成為倫敦帝國學院(The   Impe-
rial College of Science, Technology and Medicine)，成為英國著
名的科學工藝大學。

---

31 同上，page 5

32 *South China Moring Post,* 24 November 1951, 6 November 1952, 10
    December 1953, 22 December 1954 and 1955, 15 November 1956, 15
    January 1957, 30 November 1958, 18 December 1959, 21 December
    1961, 24 December 1963, 30 December 1964, 21 January 1967, 20
    March 1969.

33 F.E. Foden, Sir Philip Magnus and the City and Guilds of London
    Institute, *the Vocational Aspect of Education*, 14:29, 110, 21962

四、香港科學工藝教育

1. 早年實業教育

1863年，拔萃本地培訓女校 (Diocesan Native Female Training School)在般咸道和東街交界處成立。[34]翌年，羅馬天主教會在西角成立華人日校 (West Point Chinese Day School)，教授造鞋、木工、裁縫和釘書。[35]1866年開始接受政府資助，名西角養正院 (West Point Reformatory)。[36]1877年加開印刷術。其學生多來自裁判官的轉介，希望兒童學一門手藝，有一技旁身，不再流連街上或犯事。[37]及後於1900年成立的庇利羅士養正院，亦負起同一責任，相似今天的兒童感化院。

1878年，港督軒尼詩 (John Pope Hennessy)於大書院 (Central School)頒獎典禮上提出延伸養正院的功能，成立工業學校 (Industrial School)，希望兒童有另一出路。[38]他走後，事件隨他而去，不了了之。差不多同一時間，庇利羅士捐贈一千英鎊以豎立拱北銅像(Beaconsfield Statue)，可惜被婉拒，他於1880年將捐款轉而成立一供讀醫學獎學金的基金，有四名額，兩個供華人，兩個不限國籍。[39]但東華醫院認為

34　Anthony Sweeting, *Education in Hong Kong Pre 1841-1941:Fact and Opinion,* (Hong Kong: Hong Kong University Press, 1990)page 152

35　夏其龍著，蔡迪雲譯：《香港天主教傳教史1841-1894》(香港：三聯書店，2014) 頁308

36　同上，頁309

37　同上，頁311-313；CO129/130, page 132

38　Supplement to the Annual Report of Government Education, address of John Pope Hennessy at the Central School, 28th January 1878 at the annual distribution of prizes, Uneducated children

39　David Faure, Society (Hong Kong: Hong Kong University Press, 1997) page 22 ; *China Mail* 22 July 1880

華人可先讀中醫，後讀西醫，[40]結果到1883年基金改名庇利羅士獎學金，只提供兩個攻讀西醫獎學金。[41]其後轉輾成為入讀香港西醫院的獎學金，今天，香港大學仍頒發此獎學金。[42]相信這是早期香港推動科技教育的嘗試。1884年，港督寶雲 (George Bowen)成立政府獎學金，供學子前往英國攻讀工程、醫學和法律學位。寶雲親歷香港基礎建設的突進(大潭水塘)，切身體驗資訊的突破(香港廣州電報網開幕禮)，又認識到本地衛生環境的惡劣(潔淨局初期運作)，更經歷到民間與政府誹謗官司(《士蔑西報》與裴樂士訴訟)的重要，開始培訓本地人才，打下「發三師」的基礎。本地專業團體如工程師學會早於1882年成立，醫學會亦於兩年後成立。由於受惠人士少，開支大，加上大部份學生畢業後不回饋香港，獎學金於1894年停止。[43]獎學金得主只有一名來自男拔萃學生回港工作，就是1890年得獎的蘇父里(F. Southey)往英國修讀工程，他於1906年回港任九廣鐵路筆架山隧道測量師，成功連貫隧道。[44]

2. 民間科學工藝教育的嘗試

　　1904年的香港是怎樣？香港新地標已從畢打街鐘樓移至新填海的中環皇后像廣場，廣場周邊新一代建築物工程亦依新的建築物條例進行得如火如荼。新建築物內裝有香港首部電動梯，九龍亦剛有電力供應。馬可尼最新的無線電專利在港註冊。不單建築工程蓬勃，大潭篤水塘亦在籌備以解水荒之苦。路上有新落成的電車，火車亦在籌備階段。黃埔船

40　Hong Kong Government Gazette No 149 of 1880; *China Mail* 22 July 1880, 10 December 1881

41　Hong Kong Government Gazette No 423 of 1883

42　https://www.med.hku.hk/images/document/03edu/prizes2005-06.pdf 28 October 2017 閱

43　Report by Inspector of School for 1895, item 21

44　拙作：《車水馬龍》(香港：三聯書店，2016) 頁248-255

塢的火船越造越大，太古船塢在港島展開移山填海工程，準備與黃埔平分天下。軍部在金鐘的世紀船塢工程就近尾聲，將香港船務業推向高峰。其他工業如紡織、漂染、造繩、麵粉、造糖和肥皂業等生意亦蒸蒸日上。商業往來繁密，會計、部記、速記和打字等需要大量人才。香港樓市亦隨之而上，政府和大企業急忙興建宿舍給員工，但中小型外資就要面對招聘外籍中層員工的困難，紛紛尋找解決辦法，培訓本地中層員工是出路之一。香港工程師和造船師學會是香港最早的專業團體，十九世紀已舉辦同業研討會，互相交流和分享專業經驗，以改善和提升業界專業水平[45]。她們大部份會員是中小型外資公司老闆，踏入廿世紀，她們首次舉辦專業課程給公眾。來自英國伯明罕工業學院的威廉士(W.H. Williams)，於1904年1月4日晚上八時在德輔道中的工程師和造船師學會開課，每週兩晚，教授實用數學。分基礎和高級兩班，學徒半價。基礎班教代數、量度數和方格紙，高級班教代數、三角、幾何、量度數和初級力學。課程屬工科，力學更是建築和造船必備的基礎知識。同年9月，課程伸延至應用力學、機械繪圖、實用幾何和電力學。課程完畢，學會更安排學員應考貿易委員會科學和藝術部門(Department of Science and Arts under Board of Trade)的相關課程考試，合格後可獲證書。[46]威廉士引入英國的科學工藝教育，以半價學費吸引學徒，又安排在晚上上課，創科學工藝夜學，將理論和實踐結合，是香港公開教授科技課程的首人。香港戰前有很多新事物都始自民間，教授科學工藝課程只是其中之一。[47]

45　拙作：〈初探香港最早專業團體 - 香港工程師和造船師學會〉載《根本集》(香港：雅集出版社，2012) 頁166

46　*China Mail* 5 January 1904; *South China Morning Post* 29 February, 17 September 1904; *Hong Kong Telegraph* 14 September 1904

47　拙作：〈戰前私人組織〉載劉蜀永：《香港史話》(香港：和平圖書有限公司，2018) 頁174-181

3. 香港李陞格致工藝學堂 (Li Sing Scientific and Industrial College)

英國人通過專業團體帶來了英式夜學科學工藝班，翻開香港科學工藝教育第一篇。真湊巧，中國的自強運動令華人在美國學得科技知識，只差一個月時間，亦為香港帶來美式的科學工藝教育。世紀之交，香港華商組織商會，響應自強運動。商人李伯(紀堂)，見圖3，

圖3　香港商人李紀堂像

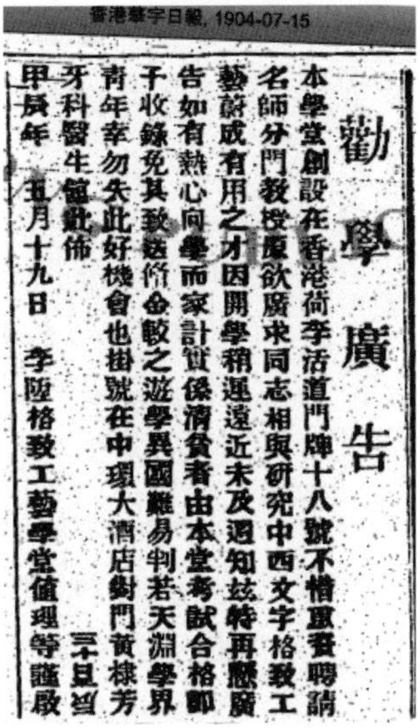

富豪李陞之子捐出五萬元，連同譚子剛、黃棣芳和尹文楷醫生成立華人科技學校。剛巧鄺華汰完成史丹福大學碩士課程，欲回饋祖國，接受了校長一職。學校改名李陞格致工藝學堂，除紀念李陞外，「格致」二字出自《大學》：「致知在格物，物格而後知至。」梁啟超曰：「……形而下學，即質學、化學、天文學、地質學、全體學、動物學、物學等是也。吾因近人通行名義，舉凡屬於形而下學，皆謂之格致。……」[48] 今人所謂之科學是也。顧名思義，是一所培訓華人的科學工藝學校。圖4是學堂招生廣告。

圖4　李陞格致工藝學堂招生廣告

1904年3月15日，李陞格致工藝學堂以月租一千六百元

48　梁啓超：飲冰室文集之十一，〈格致學沿革考略〉，導言，《飲冰室合集(第2冊)文集10-19》(中華書局，1989年3月)，頁四。

在荷李活道18號 (舊中央警署原址)開課。當時老師四人,中文兼翻譯科學老師楊襄甫,還有陳之和宋良弼,英文由鄺華汰主講。學生40人,全未能通過英文測試。英文分初中高三班,中文分初高兩班。早上有禱告會20分鐘。由於英文未達預期水平,實驗室要延遲使用。[49]第一學期完結,7月15日學堂在華商會所禮堂作結業禮,先由同學作體操示範,再英語誦文。譚子剛、黃棣芳和尹文楷醫生回應後,鄺校長介紹化學科,展示小考課卷和同學答案。小考有十題,其中兩題是從生活中解釋化學原理,現列如下:

1. 譬有極大房屋失火燒為平地,凡有形之物,變為無形,依化學理,此屋中有形之物,果如佛氏所謂一切皆空否?

2. 如生鹽白糖等化於水中,其實是化合否?其糖等化於水中何處?

學生莫耀的答案:

1. 房屋被燒,物類有形變為無形,因拆爛其物之質點,變為別種雜質,或為氣質而上升,或為本質,或為配質,不過種種變化耳,何得謂之一切皆空,觀於化學鑑原第一圖,用玻璃瓶燒棉花火藥,其理亦可借喻。

2. 生鹽白糖等化於水中,非化合也,實消化也,其鎔化後,此質藏在於水之微點隙中,即所謂水中之吼也。[50]

　　鄺校長懂利用傳媒曝光,在11月發表文章談科學工藝教學在中國的困難。他感嘆香港學生易教,但家長的影響就難以改變。百年如一日,相信今天老師亦有共鳴。他指出早

49　嶺南學生界第一卷,1904年6月刊,頁30;1904年10月刊,頁37

50　嶺南學生界第一卷,1904年10月刊,頁38-41

婚令學生無法專心學業，家庭負擔和孝道使學生經常曠課。科舉十年寒窗，一朝高中便可衣榮祿。科舉重背誦，不重思考。西方是全面教育，英文是工具。但學懂英語，便可立刻進身商界，從文員到買辦，功名富貴隨即而來。華人讀書不是求學問，是求工作。酈校長認為中國正處於過渡期，要慢慢適應。西方教育剛在中國起步，遇到師資、圖書館和儀器等問題。又沒有管理經驗，所以經常受騙。[51]酈校長亦不忘傳道，在衛斯理衛理公會講道。[52]

　　1905年1月，學堂舉行第一學年結業禮，28號晚在新校址皇后大道66號舉行。譚子剛致詞後，學生分別以中英文致詞，又以兩語辯論。酈校長總結學年報告，說明學堂宗旨是培訓「有思考的雙手」，讓學生明白到工藝背後的意義，在操作熟練之時，亦能掌握設計。最重要是要將知識應用到生活上，不淪為紙上談兵。學堂同時推行全面教育，除英文和數學外，地理和歷史亦需學習。在學堂趕追下，學生的英文亦漸追上，可應付科學課程。以中文教授科學，學生比較易吸收，但缺點是行人止步，未能進升科學另一境界。酈校長引傳媒參觀化學實驗室，由學生示範做實驗。隨著現有進度，下學年預算開三角、微積分、土木及機械繪圖課程，一位來自美國的教授將於三月抵港。他再次批評學生功利態度，不決心學習科學，只求做翻譯。70學生只得35人考試，因此平均分高達87%。酈校長稱下學年將收緊紀律。他亦提到校舍擠迫和缺乏學生宿舍。其後黃棣芳醫生主禮頒獎。[53]1905年2月，學院遷至皇后大道66號。同年8月，酈校長將他在港的教學經驗寫成文章，發表於美國的《當代科學月刊》 (Popular Science Monthly)，名〈中國教育問題面面

51　*South China Morning Post* 10 November 1904

52　*South China Morning Post* 14 December 1904; *China Mail* 15 December 1904

53　*Hong Kong Telegraph* 30 January 1905; *Hong Kong Weekly Press* 6 February 1905

觀〉。文章引用李陞格致工藝學堂
學生例子，從零開始到走入實驗室
之路。[54]

圖5　鄺華汰像

　　1906年1月，學堂舉行第二學
年結業禮，在薄扶林道31號新址舉
行。在頒獎典禮前，學院舉行軍事
演習。中文系楊襄甫老師在滙報中
提及科學工藝教育學費比中國傳統
教育高。在校董鼎力支持下，學生
亦見掌握知識，表現令人興奮，學
堂他朝將可成為香港高等學府。數
理系教授格芬(Allan T. Griffin)就將
本地學生與美國學生比較，認為本
地學生吸收新知識能力比美國學生
強，對學堂前境充滿信心。校董李
伯強調軍事和體操訓練，鍛鍊身體
的重要。並鼓勵學生，老師會是學
生的真朋友。鄺校長總結當前困難
是語言，但學堂堅持雙語學習，在
輔以中文學習後，學生已可走入實
驗室。[55]

圖6　鄺華汰墓碑

　　好境不常，鄺校長於同年5月
突然去世，圖5是鄺華汰像。鄺華
汰死後葬於跑馬地墳場，圖6是鄺
的英文墓碑，自始學堂亦無消息，
直至1908年校董會通過停辦，由主席譚子剛代表李陞格致工

54　Walter N. Fong, Some Phases of the Educational Problems in China,
　　Popular Science Monthly, August 1905; *South China Morning Post* 29
　　July 1905

55　*China Mail* 24 January 1906; *Hong Kong Daily Press, South China
　　Morning Post* 25 January 1906

藝學堂成立基金，每年捐贈1,100元作獎學金之用，連同學堂
傢私、儀器和書籍轉贈香港實業專科學校，由輔政司梅含理
代收。[56]《嶺南學生界》曾經訪問鄺華汰，誰也估不到這篇
訪問文章竟成為他的小傳，而他在美國各大雜誌所刊登的論
文亦名留千古。現將他的小傳記錄於下。

3.1 鄺華汰生平事略

　　1848年1月24日，美國加利福尼亞的蘇特磨房　(Sutter's
Mill)發現金礦，引起一場淘金熱。在太平洋另一方的中國
則發生太平天國動盪，尤其在廣東四邑爆發「土客之爭」，
香港商人譚才和郭松被捲入事件。在這時代背景下，大多廣
東人都夢想到舊金山(三藩市)掘金，鄺金龍也不例外。鄺金
龍1866年4月1日生於廣東新寧，15歲前仍是一名赤腳鄉村兒
童。每天採樵、牧牛、耕田和在村塾讀書。閒時接寫書札，
替婦女與放洋丈夫通訊。亦有在市集做買賣，懂理財。每逢
喜慶之日，皆造公仔自娛。金龍不甘這生活方式，早聞加州
可闖天下，毅然於1881年獨往加州。父母在不願意下答允要
求，其行裝衣服皆其慈母所做。

　　金龍到達舊金山後，寄居遠親的中國商店，並返長老差
會　(Presbyterian　Mission)。獲一名老婦人教授英文字母，在
教會首次聽到風琴奏西樂，但以華文唱頌。一星期後，金龍
在洛杉磯一間中國飯店找到一份管數工作，並入長老差會夜
學攻讀。禰雲牧師(Rev. J. C. Nevin)以廣東話傳道，兩年後，
金龍決定受洗。其後他剪辮和易服，考入政府夜學進修，巧
遇女老師，並為他改名華汰(Walter)，將華汰放在龍之前，英
文是Walter　Ngon　Fong。華汰日後赴港時，依舊與女老師通
信。輾轉在天使城打滾了七年，其間曾做過牧豬、修理時鐘
和打磨首飾等工作。

　　由於舊金山首飾店招聘人手，華汰決定轉變環境，但當

56　*China Mail* 2 March 1908; Report of the Inspector of Schools for the
　　year 1908 & 1910, Appendix A Hong Kong Technical Institute

抵達舊金山時，東主未能安排適合職位。幸好他拿著禰雲牧師的介紹書往見馬士篤牧師(Rev. F. J. Masters)，馬士篤牧師安排了華汰在當地教會幫手。人工雖少，但他可有更多時間攻讀。馬牧師介紹他入了太平洋大學(University of Pacific)，三年後畢業。其間他在教會每星期教五晚夜學，星期六清潔教堂，禮拜天協助傳道。

其後華汰考入史丹佛大學，起初兩年經濟緊絀，他還勉強應付得來。每天早上乘坐20英哩汽車上學，晚上又教夜學。如是者渡過兩年，由於學費實在高昂，他已感無能為力。幸好獲一班好友集資，籌得500元，免息借款，亦無指定日期歸還。終於在1896年畢業，主修經濟，副修法律和歷史，成為首位在史丹佛大學畢業的華人。在大學其間曾當大學文學會領袖(President of the Nestorian Literary Society)，並出版著作，最早一篇名〈中國六公司〉(The Chinese Six Companies)，刊於1894年五月的 Overland Monthly of America。最為著名的著作是〈中國的工會〉(Labour Unions in China)，刊於當時美國著名的成人教育運動刊物《學托擴》(Chautauquan)1896年六月和七月號。華汰的志願是回國教授經濟和法律，可惜找不到門路。他唯有留在舊金山發展，開了一間房屋貸款代理公司，並成為舊金山律師行會員，不愁生意，收入不錯。其間成為興中會會長。[57]雖然經濟轉好，他認為中國需要的不是經濟，而是科學，他轉向尋求科學知識。

1897年6月，他與史丹佛大學同窗柯斯小姐 (Miss Emma E. Howse)結婚，並居伯克利 (Berkeley)，方便攻讀加州大學(University of California)科學系。修化學、物理、地質、材料學、冶金學、分析及化驗學等，三年後畢業，打算回國教授科學，可惜他第二次嘗試又失敗，令他心灰意冷，一度打消回國念頭，在加州大學任東方語言和文學助理，並專心傳

57　*Hong Kong Daily Press* 20 October 1896

道。在伯克利，他建造自已的房屋、花園和家庭，學術就專注東方法律、生活和文學。1902年，華汰在加州大學東方語言和文學系出版了一書名《廣東話入門》(Introductory Notes on the Cantonese Language)，成為加州大學的教科書。1903年他又取得文學碩士學位，在取得學位兩月前，香港的李紀堂、譚子剛、黃棣芳和尹文楷等籌組香港李陞格致工藝學堂，邀請華汰任校長。他渴望以久的夢終於實現，帶同太太和兒子到港，執教鞭。除了辦學外，華汰不忘傳道，1904年12月14日，他在灣仔循道衛理會堂講道。[58]1905年5月22日，他第二名兒子在港出生，取名車士打羅蘭士 (Chester Lawrence)。當時他住在跑馬地黃泥涌道35號 (今愉園大廈)。圖7是鄺華汰闔家照。

鄺金龍未能回國執教鞭，卻偶然在港創立首間全日制科學工藝學院，從美國請來科學教授和添置實驗器材，以雙語講學，雖然未能開花結果，亦為培訓華人工業領袖播下種籽，算是完其回饋國家之夢。其後港督彌敦 (Matthew Nathan)和盧吉 (Frederick Lugard)所創的香港工藝學院亦只是夜學模式，以皇仁書院老師為骨幹，夥拍兼職專業人士。其發展又被香港大學工學院成立所影響而未有建樹，到

圖7　鄺華汰闔家照

58 *South China Morning Post* 14 December 1904; *China Mail* 15 December 1904

1931年貝璐 (William Peel)將香港科學工藝教育分專業、技術和中學三級，奠定全日制度，才真正延續李陞格致工藝學堂的辦學宗旨。

4. 政府的實業專科學院 (Hong Kong Technical Institute)

自從寶雲的獎學金計劃停止後，香港教育發展仍然停留在中學階段。到1901年8月，一群香港外籍精英致函港督要求成立英童學校，其主要理據是在港英童人數不斷增加，在100間學校中，只有四間適合他們，教育除了知識外，最重要是培訓優良性格，文化差異令英童沒法在這環境下培養出英國的傳統文化和宗教，家長亦無能力送子女入讀私人學校又或送返英國。當時聯署的幾乎是整個上層社會人士，當中有加士居(William Julius Gascoigne)少將、包和(F. Powell)代將、高官史勿夫(Thomas Sercombe Smith)和梅含理(Francis Henry May)、滙豐和渣甸大班昃臣(Thomas Jackson)和奇士域(James Johnstone Keswick)、首富遮打(Catchick Paul Chater)等。[59]其實華人早於3月已提出同樣要求，由何啓、韋玉、馮華川、周東生、阮荔祁、盧冠廷、曹善允和韋安聯署上書要求成立的卻是私人高級華人學校，學習西方知識，聘高薪專業老師，收高學費，建議自給自足方案，不動分毫公帑。[60]政府因此被迫成立調查委員會跟進，報告於1902年出爐。委員會建議成立英童學校；而成立私人高級華人學校則有待華人社會的建議；歷史和地理科增加本地原素；並著手培訓師資。委員會認為暫時無需設立大學，但不同意政府設立獎學金供尖子往英國修讀大學。報告內容無半隻字提及科學工藝教育。[61]可見香港

59　CO129/306, p. 312-317

60　CO129/306, p. 672-678

61　Hong Kong Government Gazette No. 207 of 1902, Report of the Committee on Education

教育發展在1902年仍然停留在中學階段。

　　港督彌敦1904年中抵港，民間已有科學工藝學堂，他在任處理過不少本地大型工程，最重要的一項是接手處理九廣鐵路前期規劃，他是工程師出身，對龐大工程自然感興趣，尤對工務司漆咸所提的西線不認同，親自勾畫出東線，並解釋其好處。[62]他亦親身經歷過太古和海軍船塢、大潭篤水塘、高等法院、中央郵局和海事處等艱巨工程。不知道他是否因此而覺得本地缺乏科技人才，要從培訓入手提升本地人才質素。皇仁書院校長於1905年報告中透露他曾在2月建議在第一班（相等於今天中學畢業）上設一學院課程（Collegiate Class），可惜未獲華人支持，他寄望夜學方案可行。[63]視學官的同年報告亦提及高等和工業教育的困難在於華人技工缺乏基礎教育，而一般學生亦甚少修讀理科課程，要他們讀化學、高數和電學是不設實際。[64]這道理顯淺不過，華人讀書目的主要是謀生，當他們掌握英語，馬上可當文員，進而升買辦，當其「白領」[65]，收入可觀，那會再花金錢和時間學習科技，到頭來在船塢或地盤當監督，俗稱當其「藍領」[66]，收入一般。連《士蔑西報》都認為香港沒有科學工藝教育的必要，足夠的實用商業教育才合適香港實況。[67]但彌敦透露兩廣總督秘書曾向他查詢香港可否借調一些華籍工程師供廣東興建鐵路，他直言沒有，因此建議在皇仁書院加強數學科。在彌敦的提議下，皇仁書院終於開了衛生必修科和三角科，加強了科技基礎教學。[68]1905年底，清朝廢科舉，西方科技抬頭，開始取代舊制度。彌敦就在此刻

62　拙作：《車水馬龍》(香港：三聯書店，2016) 頁244-246

63　Report of the Queen's College for the year 1905, Paragraph 14

64　Report of the Inspector of Schools for the year 1905, paragraph 45

65　文職人員在寫字樓穿白恤衫上班，白色表示斯文清潔

66　技工通常穿藍色工衣，俗稱「蛤乸衣」

67　*Hong Kong Telegraph* 23 January 1906

68　*South China Morning Post* 23 January 1906

成立夜學籌備委員會提供科學工藝課程。籌備委員會成員包括註冊官(後稱華民政務司)、視學官(後稱教育處長)、皇仁書院校長、助理工務局長和威廉士先生。[69]5月，委員會提交報告，建議設三組，分商科、工科和理科。商科課程包括速記、語文、尺牘和高級英語；工科課程包括實用數學、應用力學和機械繪圖；理科課程包括化學、電學、熱力學與蒸氣和衛生。課程規定最少五人成班，晚上六時至八時授課，每年兩學期，即10月至農曆年和農曆年後至5月。學生不論國籍，最少 14 歲，少於17 歲要身份證明，日校生免問(除校長批准外)。學費分註冊費五元，上足堂全退；每科每月一元，第二科五毫；理工學生另收三元儀器按金，儀器無損全退。書籍可向圖書館借用。功課：獎勵根據成績，考試每年最少一次，又或看老師和考官決定。校外試免費，鼓勵學生參加，例如大學入學試，學校頒發証書給合格學生。[70]彌敦向殖民地部申請時用試驗字眼，一年後檢討，獲殖民地部批准，政府正式開辦科學工藝教學，上課地點在皇仁書院，老師全是兼職的老師或專業人士，課程稱「進修夜學班」(Evening Continuation Class)，並委任華富士(Edwin Ralphs)為監督，見

圖8　香港實業專科學院首任校監華富士

69　CO129/334, p.183-185
70　CO129/334, p 188-205

圖8。華先生剛升常務老師，專長培訓老師，他亦是兼職並獲額外津貼。進修夜學受港督委任的委員會監察，由註冊官任主席，向港督滙報。[71]籌組秘書是威廉士，8月已編制好簡介小冊子，並派發傳媒。[72]再在報章刊登廣告招生，見圖9，預算在10月3日開課。10月3日，師生齊集皇仁書院四號房，可

圖9　香港進修夜學班招生廣告

惜未能開課，四號房將用作辦事處和自修室，成威廉士常駐地。[73]10月6日，終於依期開課，以法文班最受歡迎，有25學生，可能要分班上堂。老師來自皇仁書院。[74]

　　一年檢討期到，七位委員[75]組成的委員會交報告，內容包括為進修夜學定位，成為高等教育的基石，課程結合理論和實踐，為發展高等教育鋪路；將過去一年經驗總結而微調課程和科目；確定學年時間；規定課程修讀時間；確定每週上課時間；確定學費；規定老師薪酬；制定入學資格；規定開班人數；聘請長期老師；籌組秘書職能；進修夜學名稱；入學試；支出；畢業証書；認可資格等。[76]其中入學資格可收女生，聘請長期老師從皇仁書院入手，規定書院老

71　Report of the Inspector of Schools for the year 1906, paragraph 54

72　*China Mail, South China Morning Post* 17 August 1906

73　*South China Morning Post* 4 October 1906

74　*South China Morning Post* 6 October 1906

75　主席註冊官班雲，皇仁校長韋士，立法局議員何啓，皮雅士醫生，政府化驗師班尼，副工務司實頓和助理註冊官胡夫。

76　CO129/341, p. 640-654

師必須兼職夜學，將夜學正名為香港實業工業學院(Hong Kong Technical College)和政府確認畢業証書資格是突破。報告到新港督盧吉手上，盧督只將香港實業工業學院修改為香港實業專科學院 (Hong Kong Technical Institute)一項，連同校規，[77]於1907年10月向殖民地部申請批準。[78]專科學院一詞比工業學院更高一等，而畢業証書將是文憑(Diploma)級，比証書(Certificate)又高級些，盧吉心中不知是否為成立港大而鋪路就不得而知。1907年12月成立香港實業專科學院獲殖民地部批准，[79]但盧吉急不及待在1907年10月以香港實業專科學院招收新生，[80]胸有成竹地偷步，圖10是招生廣告。華富士被委任為香港實業專科學院總監(Director)，上課地點仍在皇仁書院。當時的老師，教物理的曲斯(Alfred Herbert Crook)、英文的嘉域(Herbert Leonard Garret)和馬田(Gaston Pacros de Martin)及數學的辛打蘭 (Arthur Robert Sutherland)皆來自皇仁書院。工科老師就是後來的工務司白建時(Thomas Luff

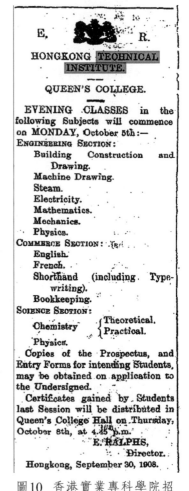

圖10　香港實業專科學院招生廣告

77　CO129/341, p.660-667

78　CO129/341, page 634, 652, 660

79　CO129/341, page 668

80　Report of the Inspector of Schools for the year 1907, Appendix C, Report of Technical Institute

Perkins)，他的名字現今還在渣甸山的街道上見到，伙拍他是助理工務司寶頓，還有黃埔船塢的杜立(Wilfred Tulip)。理科老師是政府化驗師(Government Chemist)班尼 (Frank Browne)教授化學，師資陣容鼎盛。1908年，總商會便率先承認商科畢業生資格。[81]同年實業專科學院尋求頒發文憑證書，學院亦接收了香港李陞格致工藝學堂所有硬件包括傢俬、實驗室儀器和藏書。[82]1909年成立香港大學籌款並不理想，盧吉透露將來的香港大學可先容納西醫院和實業專科學院兩所專上學院，然後才發展。[83]原來盧吉心中有數，萬一籌款不理想，西醫院和實業專科學院是後備方案。學院為了尋求認可資歷，總監華富士四出要求大學承認其部份課程。[84]情況與戰後的工業學院相同。同年，皇家衛生學會 (Royal Sanitary Institute)香港分會將其舉辦的專業課程和考試與實業專科學院合併，學院又接收了其儀器和藏書，[85]發展理想。

4.1 香港大學對實業專科學院的影響

　　上文提及港督盧吉曾建議將香港實業專科學院納入香港大學，其主因是籌款不理想，麼地 (Hormusjee Naorojee Mody)雖然願意負擔興建所有大學建築物，但條件是要政府籌足款項供儀器和裝修及每年營運經費。[86]何啟支持先建校社，以安頓醫學院和實業專科學院，待日後籌得足夠款項才擴展香港大學。當時輔政司梅含理對籌款並不樂觀，他以西

---

81 *South China Morning Post* 11 April 1908

82 *South China Morning Post* 9 October 1908; Report of the Inspector of Schools for the year 1908, Appendix A, Report of Technical Institute, paragraph 6

83 *South China Morning Post* 11 January 1909

84 *Hong Kong Daily Press* 12 October 1909

85 Report of the Inspector of Schools for the year 1909, Appendix C, Report of Technical Institute

86 Peter Cunich, *A History of the University of Hong Kong Volume 1, 1911-1945* (Hong Kong: Hong Kong University Press, 2012) page 113

醫院籌款經驗，認為一旦建成校社，籌款更為艱難。[87]轉機來自1908年底佛山號事件，太古一名外籍員工踢死一名華籍老乘客，為平息民憤，太古在港三間公司因此合共捐出四萬英鎊(約457,000元)，[88]而香港大學首個講座教授位(Chair Professor)就冠名太古講座教授，得主是工程學院的史密夫教授(Professor Cades Alfred Middleton Smith)。有了太古的支持，加上海外華人捐款，香港大學基金成立，原本西醫院和李陞學堂捐贈實業專科學院的基金亦轉至香港大學。[89]

1911年在香港工程師及造船師學會一講座上，講者提議成立委員會研究香港科學工藝教育方向。[90]1912年香港大學工程學院開課。教育處長的報告指出香港大學不單拿走實業專科學院的錢包，在某程度上亦搶走他們的學生，學院無需沮喪，這只是証明他們過去的表現理想，物理和機械繪圖課程亦於同年轉在香港大學上課。[91]實業專科學院有見及此，只有轉攻其他香港大學沒有的課目。由於總監是培訓老師出身，自然加強培訓老師課程，創幼稚園老師課程。[92]在1910年開始課程，專心師訓。華富士又是聖約翰救護隊活躍份子，1911年學院開辦急救課程，政府亦承認學院頒發的三年師訓証書為認可教師的專業地位。[93]翌年，聘老師主講實地衛生課程。[94]1913年，學院轉專注輔助大學入學試課程，扶助學生考入大學。商科課程保持水準，電力學人數減少。[95]工科只保持建造工程和實地測量課程，其他的收生未如理

87　ibid, page 112

88　ibid, page 120

89　Report of the Director of Education for the year 1912, paragraph 51

90　*South China Morning Post* 23 January 1911

91　Report of the Director of Education for the year 1912, paragraph 53 & 54

92　Report of the Director of Education for the year 1910, paragraph 55

93　Report of the Director of Education for the year 1911, paragraph 26

94　Report of the Director of Education for the year 1912, paragraph 68

95　Report of the Director of Education for the year 1913, paragraph 86

想。1916年,學院圖書館使用率低,與皇仁書院合併,減低
開支。[96]1917年,開辦家政課程,非常受歡迎。[97]1920年11月
2日,教育處長艾榮 (Edward Alexander Irving)在香港大學講
述香港教育廿載轉變,認為實業專科學院是香港高等教育的
源頭,其師訓証書獲政府認可教師的專業地位。[98]

　　1921年,《德臣西報》批評實業專科學院委員會近年
無所建樹,建議善用香港大學晚間資源如實驗室和課室。[99]
同年發生童工問題,社會上成立工業學院的呼聲又舊事重
提。華人精英籌得十萬元,向政府提出成立工業學院。[100]
《南華早報》指出政府每年用於實業專科學院的支出只一萬
元,所提供課程有限,未能招聘適合老師是主因。再看學院
老師,不少是來自皇仁書院,因為他們合約都訂明要兼職夜
學。[101]早報認為實業專科學院只是一所皇仁書院夜學,船塢
的學徒只授手工藝,並不理解背後的理論。事實上,香港是
缺乏實地學習的工具,大學和實業專科學院完全沒有聯系,
現有是時候三方坐下商討香港科學工藝教育的去向,讓有志
的年輕一代,有機會學習當代科技。[102]政府調查童工委員會
並沒有建議成立或改善工業學院,只有周壽臣提議在晚上或
星期日提供自願性教育給童工。[103]1923年,華人在油麻地
辦了一工業義學,免費教授一般課程和手工藝。[104]同年,房

96　Report of the Director of Education for the year 1916, Annex B Report
　　of the Director of Technical Institute

97　Report of the Director of Education for the year 1917, paragraph 42

98　*South China Morning Post* 8 November 1920

99　*China Mail*, 15 April 1921

100 *Hong Kong Telegraph* 15 July 1921

101 *South China Morning Post* 17 January 1922

102 ibid, 21 July 1922

103 Report of the Commission appointed to enquire into the conditions of
　　the industrial employment of children in Hong Kong, and the desirability
　　and feasibility of legislation for the regulation of such employment,
　　1921, Appendix 4.

104 *China Mail* 5 March 1923

屋建造質素被評劣等。[105]翌年，實業專科學院開辦的建造課程包括建築歷史、建築繪圖、鋼結構和鋼筋混凝土設計等科目。高級應用力學和物料力學就須依賴港大的課程。電機工程學亦須在港大上課。[106]1925年實業專科學院的突破是在九龍居民協會 (Kowloon Resident Association)的要求和跟進下完成，九龍開辦的課程包括實驗和理論化學、物理、數學、法文、部記、速記和家政。[107]上課地點在彌敦道九龍英童學校(今古蹟辦事處)，同年，學費加至每月十元。[108]1929年，上課地點增加了英皇書院和庇利羅士女校。[109]

4.2 史密夫教授的貢獻

香港大學工程學院院長太古教授史密夫創立香港大學工程學院，亦是第一位有客席教授銜的香港大學教授。他不但桃李滿門，亦活躍香港工程界，曾任香港工程師和造船師學會主席，經常在公開場合講授香港和中國工程發展，他善於寫作，除工程學術書籍外，亦寫下他在香港和中國的生活和對華人的感受。書名《英人在中國及遠東貿易》(The British in China and Far Eastern Trade)。他關心中國和香港的科學工藝教育，到港後不久，就向教育處長提出開辦香港基礎科學課程，但政府拖了13年皆無反應。他唯有在1926年4月29日將多年來的提議寫下，並去函教育處長，留下記錄。[110]他認為雖然實業專科學院有些工科課程，但整體上學院太側重商科，只培訓文員。他指出社會對中層技術員需求很大，必須重視此問題。事實上，司機和鉗工每月人工60至100元比文

---

105 *South China Moring Post* 30 August 1923

106 ibid, 8 October 1924

107 ibid, 2 September 1925

108 Report of the Director of Education for the year 1926, Annex B, Report by Director of Technical Institute

109 *South China Morning Post* 2 October 1929

110 Training Engineers and Artisans, *Hong Kong University Engineering Journal* Volume II, June 1930, p. 40-42

員每月30至40元高。港大何東工場落成後，工程系可容納一些在初級考試合格的學生成為大學學徒。他們在工場跟工人學習機械操作，情況有如海軍船塢學徒。一般學徒工資為每月6至10元。香港亦需要更多夜學課程去協助三大船塢，香港大學工程畢業生在這方面可擔當導師和課程設計。他稱華人機工會會員雖然忠心，但他們手工藝出眾，是可做之才，亦可改善他們的生活。但此信亦石沉大海，從未有回應。

5. 特別的一年

　　對實業專科學院的轉變，1930年是重要的一年。先有港督貝璐 (William Peel，圖11) 上任接替金文泰。世界經濟蕭條，貨幣大跌，政府要節約開支，貝璐上任立刻成立裁員委員會(Retrenchment Commission)。英國經濟代表團 (British Economic Mission)訪華促進兩地經濟。1929年大旱災記憶猶新。雖然無線電直播港督貝璐在大會堂上任時的演說因山頂發射台故障而被迫放棄，有如食了「詐糊」。[111]然而三日後，九龍居民在九龍西洋波會歡迎貝璐夫婦時的演說就如常直播，[112]貝璐依然成為

圖11　港督貝璐像

首位與市民在空氣中見面的港督。從未簽署的香港至廣州

---

111 *Hong Kong Telegraph*, 9 May 1930
112 *Hong Kong Daily Press*, 13 May 1930

直通車協議開始協商重簽。競投汽車渡海小輪專利正如火如荼。啟德機場工程接近完成，九龍發展備受關注。自撥電話剛啟用。冷氣亦在娛樂戲院登場。本地保護兒童協會成立。

　　上文提及因童工問題華人籌得巨款倡議成立工業學院，但政府堅持學生必須是居港兒童，否則便是浪費公帑。但由於大部份犯事兒童來自廣州而令事件裹足不前，後在1923年至1925年間，聖類斯工業學校的慈幼會找到一合適地，已獲政府批准，準備與華人商討合作開辦工業學校，可惜1925年大罷工和跟著的經濟衰退，事件擱置。事件於1930年重提，貝璐批准空置的香港仔紙廠作為工業學校校社，仍然堅持學生必須是居港兒童，同意華人與慈幼會繼續商討合作開辦工業學校。在經濟低迷下，香港大學的入不敷出更加嚴重，又要四出籌款，先找當年捐款最多的太古。但太古在1929年底致函港督清楚説明他們支持香港大學工程學院的目的是培訓更多華人工程師明瞭英國做法和其標準。其實入不敷出最大問題是工程學生下降，工學院四年課程頭三年是沒有分科，到第四年才選收土木、機械或電機工程。這做法是仿照英國大學模式。問題出於若要成為執業工程師，大學畢業後必須經過在職實習，才可進升執業工程師。香港在土木工程有很多大型基礎建造供畢業生實習，但機械工程只有兩間大船廠，而電機亦只有兩間電力公司，無力提供足夠實習機會。畢業生唯有往英國或中國尋找機會。故此機械和電機工程就無學生問津。1930年，土木工程有13學生；機械工程3學生；無電機工程學生。過去畢業生中土木工程佔84人；機械工程27人；電機工程39人。情況強差人意。[113]不單學生人數不足，太古坦言指出她們要求的員工非港大畢業生，因為他們亦要通過實習才可發揮作用，她們要的是從下而上的技術員工。[114]在實業專科學院做了廿多年總監的華富士亦

---

113 Report of the Committee on Practical Technical Education, 1931 , Para-
　　graph 16

114 ibid, paragraph 37; Appendix A

退休，圖12和13是華富士最後一年發出的實業專科學院簡章。在這大環境下，貝璐不得不成立檢討委員會，尋找解決方法。檢討委員會的職責範圍很清晰：滙報加強實用專科教育和成立職業學校的可行性。[115]答案呼之欲出。港大校長韓魯 (William Woodward Hornell)被委任為主席，委員為曹善允、教育處長、周俊年、黃埔船塢經理戴亞 (Robert Morton Dyer)、太古船塢經理邵馬土 (Thomas Henry Robert Shaw)、利安建築師麥健清 (Alexander Somerled Mackichan)和港大工程學院太古教授史密夫。《南華早報》八年前的提議終於被接納。

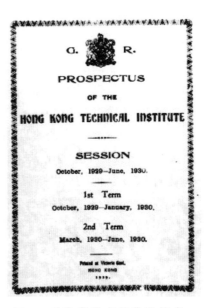

圖12　香港實業專科學院簡章

5.1 檢討實業專科教育委員會報告

　　實業專科教育委員會於1931年6月11日完成報告，12月才公開報告，有119段，兩附件。《南華早報》在7月介紹科技教育之父安達臣，[116]在報告公開後又以「學校為學

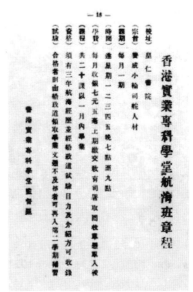

圖13　香港實業專科學院簡章

115 Hong Kong Government Gazette No. 615 of 1930

116 *South China Morning Post* 14 July 1931

徒制而設」和「輔助學徒」為標題分別評論報告書。[117]其一連串評論如基礎教育直接影響實業專科教育的成敗，香港大學與市場的鴻溝必須收窄，委員會只側重於建造和造船業而忽略其他工業領域等，都一針見血。[118]顯示出記者熟悉英國的實業專科教育經驗和本地實業專科教育的不足。[119]查《南華早報》當時的經理是衛理(Benjamin Wylie)，他是教育和廣播委員會成員，亦是九龍居民協會活躍份子。他死後，九龍衛理道就冠以他的名字。其對記者評論的影響不可忽視。報告書對實業專科學院最致命的影響是在第76、77、80和116段。委員會指出實業專科學院沒有自己校社和固定員工，其有關的課程可轉至將來的工業學校，在籌備階段中，實業專科學院要在黃埔和太古船塢附近開辦夜學給其學徒，並算出費用不少於每年四千元。明顯地，新的工業學校要取代實業專科學院，而興建和成立初級工業學校(Junior Technical School)是第一階段，到初級工業學校有了畢業生後，工業學校 (Hong Kong Trade School)就可成立，完成改革香港的實業專科教育。事實上，到1935年，實業專科學院正式易名為「香港夜學院」(Hong Kong Evening Institute)[120]，課程由初級工業學校校長韋佐治(George White)管理，[121]從1906年夜學到1907年的實業專科學院，再在28年後返回夜學名稱。當中造就不少人才，有商界、建築、造船、衛生督察、聖約翰救傷隊和老師。真湊巧，華富士的退休好像是實業專科學院的結束，而在歡送他榮休的宴會中，以全港校長和老師合辦的歡送會最為感人，[122]但以實業專科學院的的名稱舉辦就顯

---

117 Ibid 10, 22 December 1931

118 ibid 10, 11, 22 December 1931

119 ibid 21 December 1956, 18 December 1981

120 Ibid 4 September 1935; Report of Director of Education for the year 1934, paragraph 63;

121 George White, Proposed General Scheme for the Inauguration of a system of Technical Education in Hong Kong, September 1934, paragraph 8

122 *China Mail* 27 May 1930

得有點奇怪。韋佐治在1934年建議更改名稱，[123]而賓尼　(E. Burney)亦在1935年的報告中對此就有同感，並建議將師訓和大學入學試學生脫離實業專科學院，冠以其他名稱。[124]圖14是改名後香港夜學院招生廣告。提升本地技術員工的質素，關鍵是教育，按步就班地成立工業學院，培訓有「思想的雙手」，不但提高香港的競爭力，更打下香港中層科學工藝教育的基石。

6. 初級工業學校 (Junior Technical School)

　　由於報告建議初級工業學校校長需是有教學經驗的專業人士，結果畢業於格拉斯大學，後任普利茅斯和地旺甫工業學院(Plymouth and Devonport Technical College)土木及機械工程系主任的韋佐治被聘用為校長，見圖15，於1932年12月上任。[125]韋佐治的任務不但要成立初級工業學校，更重要是規劃香港工業教育的藍圖，在大學和中學間加入工業教育，培訓一班本地中層技術人才，藉扶植造船和建造業而提升香港競爭力。在管治上，增加就業機會，減少年輕罪犯，在租金高漲下，年輕華人有機會向上爬，填補外籍中層技術員的空缺，創做現代社

圖14　香港夜學院招生廣告

---

123 George White, Proposed General Scheme for the Inauguration of a system of Technical Education in Hong Kong, September 1934, paragraph 8

124 E. Burney, *Report on Education in Hong Kong* (Hong Kong: Crown Agents for the Colonies, 1935) page 15

125 CO129/544/6/page 12

會。韋佐治面對是本地基礎教育與工業教育脫軌問題，英國在十九世紀經歷過同一問題，其經驗大派用場。從實踐中學習理論是最佳工業教學法。韋校長建議兩條腿走路，一是進入初級工業學校，再入大公司的學徒訓練班，邊做邊讀「日間和晚上兼讀課程」(Part time and Evening Classes)，考取文憑資格(Diploma)，優越的可再上一層考取工程師資格。另一批是出身學徒，進修實業專科學院的夜學課程，考取証書資格(Certificate)。成立初級

圖15　香港初級及高級工業學校首任校長韋佐治

工業學校是培訓技術人才的第一步。廿多年前重「白」輕「藍」的觀念仍然牢固，韋校長建議技術員工的子弟獲優先進入初級工業學校，而選取學生時放棄筆試和測試英文程度，以防止學生學滿英文後，轉往文職或走眼了有潛質的技術人才。但他堅持學生要視力良好和身體結實，年紀太小或超齡者亦不獲考慮。結果有350人申請，挑選188人面試。取錄40人，只有11位來自非技術員工家庭。當中有22人不懂英文，校長要分兩班授課，所佔空間亦多了。剛好找到收生不足的維多利亞英童學校作為臨時校社，在加路連山南華體育會旁。他認為地點合適，鄰近空地又可發展，繪圖室、實驗室和木工場需更多室間，而圖書館藏書標準亦遠低於英國標準。到四年班全開時，學校需八間課室，還有高級工業學校和實業專科學院的課程要處理。1933年10月，學校加建實驗室新翼，由喜和盛益公司 (Hewart Shing Yick & Co) 承造，可惜爛尾，改由德興公司營造，1934年8月才完工。[126]韋校長

126 Report of the Director of Public Works for the year 1933 and 1934, paragraph 219 & 198.

稱當時教學是須要一名中文老師協助，該名老師是港大文學士，在上繪圖和工程科學課就有少許麻煩，校長要先做好筆記給中文老師翻譯，才可順利上課。這模式要持續三年，每年交下年，直至第四年。最好當然是找到港大四年級學生又或是工程師兼職。至於木工導師，他提議請老家格拉斯的木工導師，可讓學生自畫自造，導師亦可以協助校長籌組夜學課程。在儀器方面，木工工具大了少許和不足，要訂購；實驗室儀器要達英國普通國家証書水平(Ordinary National Certificate)；示範機器是重要一環，除認識實物外，教英文技術詞彙是事半功倍。學校已向潔淨局買入一汽車，將再買蒸氣器和電力摩打。校長鼓勵終身學習，圖書館除將添置教科書外，更訂了兩本易讀的業界刊物。學生畢業時分三等，優等發一級証書，可適合做管工或進船塢甲級學徒。良等發二級証書，可適合做初級繪圖員或進船塢甲或乙級學徒。合格發三級証書，可進船塢乙級學徒。校長目標是爭取被承認達英國普通國家証書水平。為此他詢查本地工程師和造船師協會可否適合當校外評審員。最後，他亦要處理歷史遺留下來的實業專科學院去向。校長認為實業專科學院最迫切是改革夜學課程，如何加重英文元素，長遠達至真正的延續課程，以課程為單位取代以科目為單位。從實業專科學院過渡至工業學校，以實業木工為試點。[127]《南華早報》以「試驗學校」為標題介紹初級工業學校，明確指出學校畢業生不是行業專才，而是提供基礎科技教育。[128]初級工業學校就此在1933年2月15日開課，而香港工業教育又轉入一新階段。圖16是初級工業學校招生廣告。

　　韋佐治安定了初級工業學校和實業專科學院，便往東南亞取經，訪問馬來西亞、檳城和星加坡工業學校，以製訂一套香港工業教育制度，即籌組高級工業學校(Hong　Kong

---

127 CO129/544/6 p20-40

128 *South China Morning Post* 18 March 1933

Trade School)。東南亞之行，他寫了一報告。[129]回港後，再撰寫高級工業學校課程銜接初級工業和夜學課程[130]，並著手預備興建高級工業學校。1934年報告名為〈開展香港科學工藝教育制度建議書〉(Report on a Proposed General Scheme for the Inauguration of a System of Technical Education in Hong Kong)，並不是成立高級工業學校建議書，見圖17。言下之意是成立香港工業教育制度之始，可見韋佐治之用心。新的香港工業教育制度包括初級工業，若初級工業學校失敗，韋佐治之合約亦同時告終，高級工業學校亦無需成立。韋先生因此經常曝光傳媒，介紹他的嬰兒，他又請教各大船塢老闆、工務局和九廣鐵路工程師，推銷他的學生。1934年政府通過興建高級工業學校，主因是港督貝璐支持和建造商會承諾以成本價興建。[131]韋先生因而順利續約，並改名為「職業及工業學校校長」(Princi-

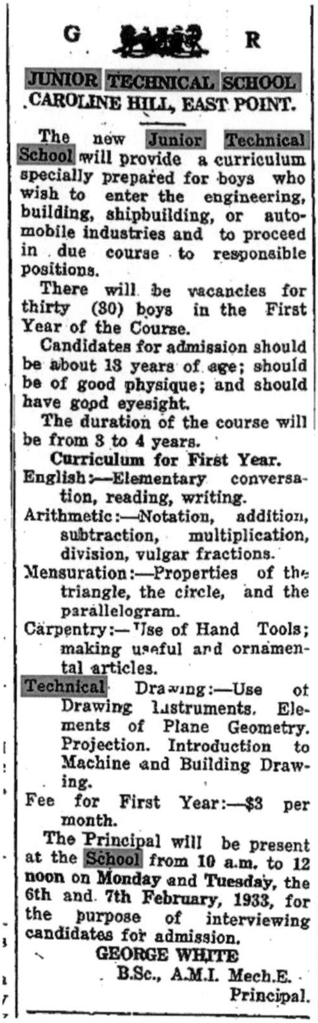

G R

JUNIOR TECHNICAL SCHOOL
CAROLINE HILL, EAST POINT.

The new Junior Technical School will provide a curriculum specially prepared for boys who wish to enter the engineering, building, shipbuilding, or automobile industries and to proceed in due course to responsible positions.

There will be vacancies for thirty (30) boys in the First Year of the Course.

Candidates for admission should be about 13 years of age; should be of good physique; and should have good eyesight.

The duration of the course will be from 3 to 4 years.

Curriculum for First Year.

English:—Elementary conversation, reading, writing.

Arithmetic:—Notation, addition, subtraction, multiplication, division, vulgar fractions.

Mensuration:—Properties of the triangle, the circle, and the parallelogram.

Carpentry:—Use of Hand Tools; making useful and ornamental articles.

Technical Drawing:—Use of Drawing Instruments. Elements of Plane Geometry. Projection. Introduction to Machine and Building Drawing.

Fee for First Year:—$3 per month.

The Principal will be present at the School from 10 a.m. to 12 noon on Monday and Tuesday, the 6th and 7th February, 1933, for the purpose of interviewing candidates for admission.

GEORGE WHITE
B.Sc., A.M.I. Mech.E.
Principal.

圖16 香港初級工業學校招生廣告

129 George White, Report on the organization, operation, cost and equipment of the Trade School etc. of Malaya with reference to the Institution of a Trade School in Hong Kong, September 1933

130 George White, Report on a Proposed General Scheme for the Inauguration of a System of Technical Education in Hong Kong September 1934.

131 Minutes of the Legislative Council Meeting, 13 & 27 September 1934

pal, Trade and Technical Schools)[132]其實香港工業教育早在民間和政府出現，因香港大學的成立而轉變，後來亦因香港大學而找到定位，韋佐治是根據1930年委員會的建議優化本地工業教育制度，成立三層制，即初級工業學校(後來的工業中學)、高級工業學校(後來的工業學院和職業訓練局)和香港大學工學院。取代了以科目為主的實業專科學院夜學，奠下了香港的三級制度。

7. 高級工業學校 (Hong Kong Trade School)

　　1934年5月，韋先生的外訪報告在立法局公開，同年9月港督貝璐在財政預算宣佈已留款項興建高級工業學校，並答謝建造商會承諾以成本價興建。高級工業課程就在1935年初在立法局公開。韋先生亦把握機會，在老師學會和扶輪社午餐例會講述香港工業教育前景。[133]他與工務局工程師鶴治(Hobbs, Charles Christie Arthur 1891 - ?)[134]商討學校設計，最初預算260,000元，[135]後減少地盤整理工程，預算約222,000元。[136]建造商會亦於同年5月與政府簽署合約營造高級工業學校，造價136,000元，另傢俬和器具60,000元。[137]圖18是學校圖則，樓宇於1935年8月完工。[138]在課程設計方面，韋先生將中層工業教學分五類，第一類是初級課程，是學徒先修

---

132 Report by the Director of Education for the year 1935, paragraph 39

133 *South China Morning Post* 15 March, 4 September 1935

134 鶴治擁有建築師和結構工程師專業資格，於1912加入孟加拉政府任助理顧問建築師，曾在印度、巴格達和尼日利亞任軍事建築師。1934年轉香港任建築師，由於具豐富軍事建築徑經驗、1938被派處理防空建築直至二次世界大戰。

135 CO129/549/7/ page 8

136 CO129/553/6/ page 13

137 ibid page 14; Report by the Director of Public Works for the year 1934, paragraph 109

138 Report by the Director of Public Works for the year 1935, paragraph 121

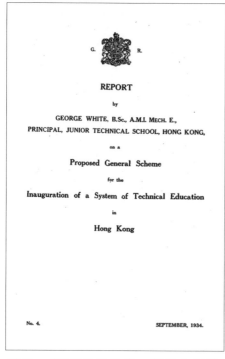

REPORT

by

GEORGE WHITE, B.Sc., A.M.I. MECH. E.,
PRINCIPAL, JUNIOR TECHNICAL SCHOOL, HONG KONG,

on a

Proposed General Scheme

for the

Inauguration of a System of Technical Education

in

Hong Kong

No. 4. 　　　　　　　　　SEPTEMBER, 1934.

圖17 　〈開展香港科學工藝教育制度
建議書〉

班；第二類是高級課程，部份或全部取代學徒課程；第三類屬兼讀課堂課程，為工程公司學徒提供理論培訓；第四類屬兼讀行業課程，為學子提供附加實用培訓，在晚間上課；第五類屬副修課程，為一些無需經過學徒制行業學生提供短期全日培訓。初級工業學校負責第一類。第二類由高級工業學校負責，校長重點放在學生的出路，他成立兩大部門，建造和工程系。工程分輕重兩組，輕的包括無線電、汽車維修、小型機器和電器，重的有海洋和火車機械工程。韋先生原先的構思是無線電班列日後發展，因為儀器昂貴，和擔心收生不足，師資亦要依賴工務局電機工程師。成立於1929年6月4日的政府無線電學校活了不足一年，於1930年3月31日因供多於求而告終。[139]到1935才重開，改名政府船隻無線電報控制員學校 (Government Wireless Telegraph School for ships operators)，歸工務局管轄。申請人必須是英籍，即香港出生，英文良好，學費每月十元，課程六至九月。船隻無線電報控制員薪金每月60至100元，政府不承諾畢業生可有聘書。[140]高級工業學校所辦的課程與工務局無異，只是定下課程為九個月，申請人英文達第二

139 Report by the General Post Office for the year 1929 & 1930
140 Hong Kong Government Gazette No. 902 of 1935

班，即前中學會考程度。算是接收了一個受人歡迎的課程。無線電班於1937年2月開課，是高級工業學校最早開辦的課程。[141]建造課程為建造業而設，學生必須是建造業公司員工，學生要通過面試挑選，是部份兼讀課程，為期三年半，完成後每月工資一百元。兼讀課堂課程的目標是考取英國教育委員會國家普通証書。亦於1937年3月開辦。剛巧天津南開大學的張彭春教授在香港大學講述中國教育，提出新「三R」觀點，以收音機(Radio, 無線電廣播)、路

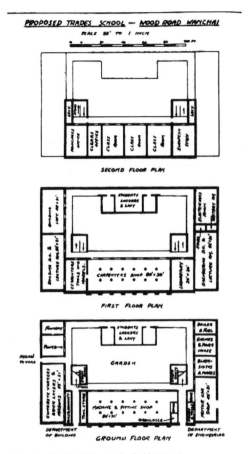

圖18　香港高級工業學校圖則

(Road)和電影　(Reel)取代閱讀(Reading)、寫作(Riting)和數學(Rithmetic)，[142]高級工業學校就開辦了兩個專科課程。至於海洋工程，學生要通過入學試挑選，目標是考取貿易委員會二級証書，人工每月三百元，非常吸引。汽車維修工程學生要通過面試和體格檢查挑選，畢業生工資約每月四十元。高

---

141 George White, A Trade School in Hong Kong, *Oversea Education: A Journal of Educational Experiment and Research in Tropical and Sub-Tropical Areas,* Volume IX, No. 4, July 1938, page 165.

142 *South China Morning Post*, 18 March 1937

級工業學校於1938年4月12日由港督羅富國主持開幕。

五. 結 語

　　西方工業革命的應用科學流入遠東，日本的明治維新和中國的自強運動均受其影響。香港亦不例外，雖然英人早了一月開辦英式夜學工科班，奇怪地由華人主辦的美式全日制科學工藝學堂竟走在政府之前推行實業教育。可惜天妒英才，鄺華汰的突然去世令李陞格致工藝學堂無法繼續。港督彌敦引入英式夜學進修班，打開政府實業教育之門，其接任人盧吉正其名為香港實業專科學院，定下制度，在中學教育之上尋求出路，除頒發証書外，還企圖頒授文憑。當時兼職老師有工務司白健時和政府化驗師班尼等，師資鼎盛，前途一片光明。其後更接收了李陞格致工藝學堂的所有硬件。盧吉在籌備成立香港大學時，亦曾考慮接收實業專科學院。香港大學成立後，確實拿走了實業專科學院的獎學金和部份學生，令她轉向其他課程發展如師訓、衛生、救傷和家政等。實業專科學院多次被傳媒和學者批評側重商科，但政府毫無反應。事實上，在香港學生未有基礎科學知識前，夜學是培訓在職人員的唯一方法，實業專科學院的工和理科都培訓了不少人才。問題是中國傳統「重文輕武」的觀念不是一代人可立刻改變。要技術人員在經濟和社會地位提升後才可改變一般人的想法。歷史往往講契機，1920年代末的經濟衰退，政府在尋找新機時，亦考慮到提升本地競爭力。本地船務和建造業的中上層技術人員多是外籍員工，除薪酬高外，宿舍租金亦高企。兩大船塢和港大工程學院教授皆認為香港有能力培訓本地中上層技術人員，取代高薪外籍員工，增加競爭力。成立工業學院取代實業專科學院訓練中層技術人員是三贏政策，因為香港正缺乏中層技術人員，又可令一些有潛質的低層技術人員向上流，填補空缺，僱主和僱員都受惠，可謂一箭三鵰。港督貝璐上任，大力發展科技教育，成立委員會進行大改革，上層技術人員，即工程師由香港大學負責培訓。由於香港中學科學知識基礎不足，訓練中層技術人員需由下層入手，即學徒。請來韋佐治校長，先成立初級工業學校，選取技術人員子弟入讀，待學生有了初級科技知識，才成立高級工業學校，培訓中層技術人員。實業專科學院就改回夜學名稱，並納入高級工業學校。香港今天的培訓技術人員三級制，就源於此。

冷戰初期兩岸的僑教政策
──對香港中學畢業生升學的影響

周正偉

珠海學院 中國文學系

一、前 言

　　二次世界大戰前，香港學生如有志深造者，除少部分進入香港大學就讀外，其餘大多採取另兩種途徑升學：（1）國外留學，多赴歐美等地；（2）因中國與香港兩地的密切關係，大部分學生選擇返回內地大學繼續學業。[1]港督葛量洪（Alexander William George Herder Grantham, 1899-1978, 15 Mar 1947 – 23 Jan 1958）曾表示，香港中學畢業生如有志繼續研究中文，會選擇返回中國的大學就讀。[2]

1　〈香港學校畢業生或肄生投考轉學辦法〉，《教育大辭典》第四卷，上海：上海教育出版社，1993年9月，第445頁。
　　譚維漢，〈二十五年來的香港教育〉，載於《星島日報創刊廿五周年紀念論文集》，香港：龍門書店，1963年，第148頁。

2　亞歷山大·葛量洪，《葛量洪回憶錄》，香港：廣角鏡出版社，1984年，第205頁。
　　《星島日報》，香港，民國45年（1956）1月18日，第五頁。
　　《香港年鑑》1952上卷，香港：華僑日報，1952年，第55頁。
　　童元方譯：《風雨絃歌──黃麗松回憶錄》，香港：香港大學出版社，2000年，第6、8頁。

　　隨著國、共內戰及韓戰的先後爆發，中國的局勢出現新的變化，臺海兩岸政府分別制訂各自的僑教政策，期望能夠吸引華僑子弟的青睞，而香港中學畢業生也是其中被積極爭取的對象。

（一）「內戰」：國府退守臺灣

　　二次世界大戰末期，美國為減少美軍登陸日本本土的傷亡，決定使用毀滅性武器，迫使日本投降。1945年8月6日，第一顆原子彈投落廣島；[3] 8日，第二顆原子彈投落長崎，[4] 先後造成20萬人的死傷。日本決定接受波茨坦宣言（Potsdam Declaration），8月14日宣布向盟國無條件投降。[5] 蔣介石（1887-1975）於同日，以及20日、23日連發三電邀請中共中央主席毛澤東（1893-1976）前往重慶面商「國家大計」。[6]

　　28日，毛澤東偕周恩來（1898-1976）、王若飛（1896-1946），在國民黨代表張治中（1890-1969）、美國大使赫爾利（Patrick J. Hurley, 1883-1963）的陪同，由延安前往重慶，開始戰後國、共兩黨的談判。[7] 經過多次磋商，雙方達成

3　《華僑日報》，香港，民國34年（1945）8月8日，第一頁；8月9日，第一頁。
　　《申報》，上海，民國34年（1945）8月8日，第一張（一）。

4　《華僑日報》，香港，民國34年（1945）8月12日，第一頁。

5　《華僑日報》，香港，民國34年（1945）8月16日，第一頁。
　　《申報》，上海，民國34年（1945）8月16日，第一張（一）。

6　《華僑日報》，香港，民國34年（1945）8月24日，第一頁。
　　國史館中華民國史事紀要組，《中華民國史事紀要（初稿）綱文備覽》第五冊上，臺北：國史館，民國85年（1996）5月，第503、510、514頁。
　　汪朝光，《中華民國史》第11卷，1945-1947，北京：中華書局，2011年，第26-28頁。

7　中共中央文獻研究室編，《毛澤東年譜1893-1949》下卷，北京：中央文獻出版社，2005年，第7、9、12、16頁。
　　國史館中華民國史事紀要組，《中華民國史事紀要（初稿）綱文備覽》第五冊上，第518頁。
　　汪朝光，《中華民國史》第11卷，1945-1947，第35頁。

12項協議（即「雙十會談紀要」）；[8]但協議卻無法有效阻止國、共雙方的衝突，且情況愈趨激烈。

同年12月15日，美國總統杜魯門（Harry S. Truman, 1884-1972）發表對華政策聲明（*Statement by Harry S. Truman on the United States Policy towards*），[9]並派遣馬歇爾（George C. Marshall, 1880-1959）為特使，專責調處國、共兩黨間衝突。自1946年初至1947年初，國、共雙方雖然經過多次停戰和政治協商，但都無法有效執行。最終馬歇爾被召返國，而國、共和解至此也完全失敗。

1947年6月底，國民政府放棄談判政策，改採軍事剿滅中共。1948年是戰局逆轉的一年，毛澤東以「農村包圍城市」的戰術，配合蜂擁而起的學潮，並建立廣泛的民主統一戰線，與國民政府進行全面戰鬥。國、共雙方經歷「遼瀋」（東北）、「淮海」（徐蚌）及「平津」（華北）三場戰役後，中共軍力不斷擴張，國民政府軍隊則兵敗如山倒。1949年10月，中華人民共和國成立。12月，國民政府退守臺灣。

（二）「韓戰」：掀起兩岸對峙

杜魯門總統在1949年8月5日發表通稱《中國白皮書》（a White Paper on China）之《美國與中國關係1944-1949》（*United States Relations with China with Special Reference to the Period 1944-1949*），白皮書的內容，把中共占領中國大

8　《華僑日報》，香港，民國34年（1945）10月12日，第一頁。
　　China Mail, Hong Kong, 11 Oct. 1945, p.1.
　　國史館中華民國史事紀要組，《中華民國史事紀要（初稿）綱文備覽》第五冊上，第555頁。
　　汪朝光，《中華民國史》第11卷，1945-1947，第47-50頁。
　　中共中央文獻研究室編，《毛澤東年譜1893-1949》下卷，第32頁。

9　*Statement by the President : United States Policy Toward China,* Public Papers of the Presidents Harry S. Truman 1945-1953, Harry S. Truman Library & Museum, 參閱於2014年8月26日，http://www.trumanlibrary.org/publicpapers/index.php?pid=506.
　　China Mail, Hong Kong, 17 Dec. 1945, pp.1,6.

陸的原因，歸咎為蔣介石自身的錯誤和弱點所造成，且美國也沒有能力改變國民政府的失敗。[10]杜魯門總統時代的初期，美國對中國是採取「塵埃落定政策」（letting the dust settle in China）的。[11]雖然杜魯門也曾希望營救撤退至臺灣的國民政府，但臺灣在美國整個東亞政策中，並非是最優先的選項，其他如阻止共黨在亞洲地區的發展、美國對日本的改造、以及防止中共繼續在東南亞的擴張，反而是較為重大的事情。

　　所以，當杜魯門仍認為臺灣國府的前途未卜，美國最終還是選擇要與中共打交道。在這種情勢下，杜魯門在1950年1月5日召開的記者會，便宣告美國目前「無意介入中國的內戰」，指出「從美國的角度看來，臺灣的資源已使其獲得足夠所需便於自衛」，美國「不再提供軍援或建議給臺灣」，[12]如此等於宣告臺灣必須獨自面對中共的軍事威脅。美國的說法相當直接，很明顯地，是為美國自己「脫身」。[13]一星期後，美國國務卿艾奇遜（Graham Allison）在國家記者協會的演講中，再一次地為美國辯護，指稱國民黨應為自己在中國大陸的失敗負責。同時指出美國在太平洋的防衛半徑，遠從阿留申（Aleutians）群島、經過日本到琉球

10　*China Mail*, Hong Kong, 6 Aug. 1949, p.1.
　　《工商日報》，香港，民國38年（1949）8月6、7日，第二頁。
　　《華僑日報》，香港，民國38年（1949）8月6、7日，第一張第一頁。
　　Robert Garson, *The United States and China since 1949* , London : Pinter Publishers, 1994, pp. 27-28.

11　Robert H. Ferrell, *Harry S. Truman : A Life*, Columbia : University of Missouri Press, 1994, p.316.

12　Harry Truman, "United States Policy Respecting the Status of Formosa (Taiwan): Statement by the President, Jan. 5, 1950,"*American Foreign Policy 1950-1955: Basic Documents (Volume II)* ,Washington, D.C. : U.S. Government Printing Office, 1957, pp. 2448-2449.
　　《工商日報》，香港，民國39年（1950）1月7日，第二頁。
　　《華僑日報》，香港，1950年1月7、14日，第一張第一頁。

13　陳啟懋，《中國對外關係》，上海：上海遠東出版社，2001年，第66頁。

和菲律賓，[14]他並未提到南韓與臺灣，等於宣告南韓和臺灣被劃在美國防線之外。

　　「韓戰」是二次世界大戰後國際關係重整過程中，最為矚目的歷史事件之一，於1950年6月25日清晨4時（美東時間為24日下午2時）爆發，[15]美國政府是在美東時間6月24日晚間獲悉這次衝突。因此，美國改變了二次大戰後放棄臺灣國府和南韓的政策，認為南韓如失，不只日本難保，其他接近蘇聯的國家也將為其囊括。所以，杜魯門總統決定派遣美國在日本的駐軍援助南韓。同時，顧慮到此刻中共可能趁機進攻撤守臺灣的國府，杜魯門又下令美海軍第七艦隊（United States Seventh Fleet）巡防臺灣海峽，確保該地區「中立化」，企圖阻止臺海兩岸的相互攻擊。[16]

　　7月7日，聯合國安理會在蘇聯代表缺席的情況下通過第84號決議，派遣聯合國部隊支援南韓抵禦北朝鮮的進攻。[17]隨著美軍於9月中旬從仁川（Incheon）登陸後，10月8日，毛澤東簽署組成中國人民志願軍命令，決定援助金日成（1912-1994），向聯合國部隊反攻。[18]　10月19日，志願軍從安東和

14　《華僑日報》，香港，1950年1月14日，第一張第一頁。
　　《工商日報》，香港，民國39年（1950）1月14日，第二頁。

15　《華僑日報》，香港，1950年6月26日，第一張第一頁。
　　《工商日報》，香港，民國39年（1950）6月26日，第一頁。

16　《華僑日報》，香港，1950年6月28日，第一張第一頁。
　　《工商日報》，香港，民國39年（1950）6月28日，第一頁。

17　《華僑日報》，香港，1950年6月27日，第一張第三頁。
　　《華僑日報》，香港，1950年7月8日，第一張第三頁。
　　《工商日報》，香港，民國39年（1950）7月8日，第三頁。

18　《工商日報》，香港，民國39年（1950）11月8日，第一頁。
　　《大公報》，香港，1950年11月8日，第一張第一版。
　　沈志華編，〈史達林關於中國出兵問題致金日成的信〉，載於《朝鮮戰爭：俄國檔案館的解密文件》（中冊），臺北：中央研究院近代史研究所，民國92年（2003），第591-592頁。
　　軍事科學院軍事歷史研究所，《抗美援朝戰爭史》上卷，北京：軍事科學出版社，2011年，第205頁。

輯安兩地渡過鴨綠江，入朝作戰。[19]

二、中央人民政府制訂優惠措施吸引僑生到內地學習

（一）教育部及粵省政府公布優待僑生回內地就學辦法

　　1949年中共接掌大陸政權後，即提出「不使華僑學生失學」的指示，[20]因此相關部門遂積極擬訂輔導華僑子弟升學的辦法，例如：採取「集中接待，分散入學」的處理方針，對到內地就學的華僑學生，先安排在北京及廣州集中接待，然後再分發至全國三十多個大、中城市的學校。[21]其中「南方大學」在第一期招生時，就特別提及「海外僑胞」也具備投考資格。且該校副校長還特別表示，要「寬取僑胞子弟」。[22]

　　翌年5月，「為了貫徹第一次全國教育工作會議的精神，開始有計劃有步驟地培養新中國的各種專門人才和建設幹部，逐步糾正過去高等學校在招生上的不合理狀態及減少學生的投考困難」，[23]教育部特公布《高等學校1950年暑期招考新生的規定》。其中對考試成績稍差的華僑學生，得從寬取錄。[24]所以，廣東省人民政府於6月隨即公布《優待僑生

19　沈志華主編，《中蘇關係史綱：1917-1991年中蘇關係若干問題再探討》，北京：社會科學文獻出版社，2011年，第129頁。

20　張泉林主編，《當代中國華僑教育》，廣州：廣東高等教育出版社，1989年3月，第15頁。

21　李修宏、周鶴鳴，《廣東高等教育》，廣州：廣東高等教育出版社，1988年8月，第363頁。
　　廣東省地方史志編纂委員會，《廣東省志・教育志》，佛山：廣東人民出版社，1995年8月，第303頁。

22　《大公報》，香港，1949年12月1日，第一張第二版；24日，第二張第七版。

23　《大公報》，香港，1950年5月29日，第一張第一版。

24　《大公報》，香港，1950年6月2日，第一張第四版。

回國就學暫行辦法》。[25]同時，華北區17所專科以上院校根據教育部的指示，組織聯合招生委員會，[26]也提供海外僑生投考的機會。

內地各級政府除擬訂各種優惠政策，期望能夠吸引更多海外華僑子弟選擇到內地學習外，在香港還透過報紙宣傳，例如：《大公報》服務版有題為「回內地升學去！」的文章，向香港中學畢業生介紹升學內地高等院校的情況，還有收費的相關資訊。[27]且報紙的專欄還附有由內地部分院校學生會撰寫「歡迎你去！」的文稿，[28]以及在「新聞版」使用一些較負面的標題，攻擊國府的僑教政策。[29]

事實上，除了華北區17專科以上院校外，東北區、中南區，包括

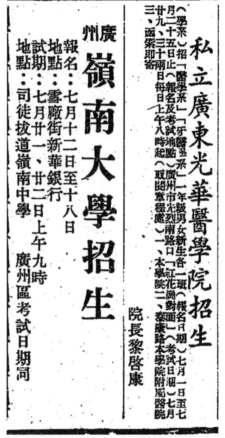

圖1　《大公報》，香港，1950年7月10日，第一張第四版。

25　《大公報》，香港，1950年6月9日，第一張第四版。

26　《大公報》，香港，1950年6月14日，第一張第二版。

27　《大公報》，香港，1950年6月28日，第二張第六版。

28　《大公報》，香港，1950年6月28日，第二張第六版。
　　〈僑胞子弟回國升學去！〉，「社評」，《大公報》，香港，1950年7月9日，第一張第二版。

29　《大公報》，香港，1955年7月5日，第一張第二版。

廣州的院校，例如：國立中山大學、嶺南大學、私立廣東光
華醫學院、私立文化大學、廣州大學、廣州法學院、華南人
民文學藝術學院，以及私立國民大學，都在香港刊登招收學
生的廣告。[30]

　　據廣東省華僑事務委員會公布，有關辦理輔導僑生升學
工作的初步統計，經由華僑事務委員會介紹投考穗市各大專
院校及中、小學校的僑生，合共177人；安排前往北京僑聯
會，轉介中央華僑事務委員會的僑生共214人；介紹到聯合
招生委員會（廣州區）投考華北17間高級學校的僑生，共21
人；全部總計420人。另由華僑事務委員會直接保送到公費
幹部學校學習的人數，則未計算在內。[31]

（二）教育部及粵省分別製訂照顧僑生暨港、澳學生入學暫行辦法

　　教育部為加強輔導海外華僑子弟返回內地升學，於1951
年頒布《關於照顧歸國華僑學生入學的暫行辦法》，其中規
定：應在確定錄取標準時，適當照顧華僑學生，還規定照顧
港、澳地區學生的原則，與華僑學生相同。[32]

　　同年7月，華北、東北、華東、中南等區高等學校，在
新學年度的報考工作上，分別宣布統一或聯合招生，並由各

30　《大公報》，香港，1950年7月5、9日，第二張第六版。
　　《大公報》，香港，1950年7月10日，第一張第四版、第二張第六
　　版；11日，第一張第二版。
　　《大公報》，香港，1950年7月14、15日，第一張第三版。
　　《大公報》，香港，1950年7月23日，第一張第二版；24日，第一
　　張第四版；27日，第二張第八版。
31　《大公報》，香港，1950年9月27日，第一張第二版。
32　金鐵寬編，《中華人民共和國教育大事記》第一卷，濟南：山東
　　教育出版社，1995年1月，第86頁。
　　徐達深主編，《中華人民共和國實錄》第一卷，長春：吉林人民
　　出版社，1994年6月，第518頁。
　　劉英杰主編：《中國教育大事典》下冊，杭州：浙江教育出版
　　社，1993年6月，第2097頁。

該區統一招生委員會統一辦理各該區招生事宜。對於華僑學生投考，仍舊從寬取錄。[33]而廣州華南聯合大學除參加全國高等學校統一招生委員會招考新生外，經文教局批准，為便利港、澳地區及港、澳地區附近的學生投考，特在澳門設立招生辦事處，接受學生報名。[34]同時，經廣東華僑事務委員會向華南分局報准後，南方大學宣布增設「華僑學院」，[35]專門培養海外華僑學生。

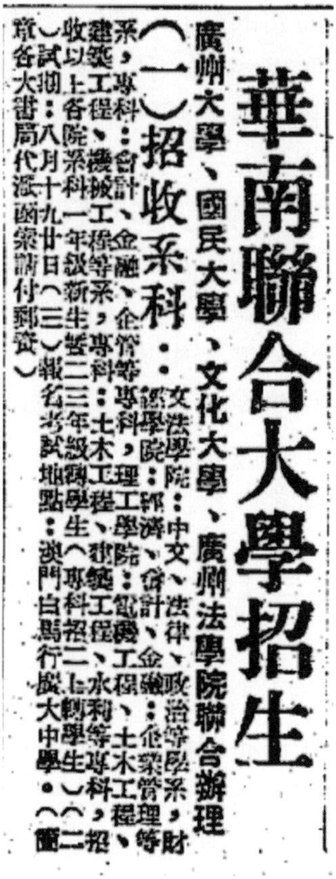

　　1952年3月，廣東省人民政府為配合教育部頒訂《華僑學生入學的暫行辦法》，以及加強對港、澳地區學生返回廣州升學的工作管理，積極準備開辦各種短期訓練班外，並頒布《香港、澳門高中學生回廣州升學暫行辦法》[36]

　　同年6月下旬，廣東省人民政府文教廳與各有關部門組成「港、澳高中畢業學生回廣州升學指導委員會」，[37]並在廣州市百靈路知用中學設立招待所，協助港、澳地區學生代辦入境、報名等手

圖2 《大公報》，香港，1951年8月11日，第一張第三版。

33　《大公報》，香港，1951年6月13、29日，第一張第二版；17日，第二張第七版。
　　《大公報》，香港，1951年7月15、16日，第二張第七版。

34　《大公報》，香港，1951年8月9日，第一張第四版。

35　《大公報》，香港，1951年7月14日，第一張第二版。

36　《大公報》，香港，1952年3月29日，第一張第四版。

37　《大公報》，香港，1952年6月5日，第一張第四版。

續,並招待住宿和安排溫習功課,又組織參觀旅行,加深學生對內地的認識。[38]據統計,約有370餘名港、澳高中畢業學生,到廣州辦理報考手續,較去年增加約三分之一。[39]

為落實對港、澳地區學生的輔導工作,同年9月,國務院電告粵省人民政府在處理港、澳地區學生的升學及照顧時,應由各省市人民政府及各級文教機關、省文教廳或市文教局負責,並出面辦理,且港、澳地區學生不能視同為華僑學生。1950年至1952年間,僅粵省即曾協助過約六百餘名僑生投考內地各高等學校。[40]

(三)教育部頒布處理僑生工作方針與方案

1953年5月,為妥善安排僑生返回內地升學,由教育部草擬的《長期收容處理華僑學生工作方針與方案》正式頒布,其中提到對華僑學生返回內地就學,應採取有積極準備及計劃的方針,以便大量招收海外僑生。且鑒於僑生的年齡一般較大,對僑生入學年齡的限制,予以適當送寬。[41]

同年6月16日,組成「香港澳門學生回穗升學指導委員會」,並擬定優待辦法,「對於志願回廣州投考高等學校的港、澳地區學生,各校按照優待規定,從寬取錄。入校後,如經濟困難,得依照規定手續,向學校申請人民助學金,各校予以優先照顧」。且為加強對港、澳地區高中畢業生提供

38 《大公報》,香港,1952年7月15、21、22日,第一張第四版;30、31日,第一張第二版。

39 李修宏、周鶴鳴,《廣東高等教育》,第375頁。
《大公報》,香港,1952年7月25、29日,第一張第四版。
《大公報》,香港,1952年8月24日,第一張第二版;30日,第一張第四版。
《大公報》,香港,1952年9月4、9日,第一張第四版。
《大公報》,香港,1952年10月31日,第一張第四版。

40 廣東省地方史志編纂委員會,《廣東省志、教育志》,第303頁。

41 金鐵寬編,《中華人民共和國教育大事記》第一卷,第155頁。
《教育大辭典》第四卷─民族教育;華僑華文教育、港澳教育,第447-448頁。

複習與必要的補習，特於7月20日，開始短期補習課程。而參加補習的學生，約有六百餘名。[42]

此外，「升學指導委員會」還公布《1953年香港、澳門高中畢業生回廣州升學暫行辦法》，協助代辦入境通行證手續。據統計，當年有逾八百名港、澳地區高中畢業生辦理入境手續。[43]最後，共有710名港、澳地區學生（香港學生約有六百餘名）參加廣東、廣州地區高等學校入學考試。[44]

翌年7月，高等教育部、教育部、華僑事務委員會決定把1953年設立的「北京歸國華僑學生投考中等學校招生委員會」遷至廣州，與「廣州歸國華僑學生投考中等學校招生委員會」合併為「歸國華僑學生投考中等學校招生委員會」。該會除負責處理升讀中等學校事宜外，並協助高中畢業返回內地投考高等學校的僑生，辦理參加廣州考區統一招生考試的手續。[45]而同年，該委員會協助八百五十多名港、澳地區學生辦理入境手續，以及抵達廣州後，安排到石牌招待所暫住，並由各大學派出應屆畢業生輔導功課，做好考試前的準備。[46]

及至1957年，為協助返回廣州投考高等學校，但未被錄取或來不及報名的港、澳地區學生，「廣州港、澳學生補習學校」於同年秋季開始，開辦大學先修班，招收學生六百名。經審查同意後，准予入校補習一年，以待來年再考，按其報考高等學校的志願分類編班。[47]

而同年經「港澳高中畢業學生升學指導委員會」安排，約有五百餘名港、澳地區學生到石牌招待所暫住。最終，共

42　《大公報》，香港，1953年6月19、24日；7月11日；8月9日，第一張第四版。

43　《大公報》，香港，1953年6月27日；7月28日，第一張第四版。

44　《大公報》，香港，1953年8月28、31日，第一張第四版。

45　《大公報》，香港，1954年7月4日，第一張第二版。

46　《大公報》，香港，1954年7月6、14日，第一張第四版。

47　《大公報》，香港，1957年6月15日，第一張第三版。

有七百多名港、澳地區學生參加入學考試。[48]據「華僑事務委員會」主任何香凝（1878-1972）在「人代會」上表示，幾年來幫助將近四萬多華僑學生進入內地各級學校學習，其中已有約百分之二十在高等學校就讀，並有將近二千名學生先後從高等學校畢業。自1949年到1955年，華僑學生返回內地升學是逐年增多，1955年比1949年增多十幾倍，1956年人數雖略減，但1957年又增多，其中有逾二千八百人參加高校入學考試。[49]

由於海外各地的學制、課程及教材內容等，都與內地不盡相同。廣東省長兼省政協主席陶鑄（1908-1969）於同年5月，在省政協第一屆委員會第三次全體會議閉幕會上，建議興辦華僑大學。其後，粵政協委員會常務委員會第25次常務會議，決定在廣州創辦專門招收華僑子弟及港、澳地區學生的華僑大學。[50]

1958年2月，粵政協常委會第28次常務會議，決定在廣州建立的華僑大學，仍沿用過去在上海的暨南大學名稱。經過半年的籌辦，選定廣州石牌歸國華僑學生中等補習學校為校址，並進行擴建工程。該校是以工科為主，兼顧文史的綜合性大學，開設五個學系11個專業；還開辦一年制華僑學生預科和兩年制工農預科。於同年9月24日正式開學，招收僑生550人。[51]

據報導，自1954年在廣州開辦歸國華僑學生中等補習學校後，就曾協助一萬八千餘名僑生考前複習，讓他們順利考

48　《大公報》，香港，1957年7月3、19日，第二張第五版。

49　《大公報》，香港，1957年7月13日，第一張第三版；15日，第一張第一版。

50　《大公報》，香港，1957年5月13、15日，第一張第一版。

51　《暨南校史　1906-1996》，廣州，暨南大學出版社，1996年5月，第117-127頁。
　　《大公報》，香港，1958年6月25、28日，第二張第五版。
　　《大公報》，香港，1958年9月19、26日，第一張第三版。

取內地各大、中城市的學校。[52]雖然中央人民政府從1949年建國開始，就積極加強僑教工作，且其後還增辦暨南大學，以便專門招收港、澳地區及華僑學生，希望集中工作，擴大效果。但由於期間發生「整風運動」、「反右」、「大躍進」及「人民公社」等事件，對香港中學畢業生選擇返回內地繼續學業的意願，造成負面的影響。

三、國府撤守在臺籌劃推動新的僑教政策

（一）國府在臺灣開始恢復籌劃僑教政策階段

　　1949年10月後，中央人民政府除了繼續對撤守臺灣的國府實施軍事行動外，還不斷向海外僑社發布對國府不利的宣傳。並且，又為了能夠與各地華僑社會建立較密切的關係，遂積極擴大推出招收海外僑生返回內地升學的優惠政策，以期爭取華僑的認同和返回中國大陸投資。所以，國府也希望能藉著「教育」，爭取海外華僑對臺灣的認同，避免僑生一面倒向內地，乃開始有計劃地招收海外僑生赴臺升學。[53]

　　「中國國民黨中央改造委員會」於1950年8月31日，發表「本黨現階段政治主張」，其中涉及僑務部分，認為：政府應儘速採取合理的措施，以解決僑胞子弟的教育問題。[54]國府僑務委員會遂於翌年6月，與教育部等相關部門修訂《

52　《大公報》，香港，1959年7月4日，第一張第三版。

53　鄭彥棻，〈無僑教即無僑務的真諦〉《華僑文教工作的方針與任務》，臺北：海外出版社，民國44年（1955）9月，第32頁。
　　鄭彥棻，〈「乃役於僑」十二年〉，《往事憶述》，臺北：傳記文學出版社，民國74年（1985）12月，第129-130頁。

54　《工商日報》，香港，民國39年（1950）9月4日，第一頁。
　　《華僑日報》，香港，1950年9月2日，第一張第一頁；3日，第一張第二頁。
　　中國僑政學會，《華僑問題論文集》第八輯，臺北：海外出版社，民國50年（1961）10月，第27頁。

華僑學生申請保送來臺升學辦法》，規定海外華僑華裔高中畢業生，得按照規定申請保送，免試分發臺灣各大專院校肄業。[55]但由於國府視港、澳地區為其一部分，赴臺升學的港、澳地區學生，並不具備僑生身分，只能以「比照僑生待遇」標準處理，故不能申請以「保送」資格升讀臺灣各大專院校。

所以，國府教育部為鼓勵港、澳地區高中畢業生赴臺升學，於同年暑假期間與僑務委員會派員到港，經洽得珠海書院同意，商借該校作招生之用，並視學生的考試成績及志願，分發到臺灣各大學院校就讀，[56]結果共有85名港、澳地區學生獲得錄取。[57]

教育部於1952年7月，設臨時辦事處於珠海書院內，專責主持招生事宜。最後，共有584人報考，而取錄入讀七所公立大專院校的學生，共有152名。[58]

同年10月21日，僑務委員會首次在臺召開全球僑務會

55　《臺灣教育輔導》月刊，第一卷第十期，臺北：臺灣省政府教育廳，民國40年（1951）9月25日，第58-59頁。
　　40年（1951）7月30日行政院臺四十外字第四○三○號令核准施行。
　　華僑革命史編纂委員會，《華僑革命史》上冊，臺北：正中書局，民國70年（1981）3月，第140頁。
56　《臺灣教育輔導》月刊，第一卷第七期，臺北：臺灣省政府教育廳，民國40年（1951）5月25日，第66頁。
　　《香港時報》，香港，民國40年（1951）8月11日，第一張第四版。
　　《中華民國年鑑》民國42年，臺北：中華民國年鑑社出版，民國42年（1953）11月，第499頁。
　　《中華民國年鑑》民國43年，臺北：中華民國年鑑社出版，民國43年（1954）12月，第546頁。
　　《中華民國年鑑》民國44年，臺北：中華民國年鑑社出版，民國44年（1955）12月，第471頁。
57　《香港時報》，香港，民國40年（1951）9月20日，第一張第四版。
58　《香港時報》，香港，民國41年（1952）7月17、18日，第二張第五版。
　　《香港時報》，香港，民國41年（1952）8月24日；9月10日，第一張第四版。

議，蔣介石致辭時，特別提到當前首要的工作中，發展華僑教育是不容忽視的，因為藉此除了可以闡揚中華文化外，並可使僑胞子弟都能為國家民族的生存而奮鬥。[59]教育部部長程天放（1899-1967）也表示，歡迎僑生回臺升學，該部將儘可能設法安置，並保證僑生無論回臺進大學或中學，都沒有問題，希望海外代表鼓勵僑生回臺深造。[60]

故翌年教育部又特別頒布優待僑生入學辦法，其中規定到臺未滿一年的港、澳地區學生，如未能進入學校者，只要持有兩地出生證或居留四年以上居留證件，並有在臺戶籍謄本可資證明，則可享有考試成績總分加20分優待；[61]使港、澳地區考取赴臺升學的學生，從1951年度的85人，升至1953年度的304人。

因此，為更有效地執行對港、澳地區學生的招收工作，且受到美國政府提出援助國府擴大招收海外僑生的影響，僑務委員會與教育部於1954年共同訂定《港、澳學生來臺就學須知》六條，正式明定臺灣專科以上學校暑期招生時間，約在每年的7月下旬至8月上旬於香港舉行，而經由港、九私立中文專上學校所舉辦的聯合招生考試，成績合格，志願赴臺升學的學生，便可獲分發升讀臺灣各院校。

在港經考試錄取的專科以上學校新生，可請由僑務委員會代辦（仍應繳付入境申請書及入境保證書）入境手續。

同年6月，國府又公布《四十三年度港、澳高中畢業生來臺升學辦法》，明確規定「報考學生以僑務委員會或教育部立案學校的高中畢業，並在港、澳地區居住四年半以上，有家長的證明書者為限」。而錄取學生，由教育部按其志願

59　《工商日報》，香港，民國41年（1952）10月22日，第一頁。
　　《華僑日報》，香港，民國41年（1952）10月22日，第一張第二頁。
　　蔣總統思想言論集編輯委員會，《蔣總統思想言論集》卷二一，臺北：中央文物供應社，民國55年（1966）10月，第195頁。
60　《華僑日報》，香港，民國41年（1952）11月2日，第一張第二頁。
61　《中華民國年鑑》民國43年，第626頁。
　　《臺灣教育輔導》月刊，第三卷第二期，臺北：臺灣教育輔導月刊社，民國42年（1953）2月1日，第43頁。

圖3　《工商日報》，香港，民國43年（1954）4月29日，第一頁。

及成績為分發標準。學校額滿不能分發時，由部參酌其成績、志願，指派其他院校相當系科或補習班，並由僑務委員會代辦入境手續。[62]

　　國府在港、澳地區聯合招生考試結束後，隨即又頒布四項對於僑生的優待辦法，協助清貧僑生完成學業。[63]經試卷評定，共取錄正取生600名，另取錄先修班學生200名，約占報考人數（1,260人）百分之七十。其後，為使有志者能獲機會赴臺升學，國府決定多錄取120名港、澳地區考生。[64]

　　臺灣方面，也好像內地一般，除制訂各項優惠政策，期望吸引更多僑生選擇赴臺升學外，在香港也透過報紙宣傳，例如：《香港時報》教育文化專欄，「升學祖國講座」；以及社會服務專欄，「僑生回國升學問題」等，向香港中學畢業生介紹赴臺升學的狀況，還有學雜膳宿等相關收費的資訊。在「港聞版」也使用一些較負面的標題，攻擊內地推行

62　《香港時報》，香港，民國43年（1954）6月22日，第一張第四版。

63　《香港時報》，香港，民國43年（1954）8月6日，第一張第二版。

64　《香港時報》，香港，民國43年（1954）8月9日，第二張第五頁；21日，第一張第四版；27日，第一張第二頁。

的僑教政策。[65]

　　1951年6月頒布實施的《華僑學生申請保送來臺升學辦法》，是臺灣有計劃恢復招收海外僑生升學之始；期間由於經費所限，故未能大規模招收僑生赴臺就學，惟人數已有逐年增多的趨勢。

（二）「美援」僑教階段（1954-1965年）

　　臺灣各大專院校所能錄取的新生名額有限，且當地學生競爭入學的情況也非常激烈，故對於擴大招收海外僑生的政策，國府並未能有效推展，有關部門乃計劃爭取美國政府的經濟援助，以解燃眉之困。

　　1953年11月8日，美國副總統尼克森（Richard　Milhous Nixon1913-1994）剛好到臺訪問，國府遂藉此機會，向尼氏說明招收海外華僑學生到臺升學的重要性。其實，當尼克森抵臺後，在與臺灣省主席俞鴻鈞（1898-1960）會面時，即曾主動向俞氏查詢有關僑生在臺升學的情況。

　　11日上午，尼克森於臺中市主持基督教會東海大學的破土典禮時表示，中共在思想方面的工作是非常積極的，目前海外已經有許多華僑子弟返回內地參與「建設祖國」的行列。所以，在未來非要先把青年教育辦好，否則影響將會十分嚴重，[66]而其中惟有積極增加招收僑生到臺升學，才可以阻止中共的影響漫延至東南亞各地。

65　《香港時報》，香港，民國43年（1954）5月4日，第一張第四頁；19日，第二張第五版。
　　《香港時報》，香港，民國43年（1954）6月8、9日，第一張第四版。
　　《香港時報》，香港，民國43年（1954）9月7日，第一張第四版。
　　《香港時報》，香港，民國44年（1955）5月29日，第二張第五版；30日，第一張第四版。
　　《香港時報》，香港，民國44年（1955）6月5日，第二張第五版；6日，第一張第四版。

66　朱匯森，《中華民國史事紀要》，民國42年7至12月份，臺北：國史館，民國78年（1989）9月，第696頁。

　　尼克森副總統在結束亞洲之行後，曾表示共產黨目前正試圖攫獲這個地區（指東南亞）；因此，尼氏認為，反共只在經濟上努力是不足夠的，應從思想教育及文化方面去根本改做，才會有完全獲勝的結果。[67]所以，尼氏希望能把華僑子弟都吸收到臺就學，且率直地提及，近年來中共派遣許多人員，到東南亞各地鼓勵華僑青年返回內地接受教育；故僑生回內地升學的是一大批一大批，而到臺灣來的只有一百幾十個，顯然國府仍需更積極推動在這方面的工作。否則，若干年後，青年一輩繼起，華人社會恐怕會全部改為認同中共政權，如此會為東南亞地區帶來動亂。至於因增收僑生到臺就讀所需款項，美國政府樂意提供支援。[68]

　　國府遂配合實施擴大號召僑生赴臺升學的政策，於1955年7月公布經修訂的《港澳高中畢業生來臺升學辦法》，其中第三項，特別規定：「香港私立專上各院校聯合招生入學試成績，在臺專科以上各學校准予認可，作為學生申請入學時成績審查的標準，審查合格者，可免試入學」。[69]此項修訂，把「港、澳區聯合招生考試」與「私立中文專科以上院校聯合入學試」合併，除減省國府在港成立辦事處，處理招生及考試等行政工作外，又可讓港、澳學生不用準備兩次考試，並可提升兩地居民對是項考試的觀感。[70]所以，共吸引1,477人報考第一次入學試，而實際應考者，則有1,468名，其中百分之九十五以上的志願，是希望赴臺升學。至於第二次報考入學試的人數為791名，缺考50人（同年香港中文中學畢業會考，共有1,491人報考，參加考試人數1,445名，及

67　許謹文譯，《和平的大道》，香港：華夏書局，1954年10月，第70頁。

68　《新聞天地》第九年第47號，香港：新聞天地社，1953年11月21日，第19頁。

69　《香港時報》，香港，民國44年（1955）7月3日，第一張第四版。

70　《香港時報》，香港，民國44年（1955）7月28日，第一張第四版。

格考生947人）。最後，獲錄取的港、
澳僑生共計1,060名。[71]

　　且為避免僑生到臺升學占去本地
學生的名額，特規定各大專院校凡新
收一名僑生，即以美援經費補助一萬
二千元至兩萬二千元（依系科決定補
助費用金額）。此外，美援運用委員
會於1954年7月宣布，教育部為招收僑
生赴臺入學，致各校現有的校舍設備
不敷應用，該會經與安全分署研議，
決撥款新臺幣867萬元作為臺灣大學、
師範學院等院校增建課室、學生宿
舍、購置書籍及設備之用。[72]故僑生的
分發，都曾受過各所院校的歡迎，[73]對
臺灣高等教育的基礎建設確有一定貢
獻。

圖4　《華僑日報》，
　　　香港，民國45年
　　　（1956）7月3日，
　　　第一張第四頁。

　　1955年9月1日，僑務委員會在臺
北市召開「華僑文教會議」，商討僑
教事宜，[74]而來自港、澳地區的文教代表，以防止華僑青年
前往內地升學為由，提出港、澳地區僑辦各高中保送成績優
良畢業學生到臺升入專科以上學校的議案；[75]僑務委員會乃

71　《香港時報》，香港，民國44年（1955）7月18、20、28日，第一
　　張第四版。
　　《香港時報》，香港，民國44年（1955）8月15日，第一張第四版。
　　《香港時報》，香港，民國44年（1955）9月11日，第一張第四
　　版；28日，第一張第二頁。

72　《香港時報》，香港，民國43年（1954）7月24日，第一張第二版。

73　張光華記，〈華僑與臺灣——鄭委員長在臺省級人民團體動員月
　　會報告〉《僑務月報》第67期，臺北：僑務月報社，民國47年
　　（1958）1月31日，第9-10頁。

74　《華僑日報》，香港，民國44年（1955）9月5日，第一張第二頁。

75　《僑務二十五年》，臺北：海外出版社，民國46年（1957）4月，第
　　178-184頁。

洽准教育部於1956年5月公布《45年港澳高級中學保送成績優良畢業生來臺升學辦法》，自同年起，凡港、澳地區立案高中僑校，得保送當年應屆高中畢業學生。[76]

此外，僑務委員會為便利華僑青年赴臺接受中等以上教育，並整合相關僑教辦法，特會同教育部於1958年5月24日訂頒《僑生回國升學及輔導實施要點》，其中包括保送及分發辦法，入學前輔導及入學後輔導等三大項。[77]

自1954年起至1965年，期間因為得到美援經費的資助，僑生教育在臺灣有著較大幅度的擴充和發展，一方面使僑生實際赴臺人數倍增，從1954學年度的738名，上升至1965學年度的1,806名。對僑教的推動，有著極大的鼓舞作用；另一方面，整個臺灣的高等教育環境，設施和資源，都得到極大的擴充和改善。

四、結 語

二次世界大戰結束後，全球民族主義思潮澎湃不已，尤其是東南亞各國的華僑，所受到的迫害，尤為嚴重。所以，當大陸易幟，新中國成立後，中央人民政府為表達對海外華僑的關懷，華僑事務委員會主任委員何香凝於1950年元旦，特向海外華僑廣播：「國內各民主黨派，早已為此要向世界人民申訴，向帝國主義提出嚴重抗議」。而且，「我們熱烈誠懇地歡迎海外華僑，本著革命的傳統，加倍地幫助祖國，參加建設新中國的偉大光榮事業。」[78]

76　《香港時報》，香港，民國45年（1956）4月30日；5月21日，第一張第四版。

77　《工商日報》，香港，民國47年（1958）5月25日，第一頁。
　　《華僑日報》，香港，民國47年（1958）5月30日，第一張第三頁。
　　《華僑日報》，香港，民國47年（1958）6月25日，第四張第一頁。

78　《大公報》，香港，1950年1月4日，第一張第三版。

圖5 《華僑日報》，香港，民國51年
（1962）10月16日，第四張第四頁。

因此，海外華僑扶老攜幼一批又一批的返回故鄉。[79]加上中央人民政府提出「不使華僑學生失學」的指示，教育部特公布相關僑教政策，對考試成績稍差的華僑學生，得從寬取錄。[80]僑生選擇返回內地升學的人數，自1950年代初開始就持續增加，對當時的國際形勢，構成重大影響。而尼克森也為此，向撤守臺灣的國府提出在美援經費中，增加對僑教事業的撥款，期望華僑子弟轉往臺灣接受教育。

但由於內地為加強管治，推出各種政治運動，尤其在1959年時爆發「三面紅旗」，造成身處內地的僑生飽受打擊，還引發1962年夏，曾出現一萬一千餘名原本在內地升學的香港學生，藉回港探親之便留下，最後只有六百餘名學生願意再到內地繼續學業的事件。[81]

79 《大公報》，香港，1959年7月4日，第一張第三版。
　　據報導，廣東省從1949年到1958年，接待由海外歸國的華僑和華僑學生共有25萬多人（不完全統計）。
80 《大公報》，香港，1950年6月2日，第一張第四版。
81 《華僑日報》，香港，民國51年（1962）10月16日，第四張第四頁。
　　《工商日報》，香港，民國51年（1962）10月16日，第五頁。

　　及至「文化大革命」爆發，中央人民政府一方面禁止在學的華僑學生重返僑居地，並在「上山下鄉」的運動中，把僑生遣送往窮鄉僻壤「安家落戶」，從事長期勞動；另一方面又認為華僑青年生長在自由社會，存有濃厚的「資產階級思想」，對內地青年會產生嚴重不良影響，「海外關係」成為「裡通外國」的黑招牌。所以，華僑教育遭受嚴重的破壞，除拒絕僑生返回內地升學外，同時各級各類華僑學校或被迫停辦、或被迫改變名稱，使到內地的僑教工作因以停頓，香港學生也無法繼續北上。[82]其中暨南大學從1966年起至1977年，中斷招生達12年；且該校與華僑大學均同時於1970年被下令關閉，教師被遣散，校舍被占用，儀器設備、圖書資料遭其他院校瓜分。

　　在這個時期，由於國府持續推出各項僑教優惠措施，加上美援政策的支持，港、澳地區學生赴臺升學的人數，出現了逐年遞增的情況。1951學年度，共有263名港、澳地區學生報名（實際錄取85名），到1959學年度，已增至1,627名報名（實際錄取759名）。其後，「文革」期間的1967和68學年度，更分別有2,396名及2,872名港、澳地區學生報考，這明顯是受到內地停止招收海外僑生的影響。但事實上，雖然報名人數是有所增加，獲得錄取的人數卻出現下跌，相信是與國府自1958學年度起，對於港、澳地區保送與錄取的標準予以提高，推行「重質」的新僑教政策有關。

　　兩岸在冷戰初期，分別頒布了各項優惠的僑教政策，從僑生報到的數字，反映出確實吸引了許多華僑子弟和港、澳地區學生的選擇。對於部分香港中學的畢業生來說，尤其是中文中學，既然無法在港升讀本地唯一的香港大學，但又期望能夠繼續學業，兩岸給予的機會，無疑是最佳的出路。

　　事實上，兩岸在這個時期所提供的大學學位，是有效協

82　《中共年報》1978年，臺北：中共研究雜誌社，民國67年（1978）9月，第2之268頁。
　　劉英傑主編，《中國教育大事典》下冊，第2098頁。

助當時的香港年青人，解決升學上遇到的困局。

附表：1951至1959年港、澳地區
高中畢業生赴兩岸升讀大專院校人數統計表

年份	回內地 報名人數	回內地 錄取人數	赴臺 報名人數	赴臺 錄取人數
1951	約250	*	263	85
1952	約370	*	514	207
1953	710	*	858	304
1954	801	*	1,706	852
1955	四百餘名	*	2,256	1,066
1956	一千餘名	約70.6%	1,401	871
1957	718	*	1,585	999
1958	*	*	1,675	729
1959	*	*	1,627	759

資料來源：

（1）回內地升學：《大公報》，參加廣東省高等學校入學考試的港、澳地區學生。

（2）赴臺升學：珠海書院教務處及教育部僑民教育委員會編，《八十一學年度回國升學僑生人數統計資料》。

道行佛緣——
扶乩選址與建設而成的圓玄學院

游子安
珠海學院香港歷史文化研究中心

　　常云：「天下名山僧佔多」，然而圓玄學院創建，道行佛緣，三教人士與信奉基督者在老圍村一帶共建宗教勝地。先是廣州來港四五同道，得東普陀開山住持茂峰法師指引，通過扶乩選址與建築布置，再向信奉基督教的老圍村鄉賢張煥廷購地，最終成就一段宗教因緣。而三疊潭與老圍村，亦因圓玄學院帶來馬路等建設，周邊佛道寺廟紛紛建立，例如乾元洞、[1]慧園、[2]俗稱「船廟」的香海慈航、西方寺、龍母佛堂等，從旅遊熱門地一躍成為宗教勝地，寺廟道堂星羅棋布。始由扶乩選址建立，再而帶動整個地區發展之祠宇壇堂，在香港除黃大仙祠外，也無出圓玄學院其右。

　　寫此文有三個構想：首先是地標作用，圓玄學院與三疊潭、老圍村名聲互相輝映，成了滄海桑田此區的地標。1953年明性堂此圓玄學院內最古之殿堂開幕，建設不過十年，1965年吳灞陵稱譽為新界「兩個宗教大花園」：

1　乾元洞，位於老圍村138號，1958年創辦，奉玉皇大帝、文昌帝君、孚佑帝君等神祇，詳參游子安主編《道風百年》，蓬瀛仙館道教文化資料庫，香港利文出版社出版，2002，頁254-255。

2　慧園，先天道道場，地址為荃灣「三疊潭山頂」，1935年創辦於葵涌，1965年遷至現址。

「新界大陸有兩個宗教大花園，一南一北，南邊的是荃灣的圓玄學院，北邊的是粉嶺的蓬瀛仙館⋯⋯遊人就分散在這個大花園裡玩，比在兵頭花園裡還舒服⋯⋯」[3]再者是「扶乩治壇」的轉變，圓玄學院初建，由覓地、建堂和命名，皆取決自扶乩。學院命名由濟佛肇賜，意指圓融廣大、眾玄無窮。自1970年代以來，圓玄學院由扶乩為主導的道壇，演變為推動文化福利事業的團體。還有，香港具規模的壇觀，黃大仙祠、蓬瀛仙館、雲泉仙館、青松觀等，來自廣東道脈，都有清晰的表述，惟獨圓玄學院論述欠清晰。如一些論著提到圓玄學院，有不確的描述，或云其起初在沙田，或云道派溯源於羅浮山沖虛觀，更有誤認為是1946年創建。[4]其實圓玄學院，創辦源自尊奉呂祖之廣州宏道精社之道侶。

一、選址：蓮花洞之三叠潭

1950年曲江覺善道壇與廣州宏道精社王明韻、謝顯通、林光慶和杜光聖等「來港闡道，覓地建壇，蒙茂峰法師導遊荃灣蓮花洞之三叠潭，觀之而喜，認為洞天所在⋯⋯至圓玄學院之名，是由濟佛肇賜，圓代表佛，玄代表道，亦佳話之長留，此本院奠基之伊始也」[5]。圓玄學院位於荃灣三叠潭，背倚芙蓉山，為大帽山環抱，創辦人之一謝顯通描述其形勝：「斯地鍾靈毓秀、氣象雄偉、萬山環繞、亂石巍峨、兼以三叠之潭倍添流觴曲水」，誠清修之福地也（詳後）。（圖1）

3　吳灝陵〈萬松嶺下有蓬瀛〉（1965年5月10日刊），《香港勝景》，香港大學孔安道紀念圖書館整理，頁4-5。

4　見卿希泰主編《中國道教史》第四卷，頁530-531。有的記述圓玄學院：「1945年由香港著名道教界人士趙鎮東、呂重德等八人發起並集資買地建構，1946年正式成立」，於創辦年份和人物皆誤，見李養正《當代中國道教》，中國社會科學出版社，1993，頁198。1946年，圓玄學院幾位創辦人仍在廣州辦道。

5　馬紹章〈圓玄學院過去之興建及今後之展望〉，《圓玄學院三教大殿落成特刊》，1971年，頁56。

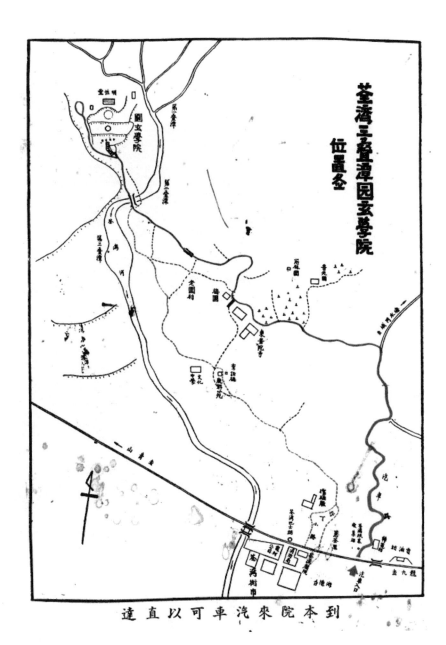

圖1　《圓玄特刊》封底所載學院位置，
　　　亦見第一、二、三疊潭之勝。

呂祖賜「萬法朝宗」牌坊聯云：

　　五嶺開來 闡教傳經 儒釋道尼乘萬法
　　三潭萃會 群機頓攝 龍獅虎象盡朝宗[6]

　　此聯由呂祖降示、創辦人之一王明韻手書。「五嶺開來」點出王明韻、謝顯通、林光慶和杜光聖等創辦道侶源自曲江覺善道壇、廣州宏道精舍；「三潭萃會」說明學院位於大帽山三疊潭；學院並兼三教，選址所具山川之氣象，牌坊橫額取上下聯綴成「萬法朝宗」。（圖2）而三疊潭地名由來，是張一麐與茂峰法師1939年遊後山溪潭，認其似廬山三疊潭，茂峰以此名其泉。[7]（圖3）《千佛山東普陀講寺碑》「……因張一麐之言，改水坑之名為三疊潭，人未知之也。上人改千石山之為千佛山，……無東普陀不足以成三疊潭之勝，

圖2　遠眺牌坊及明性堂，圓玄學院最早期建築，近景是藏龍橋（1953，謝傳清道長提供）

圖3　三疊潭第三潭在藏龍橋東，圖上方可見圓玄學院牌坊。（謝傳清道長提供）

6　詳參《（五十年來1940至1990年）呂祖靈應事蹟・玄音選刊・玄門內外修篇》，明善學院編印，2016年增訂版，頁218-219。

7　《東普陀講寺成立八十週年紀念特刊》「歷年大事年表」，東普陀講寺，2013，頁45。

無三疊潭不足以彰東普陀之盛,合之則雙美……」[8]正如1953年圓玄學院建成,更帶動老圍村地區之發展。圓玄學院背靠第一高峰大帽山,高達957米,是香港最高峰。

二、茂峰法師指引

圓玄學院源於濟佛鸞示,宏道精社弟子在港籌設佛道學院,四處訪尋佳地,而茂峰法師是關鍵的引領人。1927年茂峰法師(1888-1964)弘法香港,初駐錫於摩羅廟後街之法源堂,及後在荃灣老圍覓得佳地,1933年東普陀落成開光,與老圍村關係密切,特別是香港淪陷歲月對避難者的救助,由於法師愛護鄉民,有「慈悲王」之稱;東普陀也收容1949年大批來港的內地僧侶,東林念佛堂、西方寺多座道場得茂峰法師之助創建於荃灣大霧山麓。[9]法師和易近人,文人雅士,樂與之游。《茂峰法師事略》載,1933年東普陀寺開光後,廣州江孔殷太史、謝英伯等禮請茂峰法師至海幢寺講經。[10]或許由此結緣,16年後謝英伯兒子謝顯通來港覓地建壇,也請茂峰法師引路。謝英伯(1882-1939)廣東梅縣丙村人,自幼隨經商的父親在香港讀書,17歲考進香港皇仁書院,1905年與黃節、潘達微等人創辦南武公學,謝英伯為第一任校長。謝英伯研究佛學,組織竹林精舍於黃花崗,改組華嚴精舍於小港鄉,1938年領導成立佛教金卍字救護隊。[11]兒子謝顯通,原名景新(1911-1989),嶺南畫家高劍父與謝英伯父

8　《千佛山東普陀講寺碑》,1968年住持了一撰,石碑立於寺內大殿前,東普陀講寺,現獲評為二級歷史建築。

9　張雪松〈近代中日佛教交流──以香港荃灣東普陀寺茂峰老法師為中心〉,載游子安、卜永堅主編《問俗觀風──香港及華南歷史與文化》,香港:華南研究會,2009。

10　《茂峰法師事略》,1957年初版,2009年東普陀寺再版,頁12。

11　秦孝儀主編《中華民國名人傳》第六冊〈謝英伯〉(古鴻廷撰),台北:近代中國出版社,頁577-586。

子交往，高氏曾與宏道精社道侶於純陽殿留影。[12]

　　癸巳（1953年）三月十五日明性堂開幕，之前圓玄辦植樹節以紀慶，[13]七聖佛於植樹日降示：

> 圓融佛法
> 玄妙宏通……
> 植以玄機
> 樹人意志[14]

　　協助相地的茂峰法師，植樹日亦到賀。（圖4）

圖4　1953年圓玄植樹紀念，圖前第二排右第五位是茂峰法師，後第三排右第六位是謝顯通，背景為建設中的明性堂（謝傳清道長提供）

12　《五十年來（西曆1940年至1990年）呂祖靈應事蹟》，明善學院編印，2014，頁95。1911年廣州黃花崗之役失敗以後，曾參加起義的謝英伯、高劍父等在澳門秘密設立同盟會分會。

13　參考植麗蓮〈圓玄學院植樹誌盛〉，《圓玄特刊》，頁13。

14　《圓玄特刊》，圓玄學院，1953年，頁9。

三、圓玄學院源自尊奉呂祖之宏道精社

圓玄學院宣揚儒、佛、道三教，今天已是香港其中一所具地標作用的宗教活動場所，據網頁記述：1950年籌建圓玄學院，由前賢趙聿修等倡立。[15]《福緣善慶：圓玄學院六十周年特刊》則記載：「圓玄學院的創建肇始於呂純陽祖師於1950年（庚寅）在廣州宏道精舍（社---引者）降鸞乩述《外修篇》」；「圓玄學院創立於1953年，由楊永康、趙聿修、陳呂重德、杜光聖、林光慶、王明韻、謝顯通、黃錫祺、陸吟舫等先賢所創立」；「1950年，創院先賢在廣州宏道精舍（社---引者），請示仙聖今後闡道之方向」，呂祖、濟聖分別降乩指示。[16]有關圓玄學院的創建成員，可分為：宏道精社道侶謝顯通、林光慶、杜光聖；至寶臺道侶、百貨業商人陸吟舫[17]；同善社信徒；及營辦建築公司的楊永康等紳商。由成員組成可見，倡議創建圓玄學院的有是呂祖道堂道侶，也有先天道同善社的信徒，也有慕道的紳商支持。

圓玄學院源自尊奉呂祖之宏道精社，精社建於廣州，1948年謝顯通於宏道精社停止鸞務工作，翌年春到香江居住，隨帶呂祖肉身聖像乙張、《玄妙明聖二經合刊》及未竟完成之《玄門內外雙修篇》。據1953年謝顯通（題覺道子）《圓玄事略》筆錄這份資料，也記之甚清楚。「是院之由來，因緣於庚寅年廣州宏道精社道侶謝顯通、王明韻、杜光聖、林光慶四子，邂逅於香島，旋奉師命，籌創圓玄，於是購地興築，旋

---

15 圓玄學院網頁：事略http://www.yuenyuen.org.hk/non-flash/ch1/ch1.htm（擷取日期：2017年5月12日）。

16 《福緣善慶：圓玄學院六十周年特刊》，圓玄學院，2013，頁32。

17 陸吟舫(1897-1960)，原名詠高，道號至真，廣東三水人，百貨業商人。1943年於香港太白台「抱道堂」入道；1944年與何啟忠等人創辦「至寶台」於廣州；1950年再創「青松觀」於香港。亦任孔聖堂董事，曾任普益商會副主席。有關陸吟舫簡介，見《香港華僑團體總覽》，國際新聞社1947年刊。

囑同門陸子吟舫參加合組，自此廣徵同侶共闡法門」：

　　圓玄學院位於九龍荃灣大霧山麓（大霧山是
大帽山俗稱--引者）、三疊潭上。創於庚寅年、
鼎建於壬辰年、落成於癸巳年暮。斯地鍾靈毓
秀、氣象雄偉、萬山環繞、亂石巍峩、兼以三疊
之潭倍添流觴曲水，誠港九之名勝區，實清修之
福地也。是院之由來，因緣於庚寅年廣州宏道精
社道侶謝顯通、王明韻、杜光聖、林光慶四子，
邂逅於香島。旋奉師命，籌創圓玄，於是購地興
築，旋囑同門陸子吟舫參加合組，自此廣徵同侶
共闡法門。復得港九紳商楊永康、趙聿修、呂重
德、李唐居士、黃錫祺、林逸卿、廖輝亭、陳仲
池、佘公正暨各名流善信等先後加入乃告完成，
其中過程歷盡艱辛，非筆墨所能盡罄。今者傳經
有所，內外雙修行見
南天，法雨盡灑蒼生
也，爰集數言而略述
云爾癸巳孟冬覺道子
謹識。[18]

圖5　謝顯通於明性堂開乩
　　　（謝傳清道長提供）

　　謝顯通於1953至1961
年在圓玄學院壇務組任職，
擔任鸞生，在明性堂凌宵寶
殿左方開乩（圖5）[19]。1965
年謝顯通、林光慶等另建主
奉呂祖之玉清別館。鍾國發
指出，「圓玄學院後來沿著
同善社三教並崇的理念發展，

18　《圓玄事略》手抄本，1953，謝傳清道長藏。
19　壇務組謝顯通、林逸卿、王明韻等共7人，《圓玄特刊》頁2。

對呂祖的崇奉已不顯著。謝顯通堅持呂祖信仰，遂離開圓玄學院，另創玉清別館。」[20]1965年玉清別館臨時壇，設於三疊潭東山小築，即謝顯通家中，1966年始遷往九龍。[21]

四、扶乩對圓玄學院創建伊始的關鍵作用

1. 圓玄學院定名由濟佛肇賜

濟佛在近代角色，可從民間乩壇去說明。江蘇吳縣人包天笑追述家鄉乩壇道：

> 江南的這些乩壇，必定有一位主壇的祖師，那時最吃香而為人所崇奉的，就有兩位：一位是濟顛僧，一位是呂洞賓。大概信奉佛教的是濟顛僧，信奉道教的是呂洞賓。不過濟顛主壇的，呂洞賓亦可降壇；呂洞賓主壇，濟顛亦可降壇。他們是釋道合一，是友不是敵。吳氏這個乩壇，我知道是濟顛主壇的。[22]

1940年代以後，隨著內地局勢變化，不少高道大德輾轉來港，濟佛臨壇現象也漸多見。一些香港道堂的創立，與濟佛乩示都有直接和間接關係，如圓玄學院選址過程與濟佛指引分不開。圓玄創設，神道方面由呂祖、濟聖分別主壇執行神道教化及濟世工作。蓮花洞之三疊潭選定建壇位置經過

20　鍾國發《香港道教》，北京：宗教文化出版社，2010，頁22。

21　《玉清別館成立五十周年金刊》，元朗：玉清別館，2015，頁12-14。1949年-1951年謝顯通在老圍村家中開乩，覓地後1951-1953年在圓玄建築工地請示開乩，1953年在老圍村另建東山小築，直至1966年，十七年間謝顯通在老圍村生活及闡道，2018年1月4日，謝傳清道長訪問。

22　包天笑〈談談我的扶乩經驗〉，《春秋雜誌》第850期，1996年11月。

也甚特別,「該山地段廣闊,未知何處可稱全美。旋步行數丈,忽見一長蛇,橫繞其足,因而止步,蛇亦遠去,而該地即精華所在」〈圓玄學院籌備經過〉一文記之甚詳:

> 圓玄學院起源於庚寅年春……(王)明韻曾請示吾師,今後如何闡道?旋奉濟師見示:「我已隨風去,一路幾逍遙。明韻將我挽,暫且作留連。汝既來之,暫亦候之。能在此間組一學院則更佳。十方功德,三界方便。處處結善緣,亦即汝之般若漸見矣。一息尚存,行道豈容稍懈者。能如是,則道之成可待也。」吾師並囑:「汝等可發善心,從新闡道戍。不論境況與心情為佳為劣,祇問道之所在而行之耳。」吾等遵囑,各處訪尋,是年三月廿三日聯袂至荃灣東普陀寺,(林光慶---引者)由茂峰法師領遊大帽山三疊潭。……但需款頗巨,非目前環境所能辦者,祇有存之於心。其後再覓得九龍獅子尾之地,濟師云:「如用為養靜之室,韜光之戶,皆可為之。後因社會局以該地接近機場,未蒙允許。且是地得之亦無大益,故另尋其他」。光慶因此,遂將三疊潭之地與光聖言之。光聖心為向往,翌晨聯同往看,見地而喜。然該山地段廣闊,未知何處可稱全美。旋步行數丈,忽見一長蛇,橫繞其足,因而止步,蛇亦遠去,而該地即精華所在,捨此以外不足取也。君等遂決心用之,并請示於師,師亦謂然。惟師云:「是地按五行而論,欠木少金。若依山勢而言,可以採用。……旋濟師謂:「汝等行善功,種道德,辦學院,揚佛法,設道壇,講道經。登山涉水,追龍尋脈而不倦,歷受挫折而不懈,偉哉大矣。今地已定,至於欸之來也,汝等祇須全力以赴,當無不成之理,又

何愁孔方不自來也。……[23]

及後眾人得到趙聿修、楊永康、陸吟舫、黃錫祺和呂重德出資並向政府申請用地。1953年明性堂開幕，供奉關帝、呂祖、濟佛、觀音四聖，此亦圓玄學院內最古之殿堂。

2. 學院內外建設

圓玄學院初創，從選址到建設皆由扶乩，可說是「扶乩治壇」的時期：「是院之建築物圖則，如牌坊、正殿、明性堂、經堂……全部位置已蒙柳師（柳真君，後升格為柳天尊——引者）指示布置完妥，並經趙聿修先生請黃祖棠測師繪就，「方向及線位，亦蒙張、白兩師定妥，堪稱完善」。[24]白師即白眉祖師、與雲龍祖師、華佗先師自覺善壇（宏道精社源自覺善壇）已為該壇三師，分管堪輿、行雲化雨守禮中天，及降方施藥。[25]馬紹章一文提及圓玄最早建設，如跨越三叠潭之藏龍橋（圖2），後來已有改建或改名：「院外之永康路藏龍橋，院內之正殿、牌坊、明性堂、知止亭、會堂、道舍、寶塔、圓池、花圃等，一一如圖出現……」[26]

3. 匾聯

東普陀講寺內匾聯甚豐，除一般注意岑學呂題書，有一匾可見法師之襟懷，1949年重修圓通寶殿落成，「發菩提心」，己丑呂祖降筆，由通善壇敬奉。（圖6）佛寺內懸道教神仙乩匾，亦屬美談。圓玄學院內匾聯也甚豐，與東普陀

23　謝顯通、杜光聖、林光慶、王明韻同述〈圓玄學院籌備經過〉，分購地、名稱及圖則、發起人及籌款、建築四方面敘述，是瞭解此道堂源流的第一手資料。《圓玄特刊》，圓玄學院，1953年，頁7。

24　《圓玄特刊》，圓玄學院，1953年，頁7。

25　白眉仙翁，山西人，與黃玄憲、李志能、碧羅仙姑，為至寶台、青松觀四位鎮壇師之一。

26　馬紹章〈圓玄學院過去之興建及今後之展望〉，《圓玄學院三教大殿落成特刊》，1971年，頁56。

圖6　1949年東普陀重修圓通寶殿落成,己丑呂祖降筆「發菩提心」。(筆者攝)

來自騷人墨客區聯大異其趣的是,早期圓玄區聯多來自仙佛降筆。明聖堂各仙聖聖龕之聯句及院內門樓牌坊之楹聯皆為呂祖、濟世聖佛、觀音諸聖鸞降賜示。

丁酉年(1957)明性堂供奉觀音的神龕,聯曰:

五嶺有情欣沾甘露　　三潭無類咸被慈悲

龕聯句由呂重德恭錄乩語、黃維琚書。除了此妙聯,明性堂供奉關帝之座聯句,乃「忠蓋天地　義重山河」,而聖龕頂題欵「浩然一丕」,共十二字由岳聖書之。1953年由呂祖囑岳聖書聯,以應關聖之像,時侍鸞者謝顯通。[27]1964年謝顯通離開圓玄學院,後期落成之「三教大殿」、「養真軒」之楹聯皆由「圓玄」壇務組派人前往「玉清別舘」呈請謝顯通代叩聯句作壁,楹聯多含玄妙無窮之真諦。

五、圓玄學院創院先賢對地區貢獻

1953年圓玄學院創立,到1971年三教大殿落成,被視

27　詳參《(五十年來1940至1990年)呂祖靈應事蹟・玄音選刊・玄門內外修篇》,明善學院編印,2016年增訂版,頁128-130。

為「學院創院先賢的一個耕耘時期」，[28]1971年以後學院發展進入另一新階段。[29]圓玄學院能購地合計面積共有13萬英尺，不能不提老圍村民的支持。王明韻、林光慶往荃灣，「得林君永根介紹與地主張煥廷購買」，張君言，「該地經有數人請求轉讓，余均拒之。今與先生面晤，一見如故，豈非有緣耶？」[30]老圍是有300多年歷史的荃灣客家圍村，遷來的客家家族共有五姓，原本有五間祠堂，分屬張、曾、黃、許、鄧五族，以張氏入遷歷史最早、人口最多，仍有張姓家祠於圍村中。玉成賣地的張煥廷，自1947年擔任中華基督教會全完堂主席長達14年，老圍村望族。全完堂值理葉錦銓、張煥廷，與楊國瑞、陳永安（三棟屋村）等鄉紳領袖組成全安局。1920年成立的全安局，是鄉紳代表的組織，是當時殖民政府與鄉民的橋樑，也包括處理村民糾紛。香港淪陷，全完堂向日憲兵部申請復堂，葉錦銓、張煥廷是其中兩位復堂事宜籌備者。[31]頗難得的是，本身信奉基督教的張煥廷，沒有宗教芥蒂，樂於相助佛道有緣人：「協助建立東普陀寺、普光園、圓玄學院，並為完成圓玄學院，將其私人名下之物業數萬呎農地，以平價讓與圓玄學院。」[32]

1. 開馬路

　　1950年之前，老圍此地只是小山村。陸吟舫在《圓玄

28　《福緣善慶：圓玄學院六十周年特刊》，圓玄學院，2013，頁47。

29　1957年楊永康告病，趙聿修任圓玄學院董事會主席。趙聿修是同善社領袖，同善社儒教色彩較濃，1967年趙聿修發起籌建三教大殿。見鍾國發《香港道教》，北京：宗教文化出版社，2010，頁164。

30　謝顯通、杜光聖、林光慶、王明韻同述〈圓玄學院籌備經過〉，《圓玄特刊》，圓玄學院，1953年，頁7。

31　〈全完堂百年歷史年表〉，余煊、李興邦主編《中華基督教會全完堂百周年堂慶紀念特刊1905-2005》，中華基督教會全完堂，2005，頁11。

32　〈張煥廷先生傳略〉，《荃灣二百年》，頁52-53。張煥廷兒子張中仁，全完堂執事，2011年逝世，其後人興訟指圓玄學院2003年買地違諾索償。

特刊序》：王明韻、謝顯通四子約陸氏覓地設道場，「同人有指而告余曰：此蓮花洞也」，購地後「鑿山開道、築橋建院」。據1952年三月《老圍路開闢馬路契約》：「……荃灣大帽山麓建築圓玄學院，擬自闢馬路直達，以利交通」，由同仁、東和社司理人召集兩社開會通過，圓玄學院出資開建馬路，並捐送港幣三千元與兩社福利事業之用，張煥廷與茂峰法師等為契約見證人。[33]此馬路興築由楊永康發起，建成後冠名「永康路」：「楊公認為未開工之前，須先築一車路，以利交通，而便運輸，正所謂利人利己也。」遊人稱便：「……乘車抵荃灣市街，（原有特築汽車路直達學院門前）緩步至東普陀之背，即踏上新築之永康大道，約行里許，三疊潭在前……」[34]老圍村雖早自清初建立，但其馬路基建、學校，與圓玄學院關係密切。又如上述與荃灣墟市連貫之村路，初以村命名之鐵架牌樓暫作路標，2007年重建今貌，新舊兩座牌樓皆由圓玄學院撥資贊助、題寫楹聯。1953年圓玄學院出版《圓玄特刊》封底位置圖，標明「到本院來，汽車可以直達」，圖只寫「汽車路」仍未有路名。（可參圖1圓玄學院位置圖）

2. 老圍公立學校

　　圓玄學院創院先賢對地區教育貢獻，早期可以老圍村公立學校為例說明。1959年老圍村公立學校建成開課，校址地由老圍同和社（抗戰時由曾、張兩族成立的東和社及黃、許、鄧成立的同仁社合成）捐出，為附近各村村民提供讀書機會，1980年停辦。[35]現部份校舍已成為村公所及

33　〈老圍路開闢馬路契約〉，《福緣善慶：圓玄學院六十周年特刊》，圓玄學院，2013，頁33。文中張煥庭應為張煥廷。

34　〈圓玄學院籌備經過〉，《圓玄特刊》，頁7；及〈圓玄學院紀遊〉，頁13。

35　黃夏柏、李曉燕編《守護與傳承：荃灣鄉郊可持續發展計劃民間智慧普查彙集》，香港聖公會麥理浩夫人中心，2010，頁39-40。

聖公會麥理浩夫人中心辦事處。現存1962年所立《老圍公立學校建校捐款芳名碑》，圓玄學院主席楊永康，任建校委員主席，謝景新等為建校委員。又據《老圍公立學校建校十五週年紀念特刊》載，1959年建校委員會職員名表，主席楊永康，副主席張煥廷等三人，財務楊永康（張煥廷代）與謝景新。[36] 老圍公立學校校歌也很有地方風味：「荃灣地勝，大帽山青，老圍學校水秀山明。務耕務讀務栽培，樹人樹木樹風聲」，[37] 校旁墾地種菜，戰前，老圍以產菠蘿聞名，山上布滿菠蘿田。1970年代以後，圓玄學院建立多所中小學校，作育菁莪。

3. 醫療安老

　　圓玄學院是一所崇奉三教的道教團體，以儒的博施濟眾、佛之普度眾生、道之常善救物等精神推行善業。早在1956年，圓玄學院已註冊為有限公司，成為轄准免用有限公司字樣的慈善團體，奠定日後公益福利事業之基礎。1969年在葵涌石梨開辦福利診所，以低廉收費服務社區；1993年將西醫診所遷回學院院址。自上世紀七十年代起，顧及香港人口日趨老化的社會問題，特設立圓玄學院社會服務部，開展一系列的安老、教育、扶貧、解困等工作。黃允畋在1971年圓玄學院三教大殿落成誌慶題詞，突出兼融三教要旨：

> 儒與釋道，同源異宗。儒教明道，精一執中。
> 釋氏救渡，慈悲在胸。道家勸善，啟導群蒙。
> 三教化育，天地同功。堂皇大殿，肅穆其容。
> 虔誠奉祀，善與人同。[38]

36　《老圍公立學校建校十五週年紀念特刊》〈本校簡史〉，老圍公立學校，1974，頁31及32。

37　《老圍公立學校建校十五週年紀念特刊》〈老圍公立學校校歌〉，老圍公立學校，1974，頁2。

38　《圓玄學院三教大殿落成特刊》，1971年，頁21。

　　圓玄慈善事業歷程也有艱辛與障礙，如護理安老院的籌建即歷盡波折，1972年圓玄學院籌建，「經過悠長時間及多方波折」，1974年，圓玄學院附近的一所平房開設了圓玄安老院；1994年建成圓玄護理安老院投入服務。及後，1995年及1997年分別在粉嶺嘉福邨及深井增辦圓玄老人中心，展開社區長者服務新的一頁。[39]在1960年代末期，圓玄學院由扶乩為主的道壇，演變為推動文化福利事業的團體，先後建立診所、中小學、幼稚園、護理院和安老院，及協助擴闊馬路，贊助區內文娛康樂活動，而成為荃灣區旅遊重點和重要社區團體。據蔡志祥研究指出，總結圓玄學院的發展，是「從道壇走進民間」。圓玄學院在1960年代末期，學院「由扶乩為主體的道壇，演變為與佛教、基督教和天主教比肩的推動文化福利事業的宗教集團」，更「透過紳商的關係，進入鄉村社會」執行打醮儀式。[40]圓玄學院在宣道與社會教化亦具影響，理民府長官韋忠信曾於開放日盛讚其「此種仁慈之勢力」為「可使社會罪惡減少」之偉大建設。[41]2007年，香港回歸十周年，此鍾靈毓秀之地，香港道教聯合會在圓玄學院後山啟建羅天大醮。

六、小結

　　香港歷來是移民社會，兼容匯聚各方各業人才，才堪稱為福地，戰後南來的，還有壇堂乩手。其中何啓忠與謝顯通皆身兼乩手並創立多壇，弘道闡教：從廣州至寶台到香港青

39　《圓玄護理安老院開幕特刊》，1984年，頁9。有關圓玄學院社會服務，可參游子安主編《道風百年》，蓬瀛仙館道教文化資料庫、香港利文出版社出版，2002，頁247-251。

40　詳參蔡志祥〈從喃嘸師傅到道壇經生：香港的打醮和社區關係的演變〉，收入林美容主編《信仰、儀式與社會》，《第三屆國際漢學會議論文集‧人類學組》，臺北：中央研究院民族學研究所，2003。

41　《荃灣二百年》，荃灣區議會出版，1991，頁38。

松觀、雲鶴山房；從宏道精舍
到圓玄學院、玉清別館。大帽
山鍾靈毓秀，呂祖等神明降示
老圍，還有其他壇堂，如老圍
村乾元洞保留「當仁不讓」書
匾。（圖7）天心與道心、人心
交感，筆路藍縷，以啟山林，
圓玄學院創建，茂峰法師、楊
永康、謝顯通、張煥廷等先賢
大德，成就了一段宗教奇緣。

圖7　乾元洞保留「當仁不
　　　讓」書匾，呂祖降
　　　筆。（筆者攝）

後記：

本文得以撰成，銘感謝傳清道長大力協助，提供寶貴
資料及照片，謹致謝忱。

亡者的告退：
民國時期廣州喪葬儀式與空間的重構

潘淑華

香港中文大學歷史系

一、前言

　　1947年4月9日，以發明「發冷丸」馳名的廣州著名成藥商人梁培基（1875-1947），在順德的家中逝世，享年72歲。梁培基的家屬在報章上刊登訃文，指梁培基在「遺囑吩示火葬，毋許在家設靈開喪祈禱禮讖，子女各人如認為須有動作以盡孝思，應將欲用之歟，移往從化溫泉建築墓地點綴環境，以增地方美育之助。」家屬遵從梁的意願，在梁去世三天後，於廣州大德路的粵光殯殮公司進行家奠禮，下午「一時發引移柩小北門外白雲菴奉行火葬，擇日敬運遺灰安厝於從化溫泉區預建墓塔之內。」[1]

　　梁培基的喪禮包含了不少新式死亡文化及禮儀。儀式空間從家中遷移到殯殮公司（即殯儀館）；喪禮中有意識地排

1　梁培基訃文，見《國華報》，1947年4月17日，頁8。根據梁培基的兒子梁尚為一篇回憶文章，梁培基並沒有宗教信仰，他計劃在從化溫泉區興建佛寺，目的是吸引遊人到溫泉區旅遊。梁培基希望把骨灰安葬在從化溫泉區的心願，因「時移勢遷」沒有達成。文中沒有解釋「時移勢遷」的意思。見梁尚為：〈梁培基參與倡建從化溫泉事略〉，載政協廣東省委員會辦公廳、廣東省政協文化和文史資料委員會編，《廣東文史資料精編》下編，第4卷，《民國時期文化篇》（北京：文史出版社，2008），頁1061-1065。

除宗教元素，不再聘請僧道尼（即僧人、道士及尼姑）等儀式專家誦經禮懺為亡者祈求更美好的來生；火葬替代土葬；而放置骨灰的墓地，強調「地方美育」功能而不是保佑子孫的好風水。儘管火葬儀式在富有佛教色彩的白雲菴舉行（白雲菴位於廣州市北象崗，是一所庄房，有關庄房，詳見下文），喪禮的世俗化傾向仍是非常顯眼的。

　　應該如何面對死亡？生者應以什麼方式（或儀式）與亡者告別？應如何處理人死後的遺體？亡者在活人的世界，又應該占有甚麼空間位置、以什麼方式繼續存在？這是自古以來不同文化及不同族群皆要面對的重要課題。法國史學家阿力耶斯（Philippe Aries）有關西方死亡史的研究，對比了古代與現代的死亡態度，認為在古代，人們以坦然的態度接受命運及對待死亡，死亡因而並不顯得特別可怕。這種態度在中世紀開始出現變化，到了現代，人們一方面恐懼死亡，但另一方面，死亡似乎無處不在——墳場、送殯行列、黑色的喪服等等，有些墓園甚至成為旅遊景點。[2]雅克‧勒高夫（Jacques Le Goff）從政治角度分析死亡文化的變化，他認為法國大革命強化了生者與死者的關係。在十八世紀末的法國大革命前，亡者很快被遺忘，但革命導致生者對亡者產生前所未有的興趣，新式的紀念碑、墓園及葬儀陸續出現，新政權通過紀念亡者，保存革命記憶。[3]簡言之，在西方，死亡的宗教色彩逐漸減退，對革命有功的亡者，則被留在現世長期為革命服務。

　　中國進入二十世紀，與西方經歷了相似的變遷，處理死亡的態度同樣受世俗化及革命政權影響。當中既有來自政權及知識份子自上而下的力量，也有因民眾追求「摩登」及便捷心

2　Philippe Aries, *Western Attitudes Toward Death: From the Middle Ages to the Present* (Baltimore: Johns Hopkins University Press, 1974), pp. 104-107.

3　Jacques Le Goff, *History and Memory*, trans. Steven Rendall and Elizabeth Claman (New York: Columbia University Press, 1992), pp. 85-86.

態而日漸普及的殯儀館所帶動的變化。本文以民國時期的廣州為例，第一部分討論「反迷信」及「反禮教」等現代性論述的出現，如何促使國家政權嘗試改革舊式喪禮，以改造民眾的思想行為。文章第二部分指出，政府以「衛生」及「展拓社區」等論述作為理據，制定政策把墳山及用作停柩的庄房不斷向城市邊緣遷移，亡者空間逐漸從民眾的日常視野消失。文章第三部分，分析美國歸僑成立的殯儀館，引入「摩登」製殮方式、中西結合的喪儀及新式墳場，使位於城外的殯儀館成為新的死亡儀式空間。傳統慣習當然不會即時消失，但民國時期的變化，導引出二十世紀中國人處理死亡的新態度和新方式：在思想層面，世俗化思潮衝擊過去對「來世」的信念；在空間層面，亡者從生者的生活空間日漸退隱。

二、現代政權、死亡儀式與社會改革

　　在傳統中國，喪祭禮儀是一場帶有「轉化力量」（transformative power）的表演，擔負多項功能。[4]宗教方面，喪葬儀式為亡者的來生作準備，並且把亡者從令人不安的「鬼」轉化成庇佑子孫的「祖先」。儒家倫理方面，喪祭禮儀表達對亡者的尊敬與思念，並可擔當「教化」的工具，幫助鞏固以家族為中心的社會秩序。在影響深遠的《家禮》的序言中，宋代理學家朱熹（1130-1200）指出，「冠婚喪祭」等禮儀，可以幫助國家「崇化導民」。辛亥革命後，傳統喪葬儀式面對迷信及浪費（包括浪費資源及時間）的指摘，成為急需改革的政治及社會課題。在科學及世俗化影響下，追求國家現代化的官員及知識份子，對「來世」採取否

4　James Watson, "The Structure of Chinese Funerary Rites: Elementary Forms, Ritual Sequence, and the Primacy of Performance," in James Watson and Evelyn Rawski, eds, *Death Ritual in Late Imperial and Modern China* (Berkeley: University of California Press, 1988), p. 4.

定的態度，認為宗教儀式是「迷信行為」。[5]他們銳意通過死亡儀式的簡單化及「去宗教化」，展示改革社會的意願，以及建構反「禮教」或反「迷信」的自我形象。可見在中國，從宋代的朱熹到二十世紀的革命政權，改革死亡儀式一直是改革社會的手段。

　　傳統喪禮成為知識份子反「禮教」的批判對象。傳統喪禮一般為期數天，家屬需穿上合符禮制的喪服，披麻帶孝，再加上體面的出殯儀仗。反「禮教」知識份子指責這些禮儀鋪張浪費，更是家族對個人的壓迫，因而主張以簡單的方式與亡者告別，暗示逝世的人不應占有太多現世資源。胡適（1891-1962）為母親舉行的新式喪禮便是好例子。胡適批評古喪禮迷信、虛偽，並且認為儀式由繁複變為簡單是一種「進化」過程。1918年胡適的母親去世，胡適把母親的祭禮從原來為期七、八天的儀式，改為以15分鐘完成的「新禮」，親屬的喪服由披麻帶孝簡化為臂纏黑紗。胡適認為經過他改良的祭禮非常值得別人參考。[6]喪禮大都是後輩為長輩辦理，在強調孝道的中國社會，把表達對長輩的敬意批評為浪費時間及金錢，是對傳統家庭秩序及家長權威的挑戰。然而自清末開始，「迷信」有礙國家及社會進化的論述力量日益強大，傳統喪禮被扣上「迷信」標籤，為喪禮改革的企圖賦予了合理性。

　　改造喪禮也是現代國家建構過程的一部分。現代政權企圖削弱死亡儀式的家族色彩，並將個人納入新的國家文化規

5　有關「反迷信」論述及政策，可參考Shuk-wah Poon, *Negotiating Religion in Modern China: State and Common People in Guangzhou, 1900-1937* (Hong Kong: Chinese University Press, 2011); Rebecca Nedostup, *Superstitious Regimes: Religion and the Politics of Chinese Modernity* (Cambridge: Harvard University Asia Center, 2009).

6　胡適：〈我對於喪禮的改革〉《胡適文存》，卷四（上海：亞東圖書館，1935），頁999-1016。另外，李叔同（1880-1942）在1905年亦為母親舉行了「文明喪禮」，他除去所有繁複的儀式，改為以追悼會的方式悼念母親。見吳可為：《古道長亭：李叔同傳》（杭州：杭州出版社，2004），頁50-51。

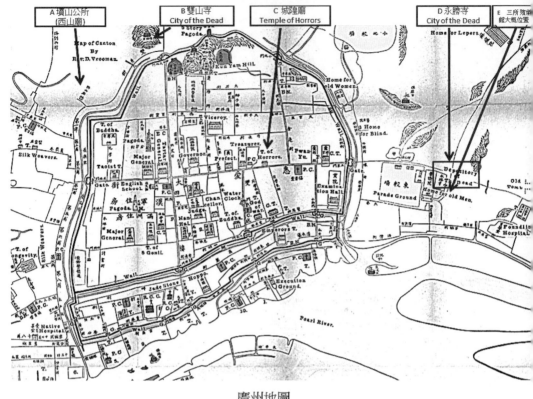

廣州地圖

範中。[7]廣州是「革命策源地」，廣州市政府及國民黨黨員在1920年代開始進行各種「反迷信」政策，期望自上而下改革民眾的死亡觀念及喪葬儀式。在中國傳統神祇譜系中，與死亡概念關係最密切的神靈，是輔助陽間官員管轄陰間的城隍神。城隍廟內描繪人死後在地獄受審判情景的「十王殿」壁畫，幫助人們具體地想像死後的「因果報應」，這在傳統中國社會發揮了勸善懲惡的道德教化力量。1920年代開始步向高潮的「反迷信」運動，令廣州大部份廟宇受到打擊，位於城市中心、與皇朝時期官僚系統關係密切的城隍廟，無可避免亦受到衝擊，「打城隍」成為「反迷信」的重要部分，城隍廟在不少中國城市中被剷除。在廣州，位於城隍廟（地圖C位置）正殿兩旁的「十王殿」壁畫，1924年遭拆卸，土地被政府充公變賣。1932年，廣州城隍廟被改建為國貨陳列

7　　Vincent Gossaert & David Palmer, *The Religious Question in Modern China, 1898-2008*, Ch. 9."Filial Piety, the Family, and Death," pp. 225-238.

館，過往幫助人們想像死後世界的宗教空間，被改造成為宣揚愛國觀念的國族空間。[8]

　　新思想否定死後世界，把死亡視為肉體與精神的終結，為引導亡者過渡到死後世界的繁複而漫長的傳統喪禮，被指為「迷信」「浪費」。過去，廣州的中上階層家庭，老人去世後，會在家中停柩四十九天（即「七虞」），每七天由僧道尼進行宗教儀式後始出殯。窮困家庭則會即時殮葬過世的家庭成員。[9]激進國民黨黨員於1929年成立的廣州市風俗改革委員會，嚴厲批評喪禮的各種「陋俗」，包括死者氣絕時，家人要手拿一炷香「引魂」；為死者換衣服後，需要把利市放進死者雙手，以表示對子孫的庇佑；入殮前，由僧、道或尼為死者念「倒頭經」，又要找南巫「開路」，「孝子」必須在南巫指引下，帶著盛有錢幣的水盆，哭著到附近水邊「買水」等等。對風改會來說，這些喪儀是「鬼神的迷信」，耗費社會有用的時間及金錢。[10]

　　1929年10月，廣州市社會局頒布新的喪禮儀式，以取代「虛耗巨資」及「含有封建色彩」的喪禮。此儀式基本上抄錄自南京國民政府於1928年訂定的「禮祭案」中的「喪禮草案」。新的喪禮儀式分為七個環節，分別為：

　　（一）報喪：以訃帖或登報通知親友死訊。

　　（二）視殮：喪主向死者行鞠躬禮、入殮、再向死者行

8　〈城隍廟禁駐兵，財局收回拆卸〉，《廣州民國日報》，1924年4月17日，頁10；〈城隍亦有此日〉，《越華報》，1931年11月19日，頁1。有關廣州城隍廟的改造，參看Shuk-wah Poon, "Religion, Modernity, and Urban Space: The City God Temple in Republican Guangzhou,"*Modern China*, Vol. 34, No. 2 (April, 2008), pp. 247-275.

9　沈瓊樓：〈廣州婚喪習俗沿革〉，載《廣州文史資料存稿選編》，第9輯（北京：中國文史出版社，2008），頁381-383。

10　〈廣州陋俗種種〉，《風俗改革周刊》，27期，載《廣州民國日報》，1930年2月24日，3張4版。有關廣州市風俗改革委員會，可參看拙作〈「建構」政權，「解構」迷信？—廣州市風俗改革委員會的個案研究，1929-1930〉，載於陳春聲、鄭振滿編，《民間宗教與社會空間》（福州：福建人民出版社，2003），頁108-122。

鞠躬禮。

（三）受吊：來賓到靈前行鞠躬禮（行禮時奏哀樂）

（四）祭式：向靈前行鞠躬禮、獻祭品（限香花果酒）、讀祭文、辭靈（行禮時奏哀樂）

（五）別靈：來賓向靈前行鞠躬禮辭靈（行禮時奏哀樂）

（六）出殯：次序為銘旌，輓聯花圈，樂隊，送殯者，喪主，靈柩（不應用儀仗）

（七）葬儀：喪主祭基禮，向墳前行鞠躬禮（行禮時奏哀樂）[11]

新式喪禮與傳統儀式主要分別是：（一）沒有僧人、道士或尼姑為亡者誦經禮懺；（二）以香花及花圈等代替香燭、冥鏹及儀仗。值得注意的是，這套儀式中包括「奏哀樂」，出殯時亦可由樂隊奏樂。不過社會局並沒有清楚説明，新式喪禮中所演奏的「哀樂」，是否沿用過去的儀式音樂。傳統喪禮中，音樂由「醮師」負責演奏，而演奏的音樂與負責宗教儀式的僧道巫配合，因而音樂本身是宗教儀式的一部分。若沒有新的音樂，新喪儀便難以有效實行。[12]

廣州政府除了規管家中進行的喪禮儀式外，亦以衛生理由規管去世親人在家中的停屍時間。1928年發出的「取締市內停柩章程」，規定「市民死後限二十四小時內收殮，七日內遷出市外」。[13]換言之，家中進行的喪禮必須在親人逝世後一天內完成，然後封棺，七日內下葬。

政府改革喪禮儀式的意圖，得到一些民眾言論上的支持。例如1932年廣州《越華報》刊登了〈喪禮亟宣改〉一文，作者從三方面批評傳統喪禮。首先是「儀仗羅列」。他

11　〈社會局規定喪禮儀式〉，《廣州民國日報》，1929年10月17日，頁5。

12　現今中國通行的葬禮音樂為1945年羅浪改編自北方民間樂曲的「哀樂」及1948年中國作曲家李桐樹創作的「葬禮進行曲」。楊浪：《老歌的發現》（太原：山西人民出版社，2015），頁179-183。

13　〈取締市內停柩章程〉，《廣州市市政公報》，1928年（第304期），頁42。

認為「鼓樂喧天」，結果「變哀為樂」，這是對先人不敬。
二是延請僧道作佛事的傳統。作者認為「人既已死，魂亦不
知何往」，即使相信輪迴之說，超渡先人假設了「先人必入
地獄受苦」，這等同「褻瀆先人」。三是焚燒紙札。作者懷
疑「先人真能收受焚化之物，則亦只能享受破爛不完之物件
而已，得物不能為用」。作者並不反對進行喪禮儀式，但認
為儀式中應「肅靜潛默」，才能表現「悲悼之深」。他建議
以馬車直接載運棺木到墳場，子孫若要表示孝道及對先人的
思念，可以「先人的名義捐助慈善事業」。[14]這位作者在文
章中表達了世俗化的死亡觀，否定死後世界的存在，主張子
孫應該幫助亡者，以慈善事業方式貢獻及服務現世，好讓先
人繼續活在世人的記憶和懷念中。

　　廣州政府並沒有積極敦促民眾執行新式喪禮，大部分民
眾亦選擇繼續傳統儀式。政府頒行的新禮儀節省時間及金錢，
但為何得不到民眾支持呢？一位作者提到廣州人對喪禮的態
度，是「生人做給生人睇」。[15]喪禮儀式也就是一場以活人為
主要觀眾的表演，是體現家族認同的場合。喪禮大多是兒子
為父母舉行的告別儀式，儀式確認生者與死者的家族關係，
同時確認子孫盡了責任，讓先人有體面地離開現世。除非父母
對自己的喪禮有清晰的安排，並寫下遺囑吩咐子孫遵行（如梁
培基），又或是子孫輩有強烈背離傳統的傾向及個性（如胡
適），不然的話，一般民眾會選擇依循其他家族成員的期望，
以社會上被視為體面的方式，舉行父母的喪禮。1934年《越華
報》的一篇文章清楚表達了後人為父母舉辦喪禮時面對的家庭
規範。文章指一位謝某，「自命為社會新進人物」，對「舊禮
教、舊道德，與及一切社會迷信，素所鄙屑」。他會不留情面
地嘲諷朋友任何「舊禮教」的行為。後來，謝某的母親去世，
謝某卻順從地遵照舊俗舉行喪禮。當朋友諷刺他言行不一時，

14　〈喪禮亟宣改〉，《越華報》，1932年9月27日，頁1。
15　〈從人力的動員說富喪的消費〉，《越華報》，1948年4月28日，
　　頁5。

謝某表現得無地自容，無奈地回答：「奈家長性頑，素守古風，難以違命，無可奈何。」[16]

雖然廣州政府沒有以政治力量，強制民眾執行新式喪禮，但在一些政治敏感時刻，政府仍會高調規管民眾的喪禮，以表現政治權威。這種情況在1936年7月陳濟棠（1890-1954）倒台後出現。自1930年控制廣東省的軍閥陳濟棠，發動推翻蔣介石的南京政權，失敗後出走歐洲，南京中央政府把廣東省納入控制後，藉著在廣州推行蔣介石於1934年發動的新生活運動，宣示其對廣州的政治主權。過去，廣州人一般在家舉行喪事，聘請僧尼及道士在家中誦經進行「功德」儀式。在廣州新生活運動中，政府下令僧尼及道士開壇打齋，必須在晚上11時前結束，而且不得焚燒紙錢。自稱為道士，但未能出示戒牒及准許證的，則被視為宣揚迷信的「巫」，他們不得為喪戶進行「功德」儀式，否則會被拘捕。喪禮中極為重要的「破地獄」儀式，也被視為迷信行為，不得進行。[17]

可見，除了滿足短暫的政治需要，廣州政府對於推行新式喪禮，並不顯得積極。然而在下文會看見，出於實質的經濟利益考量，政府對於搬遷舊墳，表現強大的決心。

三、生者與亡者爭地：從墳山到墳場

在傳統中國，墳墓皆位於城外。雖然亡者的空間占去不少土地，但生者鮮有與亡者爭地的想法（雖然侵占其他宗族的風水墓穴的例子有不少）。民國以前，廣州城牆外西北面及東面佈滿大大小小的山岡，山岡上有不少墓穴。每個山岡

16　〈出殯趣聞〉，《越華報》，1934年7月20日，頁1。

17　〈死鬼未超度，生人先被拘〉，《越華報》，1937年11月15日，頁2：1；〈違禁令執業，巫人被拘懲〉，《越華報》，1938年3月24日，頁1：4。

皆有名字，方便後人記憶先人墳地的地理位置。然而，到了民國時期，當城牆被拆去，城市不斷向外擴展，生者入侵了亡者的空間，亡者空間亦開始被視為阻礙社會發展。廣州政府以經濟及城市發展為理由，下令出售墳山及遷移墳墓，官方的話語是「展拓市區」，「推廣市民住居」，「增加公家收入」，「於公於私均有裨益」。遷移山墳，騰出原來的墳地，「化無用為有用」，日漸成為主流論述。[18]

廣州政府無視墳主及善堂反對，積極遷移山墳。1924年，西村蔡族數以千座位於石頭崗及大墳尾崗的祖墳，需要被遷移，原來的墳地由美國歸僑成立的公司承領。即使蔡族動用族產，希望領回墳山，但政府的立場是墳山所在地已劃入市區，以興建新式住宅，最後蔡族未能保留祖墳。1930年，廣州市政府計劃把大北門外三眼灶、騎龍及中心崗的墳地收回，將之發展成動植物園，亦引起墳主群起反對。[19]儘管廣東省各善堂組成的「廣東善團總所」，批評政府的政策「滅及祖骸，人心所共憤」，「孤兒寡婦，含淚收骨」，要求政府「凡有墳墓之山地，永遠禁止承領。」政府並沒有理會來自四方八面的反對聲音。[20]

廣州政府在遷移墳山的同時，答允興建公共墳場，以解決墳地問題。政府批評傳統墳山為「舊式之魚鱗疊葬」，標榜公共墳場是「公園式墳場」，當中植樹建亭，環境優美。然而官員對興建公共墳場，並不如遷移墳山熱心和積極。廣

---

18 〈箋函山墳公卹解釋展拓市區情形由〉，《廣州市市政公報》，1921年9月12日（29號），頁27。

19 〈紛紛請保留大北墳地〉，《越華報》，1930年10月13日，頁5。

20 〈呈省長據工務局長陳請擬收回東郊馬棚竹絲等崗展拓市區請示核奪由〉，《廣州市市政公報》，1924年7月4日(19號)，頁1-2；〈訓令財局奉省令永遠禁止承領叢葬墳山由〉，《廣州市市政公報》，1924年9月8日(145號)，頁21-22；〈開闢公共墳場之進行〉，《廣州市市政公報》，1924年4月21日(125號)，頁20-21；〈不准令回墳山〉，《廣州民國日報》，1924年4月11日，頁7；〈開闢新式墳場〉，《廣州民國日報》，1924年2月28日，頁6。

州政府於1922年首先提出興建公共墳場的想法，但選址一改再改，歷經12年，公共墳場直至1936年才建成。1922年政府選址燕塘後壽考嶺一帶（現位於天河區），以及橫枝、佛塔兩崗（現位於越秀區），1924年選址改為瘦狗嶺（位於廣州東北的山嶺）。1929年又提出在牛面崗、龍船崗及馬鞍山三處興建公共墳場。牛面崗及龍船崗皆位於瘦狗嶺旁，與市區接鄰。馬鞍山則位於白雲山東北角，距離市區頗遠。牛面崗本是墳山，有二百多座墳墓。龍船崗有一座畢姓大墳，而馬鞍山有余姓的一座大墳及五、六座墳墓。由於以上區域先後被徵用作其他用途，公共墳場的計劃一直被拖延。[21]

1935年，政府建議於廣州東郊的二望崗（永濟火藥庫舊址）興建公共墳場。[22]廣州首座公共墳場終於在1936年建成，可容納11,154座墓穴。根據《廣州市公共墳場管理細則》及《廣州市公共墳場葬掃規則》，墳場分為「免費區」及「收費區」兩個區域。申請「免費區」墓地，需繳納十年管理費（共四元），十年後需起墓（即執骨或「執金」），將金箱（盛載先人骸骨的箱子）移葬至另一指定區段。以上的政府規則並沒有說明「收費區」墓地的價錢，不同位置的墓穴很可能收費不同。公共墳場與傳統墳山的分別，在於掃墓者不得燃燒紙錢寶燭炮仗等所謂「迷信物品」。其次，管理細則訂明，安葬地點根據登記的先後次序，以免爭執，這

21　〈訓令工務局會同勘繪瘦狗嶺外一帶荒山作為公共墳場由〉，《廣州市市政公報》，1924年4月14日(124號)，頁32；〈籌建公共墳場次急進〉，《廣州民國日報》，1929年6月4日，頁6；〈籌建三個公共墳場之急進〉，《廣州市市政公報》，1929年，第331-332期；〈規劃公共墳場之佈置〉，《越華報》，1931年2月9日，頁4。

22　〈工務局規劃公共墳場〉，《廣州民國日報》，1935年4月2日，頁2：3；〈東郊外二望岡為本市殉職警察墳場〉，《香港華字日報》，1927年10月7日，頁2：2；〈興築公共墳場竣工〉，《越華報》，1936年1月6日，頁6。

顯然是為了杜絕過去強調風水墓穴的「迷信」概念。[23]安克強 （Christian Henriot） 在其有關上海死亡史的研究中認為，死亡並不令人變得平等，而是反映甚至強化了原來的社會階層界線。[24]廣州政府制定的新式喪禮及新式墳場，主要目的是「反迷信」及「反浪費」，但不能否認，標準化儀式及墳地的實施（儘管仍分為「免費區」及「收費區」兩大類別），會有助於打破社會階級界線。

　　廣州政府在徵用市郊墳山的同時，亦宣揚火葬的優點，認為火葬既衛生、亦節省土地資源。這種對火葬的正面態度與傳統中國思想大相逕庭。傳統中國社會視火葬為與儒家倫理相悖的佛教傳統，又或是沒有金錢購買棺木的貧苦家庭的無奈選擇。火葬的意義在民國時期被「非宗教化」──它不再被視為佛教傳統，而是合乎經濟及衛生原則的文明選擇。1923年廣州衛生局出版的《衛生年刊》，刊登了黃慶枬〈論火葬〉一文。黃認為從衛生及經濟角度考慮，火葬皆有可取之處：火葬既能讓土地物盡其用，而且合符衛生，避免屍骨暴露，傳播疾病的危險。[25]1924年6月，廣州陸軍海軍大元帥大本營建設部長林森（1868-1943），向廣州政府建議將已廢棄的永濟火藥庫舊址，開闢為「天葬場」（即火葬場）。他認為土葬是「耗有用之財，奪生產之地」。[26]但政府並沒有跟進此建議。

23　《擬建二望岡公共墳場說明書》（廣州市政府工務局編，1935），廣東省會公安局統計股編，《市民要覽》，〈公共事業〉（1934），頁64-67。

24　Christian Henriot, *Scythe and the City. A Social History of Death in Shanghai* (Stanford: Stanford University Press, 2016), p. 363.

25　黃慶枬，〈論火葬〉，《衛生年刊》，（1923），頁82-84；宋國賓，〈火葬〉，《越華報》，1930年6月18日，頁8。

26　〈飭將永濟藥庫廢址撥為天葬場所令〉，1924年6月9日。林森雖然對火葬推崇備至，但他並沒有為自己安排以火葬方式處理自己的遺體。他於1943年在重慶去世後，國民黨為他進行國葬禮，並在其重慶的官邸前方修建陵墓，安葬其遺體。劉曉寧：《無為而治的國府元首：林森傳》（北京：中國文史出版社，2002），頁343-346。

　　由於火葬被視為改革精神的體現，一些官員以身作則，寫下遺囑要求去世後火葬。最有名的例子是1922年6月去世、曾任駐美公使及外交部長的伍廷芳（1842-1922），在廣州河南的南石頭的火葬場（由居留廣州的日本人建立）進行火葬。[27]另一官員林直勉（1888-1934），1934年去世後於小北外江西義地的荼毘爐火化。報導指其葬禮儀式中，有白雲庵主持唸經咒，爐前供奉香燭果品，因而林可能是因為篤信佛教而選擇火葬。然而選擇火葬的人仍屬少數。直至抗日戰爭時期，簡便的火葬變得比前盛行。到了戰後，有廣州人提出應把火葬從城市推廣至鄉間，但首先需要將火葬場普及化，推行「一鄉一火葬場」。[28]

　　除了遷移墳山外，廣州政府亦銳意取締城內的「死人旅舍」——「庄房」。庄房的作用是「停柩」，是亡者從喪禮到安葬的過度空間。所謂停柩，是把盛有遺體、未殮封或已殮封的棺柩，暫時安放在庄房，為期數日、數月、數年，甚至更長時間，才進行安葬。導致延遲安葬的原因各異，有的家庭希望覓得風水寶地，有的則經濟拮据或需要等候遠方的親人歸來，而未能辦理喪禮。有的庄房設於寺廟，有的則由專人營辦，亦有不收費用的義庄。在廣州，庄房多設於城市的邊緣地帶，主要集中於市北的大北及小北外。

　　西方人把廣州的庄房稱為「死人之城」（City of the Dead），英語旅遊指南喜歡把「死人之城」列入遊覽行程。旅遊指南中的描述，並不見負面評語，可以估計當時庄房的管理應該沒有引起很大爭議。其中一所頗具規模的庄房是位於大北門外的雙山寺，建於1710年（康熙四十九年），

27　1918年，廣東日本居留民會在廣州河南南石頭開闢墓地，並附設火葬場。參曹大臣：〈日本人在中國的墓地（1871—1945）〉，《歷史研究》，2011年第3期，頁113。

28　〈林直勉遺骸今日火化〉，《越華報》，1934年8月12日，頁5；〈林直勉遺骸火化情形〉，《越華報》，1934年8月13日，頁5；〈應推行一鄉一火葬場〉，《國華報》，1948年4月24日，頁4。

分為東西北三個庄房，各有僧人為庄主，儲柩營業。[29]美國
傳教士及醫生嘉約翰（John Kerr）編撰的 *A Guide to the City
and Suburbs of Canton*，提到大北門外的「棺材庄 City of the
Dead」，相信即為雙山寺（地圖B位置）。Kerr指出雙山寺有
超過100個寄放棺木的房間，若喪戶要寄放棺木，要先繳納10
元到25元不等的費用，然後每月繳納租金。棺木前放有各種
祭品，包括仿造（相信即紙紮）的煙斗、婢女及轎子。[30]

　　廣州另一所有名的庄房是位於東門外的永勝寺（地圖D
位置）。根據英國傳教士格瑞（John Henry Gray）的 *Walks
in the City of Canton* 的介紹，此庄房有194個放置棺木的房
間，棺木前放了香燭祭品。有地位顯赫的家庭恐怕放置在先
人棺木內的貴重物品被盜，甚或遺體被挾走要求贖金贖回，
因而會派人在晚上看守棺木。除了棺木內的財物及遺體外，
需要看守的還有亡者的魂魄。永勝寺庄房建有一座庭園，
園中養了兩隻白色公雞，庭園中又有一座養了數隻白鵝的水
池。牠們負責守護亡者，防止亡者的魂魄離開遺體。[31]1870
年代曾到廣州旅遊的德國女旅行家Margaretha Weppner，記

---

29 廣州市市政廳總務科編輯，《廣州市市政概要》（廣州：廣州市
　　市政廳總務科，1922），《市政廳紀略‧財政局》，頁18-19；廣
　　州市宗教志編纂委員會編，《廣州宗教志》（廣州：廣東人民出
　　版社，1996），頁38。由於根據政府規定，載有遺體的棺木只可以抬
　　出廣州城，而不能抬入城內，西關的喪戶會把棺木抬到大北門外的庄
　　房，如雙山寺。居於城內的喪戶，則根據居住位置把棺木抬往大北門、
　　小北門或大東門的庄房停柩。沈瓊樓，〈廣州婚喪習俗沿革〉，頁383。

30 Dr. Kerr, *A Guide to the City and Suburbs of Canton* (Hong Kong:
　　Kelly & Walsh, Ltd., 1918), p.31.

31 John Henry Gray, *Walks in the City of Canton* (Hong Kong: De Souza,
　　1875), pp. 540-543. John Henry Gray 的妻子在寫給母親的信中，
　　亦多次提到「死人之城」。Mrs. Gray, *Fourteen Months in Canton*
　　(London: Macmillan and Co., 1880), pp. 71-74, 182-184, 365-366, 368-
　　369。1910年，廣州曾發生庄房棺木被盜竊事件。祖籍廣東省南海
　　縣的軍機大臣戴鴻慈（1853-1910），其靈柩寄柩於名為松蔭園的
　　庄房。兩名賊人入夜後潛入庄房，打算偷走棺木中的貴重物品，剛
　　巧守庄人經過，賊人只偷了帷帳及錫器供品，即時逃去。見〈戴鴻
　　慈庄房被竊〉，《香港華字日報》，1910年6月4日，缺頁數。

錄了庄房守門人的解説。守門人説魂魄在日間會到處遊逛，
希望見見朋友。到了晚上，守門人上床就寢前，要先叫喚魂
魄回到遺體。Weppner形容守門人把魂魄哄回來的方式，像
是哄回白鴿或家禽。[32]

　　「迷信」及「衛生」等現代話語，促使民國政府重新審
視停柩習慣及庄房的存在意義。墓穴風水被視為迷信陋習，
而市民長年累月與盛有屍體的棺木為鄰，則是對衛生的威
脅。1922年，廣州市衛生局發出「取締庄房義莊棺柩停厝規
則」，是廣州政府以衛生理由規管民眾停柩習俗的開端。根
據規定，市區內的庄房不得繼續營業；至於市區外的庄房，
棺木不可有臭味溢出，棺木入庄後必須在半年內安葬。[33]政
府的法令，把亡者的空間從城市逐出城外，強化了生者與亡
者的界線。此外，「迷信」及「衛生」話語，亦加強了徵用
庄房作其他用途的理據。1931年2月，廣東憲兵司令提出改
建上文提及的永勝寺庄房為兵房，據為己用。衛生局遂發出
佈告，要求家屬遷移及安葬停厝於庄內的先人棺木，未被遷
移的棺木，由善堂將之編號，集體安葬。[34]

　　傳統思想視死亡為不潔，需要通過宗教潔淨儀式處理，
現代政權則從公共衛生角度，視死者的遺體為污染。然而，
由於防腐技術尚未普及，政府只能規定不得有臭氣從棺木漏
出，而不能要求庄房的遺體必須經防腐處理。1920到1930年
代，廣州市政府不斷重申庄房的法令，一方面反映政府對此
問題的重視，另一方面亦説明規條並不能杜絕棺木逾期不葬
的情況。1930年代，廣州市註冊的庄房有七所，義庄九所，

32　Margaretha Weppner, *The North Star and the Southern Cross: Being the Personal Experiences, Impressions and Observations of Margaretha Weppner, in a Two Years'; Journey Round the World* (London: S. Low, Marston, Low, and Searle, 1875), pp. 444-5.

33　〈廣州市衛生局取締庄房義庄棺柩停厝規則〉，《衛生年刊》，1923年，頁33-34。

34　〈永勝寺舊棺定期叢葬〉，《香港工商日報》，1931年2月27日，2張3版；〈訓令財局佈告永勝寺內庄房〉，《廣州市市政公報》，90期。

它們一直存在至1949年新政權成立。[35]

四、殯儀館的「摩登殯儀」

　　民國時期，除了政府及知識分子有意識地改革喪葬禮儀外，殯儀館（又稱製殮公司）作為處理死亡的新式機構，亦帶動了死亡文化的變化。殯儀館同時提供殯儀服務、進行殯儀的場地及安葬遺體的墳地，為亡者家屬處理喪葬的各個環節，對亡者家屬來說是頗為便捷的。我們也可假設，民國政府逐步打破民眾處理死亡的慣習，包括規管遺體在家中的停柩時間、充公墳山及取締庄房，令殯儀館提供的包含喪葬各個環節的整合式服務，更能受到民眾接受。

　　廣州有三所殯儀館，包括粵光、樂天及別有天，總辦事處皆位於廣州東郊東川路（地圖E位置），由曾僑居美國的中國歸僑成立。粵光製殮公司是集股經營的股份有限公司，成立最早，亦最具規模，於1925年成立，1926年於廣州市中心的大德路增設分行。負責人是美國歸僑吳文波，他祖籍台山，為基督教牧師。有別於過去以冰塊冷藏屍體的處理方法，粵光公司提供先進的屍體防腐技術，可以讓屍體保存更長時間。粵光亦擁有墳場及暫時停放棺木的庄房，粵光墳場位於

35　七所庄房分別是慈蔭仙館（大北外）、裕德（大北外）、環雲仙館（小北外）、福裕堂（西門外）、鳳梧仙館（西門外）、白雲蓉（象崗）及廣福（河南庄巷）。九所義庄為本仁堂江蘇義庄（西門外）、敦仁堂寧波義庄（大北外）、浙紹義庄（小北外）、湖南義庄（小北外）、雲貴義庄（小北外）、福建義庄（小北外）、江西義庄（小北外）、安徽義庄(小北外)、杭嘉湖義庄（小北外）。見廣東省會公安局統計股編輯，《市民要覽》，（1934），頁70。1948年，廣州仍有庄房及義庄共16所。見廖淑倫編，《廣州大觀》（廣州：天南出版社，1948），頁90-91。

廣州東郊田心崗等4個山崗。[36]1931年成立的樂天殯儀館與粵
光相似，同樣是股份有限公司，也是由台山籍的美洲歸僑設
立。樂天亦擁有墳場及製殮地方，位於太和崗。1944年開始
營運的別有天殯儀館，墳場設於玉子崗及淘金坑等地。[37]

　　殯儀館在廣州出現，與基督徒及外國人數目日漸增加，
以及愈來愈多海外華人回國後定居廣州有關。由於資料缺
乏，我們未能了解民國時期殯儀館內的佈置及儀式，與過往
在家庭進行的家奠禮有何不同。不過1935年報章上一篇名
為〈摩登殯儀〉的文章，為我們提供一些線索，了解殯儀館
的喪禮與傳統喪禮的分別。作者指出殯儀館的顧客，皆是「
有錢而又思想清新之家」，而且形容殯儀館的服務為「摩登
殯儀」。所謂「思想清新」，相信是指這些顧客，並不聘請
僧道尼誦經禮懺，而是追求簡單省時的禮儀。至於「摩登殯
儀」，是把棺木放置於汽車內，無論是披麻帶孝的孝子，或
是執紼的親友，皆坐在尾隨的車輛上。這與傳統喪禮由八個
或十六個仵工肩抬棺木，再加上儀仗隊伍在街上邊走邊進行
喧聲震天的表演非常不同。作者認為「摩登殯儀」讓「時間
極為減省」，仵工及死者親屬亦可減少勞累。[38]這位作者對
殯儀館持正面態度，認為處理死亡變得比以前簡單省時，是
殯儀館最可取之處。不過我們亦可以説，以汽車（即殯儀館
的靈車）而非仵工運送棺木，也是財富與「摩登」身份的宣
示。殯儀館對城市喪葬禮儀帶來的最大變化，是殯儀館承辦

36　根據粵光製殮公司註冊資料，登記註冊人為台山人劉五明，1925年集
　　合股份2800股，每股價值50元，資本金額為14萬元。〈粵光製殮公司
　　（廣州）〉，中央研究院近代史研究所檔案館藏，《實業部檔案》，
　　檔號03-41-013-01-031。1952年，吳存義及吳文波被政府指控「利用宗
　　教欺騙財物及瞞騙稅款」而被關押在獄中。吳存義同年死於獄中，
　　時年87歲。見〈穗粵光製殮公司資方被清算〉，《香港工商日
　　報》，1952年5月2日，第3頁。

37　《廣州百科全書》，頁829，廣州市地方志編纂委員會編，《廣州市
　　志》，卷十（廣州：廣州出版社，2000），頁595-598。

38　〈摩登殯儀〉，《國華報》，1935年10月8日，頁1：4。

的喪禮，家奠禮（即家祭）於殯儀館的
禮堂舉行。換言之，位於郊外的殯儀
館取代了家庭，成為喪禮的重要儀式空
間，喪禮的死亡氣息，逐漸自城市隱
退。

　　雖然殯儀館初期的主要服務對象是
基督徒、外國人及社會上流人士，但其
後業務逐漸擴展，跨越了社會階層，強
調為不同宗教及階級的顧客，提供中式
及西式喪葬服務。例如曾任廣東省警務
處長的魏邦平（1884-1935），1935年去
世後，由製殮公司承辦喪禮。報導指魏
的棺木為西式，但喪禮採用中式殮儀。
下葬前，魏的家屬於城北雙山寺的庄房
開喪，接受親朋吊唁。[39]中日戰爭令殯
儀館打破原有的社會階級分層及地理空
間邊界。首先，殯儀館提供的服務變得
平民化及多元化，1943年粵光製殮公司
的廣告，標榜「豐儉由人」、「信仰自
由」，提供中西式壽具和儀仗，而且備
有山地及禮堂。[40]其次，殯儀館主要的業
務經營從城市邊緣（市東郊東川路）遷
移到市中心大德路。在戰事的陰影及朝
不保夕的情況下，民眾對亡者的處理更
為簡化。

粵光製殮公司廣告
《越華報》，
1946年2月26日

　　戰後，殯儀館的服務持續平民
化。1946年粵光製殮公司的廣告，指「為適應目前社會環境
之需要，特設儉喪部分，務其以節儉為主旨……豐儉由人，

39　〈魏邦平逝世昨日大殮〉，《國華報》，1935年10月20日，頁2：2。
40　(廣告)〈粵光優待貧喪者〉，《中山日報》，1943年4月12日，頁4。

貧者酌贈，以符本公司慈善營業之本旨」。[41]但民眾不滿殯
儀館遷移到市中心，要求它們搬回城外。政府亦認為殯儀館
位於市中心，有礙衛生及「觀感」，1947年4月下令各殯儀
館搬遷。殯儀館奮力請願，但最後招牌被警察強行拆走。[42]
我們可以推想，在紛亂的歲月，生與死的界線變得模糊，但
戰事過後，民眾開始重新強化生者與亡者的邊界。

　　殯儀館的「摩登」亦表現於其新式墳場的模式及管
理上。當中規模最大的粵光墳場位於東郊田心崗等4個山
崗。1940年代末，粵光墳場埋葬約六千人。殯儀館墳場的經
營管理比傳統墳山優勝，雖然廣州在1881年（光緒七年）成
立了名為「墳山公所」（地圖A位置）的慈善組職，負責看
管墳山，但因廣州墳山眾多，墳山公所能夠處理的，不過是
在清明及重陽等掃墓時節，向政府要求派警察保護掃墓者安
全。[43]墳山上的墓穴不時會被俗稱為「山狗」或「山老鼠」
的不法分子破壞，他們故意把墳墓的界石移走，賣給石行圖
利，有時甚至把墳地自行出售。若沒有其他標記作識別，界
石被移走後，家屬難以找回先人墓地的確實地點。「山狗」
或「山老鼠」會在掃墓時節出現，向掃墓者表示知悉墓地位
置，並要求打賞。[44]殯儀館的墳場設有管理人，墓碑上不單
有亡者的姓名、籍貫及生卒年月日，還有其照片。[45]到殯儀
館經營的墳場與過往到墳山祭掃的經驗，因而有很大差別，
尋找先人墓地變得較為容易。此外，與過往的土丘相比，附

41　(廣告)〈粵光製礆公司總行國土重光恢復營業〉，《越華報》，1946
　　年6月9日，頁2。

42　〈殯儀館緩遷市府不准〉，《國華報》，1947年4月2日，頁2。

43　民國《番禺縣續志》，卷五，建置志三。墳山公所位於廣州西門外
　　的西山廟，成立目的是清查及注冊廣州城外的墳山，以防止山狗侵
　　盜墳地。

44　〈石行集議保存山墳之善法〉，《華字日報》，1909年8月17日，
　　頁4；〈山狗毀墳詭計〉，《越華報》，1930年6月26日，頁1；〈死
　　人的故事〉，《國華報》，1948年4月5日，頁7。

45　〈粵光墳場中所見〉，《越華報》，1948年3月2日，頁4。

有照片的墓碑，更能幫助後人感受與先人的聯繫。

五、結　語

　　民國時期，新概念及新力量以不同方式改變人們對死亡的態度，以及對死後世界的理解，從而形塑新的處理死亡的方式，以及生者與亡者之間的關係。二十世紀初開始對現代性的追求，對死後世界的否定，喪禮儀式不再是為亡者下一段旅程作準備，而是對亡者的最後致敬，因而主張以「非宗教」的「文明」方式與亡者告別後，亡者亦應該從活人的空間徹底地告退，不應阻礙社會發展。然而，對大部分民眾來說，在喪禮中聘請僧道尼為亡者唸經禮懺，焚燒紙錢，仍是他們對先人應負的責任。他們並不接受政府的新式喪禮，但歡迎殯儀館提供的簡便的、可彈性選擇的中式及西式殯儀服務。死亡儀式亦因此從家中遷移到位於市郊的殯儀館。過往在城內及城市周邊的死亡空間，包括庄房及墳山，因衛生理由不斷向外圍遷移，城隍廟的十王殿亦被拆卸，展示死亡的景觀逐漸在民眾的日常視野中消失。死亡從過去的無處不在，變得愈來愈隱蔽。

　　值得注意的是，當平民的死變得愈來愈隱蔽，愈來愈快地從生者的生活中告退，以減輕對在世者的滋擾與負擔時，偉人的死則被歌頌得愈來愈偉大。自民國時期開始，偉人的葬禮、屍體及陵墓被賦與嶄新的意義，圍繞著革命烈士及偉人遺體的現代中國國家死亡文化，包括新式的死亡儀式、墓園及紀念碑，亦陸續出現。製造偉人及英烈的國葬禮、展示政治領袖遺體的中山陵及毛主席紀念堂等，標示著革命英烈的永生。[46]在現代國家建構過程中，平民與英烈的分別，在死亡中得到彰顯和強化。

46　有關民國時期的國葬禮，可參考拙作〈國葬：民國初年的政治角力與國家死亡儀式的建構〉，《中央研究院近代史研究所集刊》，vol. 83 (Mar. 2014)，頁47-87。

客家人遷莞歷史以及遷徙原因初探

麥淑賢

東莞市博物館

　　不為人所熟知的是，在今天東莞境內生活著許多客家人。1988年，侯國隆對廣東客家人口進行調查時發現，當時東莞的人口總數為1,239,381人，其中77,513名為客家人，占總人口的6.25%；[1]2009年，東莞戶籍人口為1,787,288人，其中285,966名為客家人，占當時總人口的16%。[2]但東莞客家人的具體狀況較少得到學界關注，目前只見若干零星材料。為了更加全面深入地瞭解認識東莞客家人，東莞市博物館結合田野調查與文獻釋讀，自2015年3月起對其進行研究，本文是初步成果之一。在此，為明確概念以及方便敘述，本文所提及的東莞客家人是指1978年以前陸續遷入並定居於今東莞境內的客家人。

一、客家人遷莞的歷史

（一）東莞客家人的分佈與來源

　　據實地調查，客家人如今分佈在東莞市的12個鎮（街），

1　侯國隆：《關於廣東客家人分佈情況的調查》，程志遠編：《客家源流與分佈》，香港天馬圖書有限公司出版，1994年，第123頁。

2　詹堅固：《廣東客家人分佈狀況及其對客家文化發展的影響》，《探求》2012年第4期，第89頁。

即謝崗鎮、樟木頭鎮、清溪鎮、鳳崗鎮、塘廈鎮、黃江鎮、大嶺山鎮、莞城街道、東城街道、南城街道、厚街鎮和虎門鎮。除了樟木頭鎮為純客住鎮[3]之外，其餘均為非純客住鎮（街）。東莞客家人所在的67個行政村（社區）、305個自然村（居民小組），絕大多數是「純客住村」[4]，部分是客家人與廣府人共處的村落。而從地形上看，謝崗、樟木頭、清溪、鳳崗與塘廈大致位於東莞東南部低山盆地區，黃江、大嶺山、東城大部分以及南城小部分位於中南部丘陵崗地區，厚街與虎門大部分位於西部三角洲平原，小部分（含客家聚居地）位於丘陵山地地帶。由此可知，東莞客家人的聚居地絕大多數處於丘陵或山地，與他處所見的「客家山居」情況相似，而且同樣是由於客家人相對較晚遷入所導致。

關於客家人遷莞的最早時間，有較多且可靠的材料證明確切年代在明代。此後，東莞境內的客家人漸次增多，而清代則是最主要的遷入時期。從收集而來的相關的資料[5]（詳見附錄）260例來看，清代遷入的共計165例，占總數的63.5%，其中又以康熙（34例）、乾隆（31例）和光緒（20例）三朝為主；明代遷入的共計56例，占總數的21.5%，集中在萬曆（21例）和崇禎（13例）兩朝；民國及以後亦有遷入，共計37例，占總數的14.2%。

客家人遷莞后，最初居住於今東莞謝崗、清溪、鳳崗和樟木頭等地。在（康熙）《東莞縣誌》卷一《圖考》中附有《京山司圖》，該圖中有兩處特殊的標注，即「三峰客家」和「山豬棚客家」（詳見圖1[6]）。「三峰」今為清溪鎮三中村，含兩個自然村，即「三峰上圍」和「三峰下圍」；「山

3　所謂「純客住鎮」，指戶籍人口95%以上為客家人的鎮（區）。

4　所謂「純客住村」，指戶籍人口95%以上為客家人的村落（居民小組）。

5　資料包含縣誌、鎮志、村志以及部分族譜、訪談資料。

6　郭文炳：（康熙）《東莞縣誌》，康熙二十八年（1689）刻本，東莞市人民政府辦公室據日本內閣文庫藏本影印，1994年，第32B頁。

圖1　《京山司圖》（選自【康熙】《東莞縣誌》）

豬棚」今為樟木頭鎮石新社區，現寫作「珊珠棚」。由此可
以推測，清康熙年間，三峰和山豬棚兩地已有客家人的聚居
甚至出現村落，為使其區分於本地土著廣府人而特作説明。
從清初到清中期，客家人的定居地逐漸發展至今黃江、大嶺
山、東城、厚街、南城等地；到了清晚期，今東莞虎門、莞
城、塘廈也出現了許多客家村落。

　　通過整理分析發現，今東莞客家人的直接來源地較為
集中，具体可參見表1。由表1可知，東莞客家人的祖籍地即
遷出地，小部分位於福建境內，如平和、上杭和寧化等地，
三者當時分屬福建漳州府和汀州府。絕大多數的東莞客家人
都是從省內各處遷入，如長樂（五華）、惠州（含歸善、惠
陽、惠東、海豐、陸豐）、新安（寶安）、興寧、龍川、揭
陽（含揭西）、增城、紫金和程鄉（梅縣）等地，這些遷出
地位於粵東與粵中，而這兩個區域也是明清以來廣東客家人
最主要的聚居地。

　　據已有的資料，我們可大致勾勒客家人遷莞的三條主要
路線。其一，由閩西出發經粵東某地停留長短不一的時間後
再遷東莞，這條路線大致又可細分為兩條支線：第一條支線
從福建上杭、武平等地出發，經興寧、長樂（今五華）、永
安（今紫金）並停留一段時間後再遷東莞；第二條支線從福
建平和出發，經揭陽、陸豐、海豐、歸善（今惠陽）並停留
一段時間後再遷東莞。其二，直接由粵東（含興寧、長樂、
永安、揭陽、陸豐、歸善等）遷入東莞。其三，直接由南粵
（含新安、增城）遷往東莞。遷莞後，部分客家人就此定居
并生活至今，也有部分人因各種原因又在東莞境內遷移，甚
至輾轉多次，最終定居在現居地。這種在縣境內的遷徙，共
統計到72例，其中清代54例，占總數的75%，其中11例出現
在乾隆朝，8例出現在光緒朝，7例出現在康熙朝；10例發生
在明代，占總數的13.8%；民國以及中華人民共和國成立後
（至1978年）共計8例，占總數的12%。

　　分析所得的各種資料可知，因謝崗、清溪和樟木頭等地
是客家人抵達後最初的定居地，所以從這些地方再度遷至東
莞各處的案例相對較多；而客家人遷入塘廈、大嶺山、厚街
和東城等地的時間較晚，因此從這些地方再度遷往東莞各處
的案例則相對較少。

表1　東莞客家人祖籍地及遷莞時間表[7]

（二）客家人遷莞後的初期生活

客家人到來時，平坦開闊等相對較好的田地早已被先來的廣府人佔有。為了生存，初期客家人主要在山地落腳，就地取材築梯田，種植各種作物，借此度過了最初極為艱難的日子。在東莞銀瓶山山脈一帶，至今仍可見到當時修建的若干梯田與村落遺存。

據2009年

遷入時間＼祖籍地	長樂 五華	歸善 (含惠陽、惠東)	新安 寶安	興寧	龍川	揭陽 揭西	陸豐 海豐	增城	紫金	程鄉 梅縣	福建 平和 上杭 寧化
永樂											1
宣德	2										
成化		1									1
弘治			1								
正德			1								
嘉靖				2							
隆慶	1		1								
萬曆	7	1		1	1	1	3				1
天啓		1					1				
崇禎	1	1				2			1	1	1
順治	4	2		1							
康熙	10	7	2			1			1		1
雍正	1	1	1								
乾隆	3	3		4	1		2				
嘉慶		1	1	1							1
道光	2				1						
咸豐		1									
同治		2									1
光緒	1	4	1					3			
明中葉										1	
明末	2	1									
明末/清初			2								
清初	1	2		2	4				1		
清中葉	1	1					1				
清晚期			1								
清末	1	1	3	2			1				
民國		1						2			
中華人民共和國成立後	2	1			4				1		
合計	38	30	15	14	11	6	6	5	4	3	8

7　此表相關信息來源於編寫年代不同的資料，地名中有歷史地名亦有當今地名，為保留資料原貌而不作改動。

的調查所知[8]，東莞客家梯田與村落遺址主要發現於今清溪鎮、樟木頭鎮、謝崗鎮所屬的銀瓶山森林公園內（具體情況參見表2）。銀屏山森林公園總面積123.5平方公里，其中梯田分佈範圍較廣，最東為謝崗鎮界石（與惠州交界處）；最南為清溪鎮正坑；最西為樟木頭鎮關涌；最北為樟木頭鎮九棟。僅清溪鎮內，目前已知的梯田至少有2萬畝。

表2 客家梯田與村落遺址分佈一覽表

鎮區	分佈地點	梯田遺存	其他遺存	當時的生計
謝崗	銀屏嘴山脈的觀音坐蓮等地點	梯田分佈在海拔200至600米之間，坡度約為20～30度，寬度多為1～1.5米，長度多為5～10米，高度約為1.5米。主要種植稻穀、蔬菜、茶葉、黃豆、花生等作物。	房屋構造以方形為主，石壘牆基，泥磚砌牆，瓦片蓋頂。另外發現登山道遺存。	①伐木燒炭售賣；②製作竹器、藤器、木器
清溪	銀瓶嘴山脈的黃芽田、楊橋坑、十二排、爆石山	梯田分佈在海拔150至350米之間，坡度約為25～35度，寬度多為1～1.5米，長度多在5～10米，高度約為1米。過去主要種植油茶、蕃薯、木薯、芋頭等作物。因擁有比較豐富的水源，爆石山的正坑、樵窩山一帶曾種植水稻。	十二排、黃芽田、正坑等地均有房屋遺址，砌石成牆，用泥漿塗牆，以茅草覆頂（後期部分有泥磚砌牆、瓦片蓋頂）	①種植油茶榨油等售賣；②伐木燒炭售賣；③就地取材製作鋤頭柄售賣；④售賣獵物、藥材、木材
樟木頭	樟木頭觀音山森林公園、樟木頭林場的九棟和樟洋	梯田分佈在海拔250至550米之間，坡度約為30～40度，寬度約1～1.5米，長度多在5～10米，高度為1米以內。主要種植旱地作物。多用有棱角的塊狀石料。	九棟、樟洋附近有民居遺址，牆體砌石，用泥漿塗牆，上蓋茅草用來墊瓦；水源兩旁有石壘堤坎。	①伐木燒炭售賣；②售賣獵物、藥材、手工製品、家禽

　　客家梯田分佈在海拔150至600米山地間，多沿著山間溪水或河道兩旁而建,用當地石料壘砌，平均高度為1米，平均寬度為1—1.5米，平均長度在5—10米。梯田，在相對平坦的地方，多為水平走向；而在陡峭的地方，其走向與水平線成25—40度角，這種砌法使梯田與山體的咬合力較大，更能抵禦雨水和山洪的沖刷。因年代久遠，許多梯田已被植被覆蓋，即使可見亦只是裸露的小部分。梯田主要種植木薯、花

8　在全國第一次不可移動文物普查期間，東莞市普查辦組織專人對客家地區現存的梯田與村落遺存進行調查。相關內容參見羅斌：《東莞山區石壘梯田與村落調查報告》，《客家文博》2017年第2期。

生、紅薯、油茶、茶葉等作物。油茶抗嚴寒，耐高溫，耐貧瘠，生長期達100—200年。今清溪鎮爆石山海拔700米處，尚可見二十多畝油茶林，樹齡平均上百年。此外，在水源較為豐富的梯田亦可種植水稻。

限於旱地的條件，靠山吃山的客家人生計手段相對較少，主要有以下三種：一是種植旱地作物，二是售賣「山貨」，如獵物、藥材、木材以及就地取材製成的竹器、木器、藤器以及鋤頭柄，三是伐木燒炭售賣。

除了梯田外，客家先民還修築登山道、房舍等。據現場勘查，可推斷出當年修建的房舍為方形，有隔間，分作臥室、廚房、茅廁、豬圈，面積一般為20至30平方米。取材於當地，砌石成牆，用泥漿塗牆，以茅草覆蓋作頂（後期部分用泥磚砌牆、瓦片蓋頂）。為便於耕種與生活，房舍選址一般在依山傍水之處，直至今日當地客家人仍有「一條

圖2　今謝崗鎮銀屏山脈觀音坐蓮處的梯田遺存

圖3　今清溪鎮銀屏山脈正坑一帶的梯田遺存

坑一條圍」的說法，「圍」即村子，而「坑」則是指山谷地帶，地勢較低，多有溪流。

據《楊梅坑族譜》和《清溪客家風情》記載，楊梅坑村的楊姓於明萬曆二十六年（1598）由廣東陸豐縣遷移到清溪重木村，明崇禎年間（1628—1643）楊應龍夫婦攜子又從重木村遷至黃茅田山脈土名

圖4　今樟木頭鎮九棟發現的疊築梯田的石料

圖5　今謝崗鎮銀屏山脈觀音坐蓮處的登山道遺存

為大灣（又音「大環」）的地方居住，並在大灣、楓樹山上開墾拓土。清咸豐年間（1851—1861），楊姓從大灣下山至楊梅坑居住，立村為楊梅坑村。訪談時發現，許多楊梅坑村民都瞭解其先人曾經山居的歷史。而在謝崗鎮，當地一位60多歲的羅姓村民稱，自先祖從福建遷來謝崗後，二十三代人一直在山上生活，至1958年才搬至山下居住。[9]隨著代際的不

9　羅斌：《東莞山區石壘梯田與村落調查報告》，《客家文博》2017年第2期。

斷延伸發展，東莞客家人逐漸完成了在地化的過程。

二、客家人遷莞的原因

　　關於客家人遷徙的原因，羅香林先生認為「或由於外患，或由於饑荒，或由於匪盜，或由於兵災，或由於政府獎掖召募或安插，或由於外地經濟的引誘。」[10]而據實地調查所得，客家人遷莞的原因與羅氏所述基本相同。

1. 因遭受自然災害而遷徙

　　限於小農經濟的先天缺陷，一旦遭遇較為嚴重的自然災害，多以農業為生的普通人便會陷入困境。因此，每到災荒年景，通過人口流動以求活命幾乎成為必然的選擇。

　　分析所得的資料可知，明清時期惠州府下轄的歸善、龍川、永安、海豐、陸豐和博羅等地，是東莞客家人最主要的來源地，尤以歸善（含惠陽、惠東）和龍川為最。這些地方的人口外遷活動集中在清朝初期，與同時期惠州府下轄各縣水災或旱災頻發有密切的正相關關係。

　　清代惠州府水、旱等災害頻發（見表3），「綜合水災次數、水災連年發生、水災破壞程度等指標，歸善縣、海豐縣、龍川縣、博羅縣既是水災多發地區，也是受災比較嚴重的地區。其中最嚴

圖6　今清溪鎮銀屏山脈樵窩山一帶的房舍遺存

10　羅香林：《客家研究導論》，上海文藝出版社，1992年，第66頁。

重的是歸善縣,水災次數高達 60 次,而清代歷史上四次最為嚴重的水災歸善縣都是重災區。」[11]自然災害頻發的時間與客家人遷入東莞的時間呈正相關狀態,尤其是歸善縣的相關度最高。面對無力抗拒的自然災害,人們趨利避害,由此產生頻繁的遷徙。

表3 清代惠州府各縣水災旱災統計表[12]

州　縣	博羅	歸善	海豐[13]	和平	河源	連平	龍川	永安	長寧	總計
水災次數	29	60	34	17	14	8	31	5	6	204
旱災次數	10	18	16	4	5	4	18	2	2	79
各縣小計	39	78	50	21	19	12	49	7	8	281

2. 響應政府號召而遷入

在一定意義上說,珠江三角洲真正的開發始於明代,這一時期有相當數量的人口流入,從事軍屯、墾邊並最終定居下來。如明政府於洪武十四年(1381)在東莞設立南海衛,並於洪武二十八年(1395)頒令,「邊海衛所,七分守城,三分屯糧」。其時南海衛有屯田十二處,十二處屯田中又包含若干子屯。到了清朝,為盡快恢復珠江三角洲的社會經濟,政府同樣大力招入人口,如清世祖制定墾荒興屯令,「凡州、縣、衛無主荒地,分給流民及官兵屯種。如力不能墾,官給牛具、籽種,或量假屯資。次年納半,三年全納。」[14]順治六年(1649),政府再度重申「凡各處逃亡人民,不論原籍別籍,必廣加招徠,編入保甲,俾之安心樂業。查本地無主荒田,州縣官給以印信執照,開墾耕種,永准為

11　李志慧:《清代惠州府水旱災害與應對研究》,暨南大學碩士學位論文,2015年,第12頁。
12　李志慧:《清代惠州府水旱災害與應對研究》,暨南大學碩士學位論文,2015年,第12頁、第17頁。
13　陸豐縣於雍正九年從海豐縣析出。
14　(清)趙爾巽:《清史稿·志九十五·食貨志》,中華書局,1977年,第3501頁。

業，俟耕至六年之後，有司官親察成熟畝數，撫按勘實，奏請奉旨，方議徵收錢糧。」[15]順治三年(1646)制定屯田官制，衛所官職從世襲制改為任命制，衛軍改為屯丁。屯丁依舊隸屬軍籍戶口，作為國家的佃戶耕種屯地、運送漕糧。

不少客家人因各種原因響應國家號召而落籍東莞。立於清乾隆四十年（1775）的《義建崇烈堂碑》就記載了鳳崗當地客家人的來歷：「我土離、前黃、左黃三屯，原附南海衛軍籍，自國朝定鼎之初，世路險

圖7　義建崇烈堂碑

陂，前民逃散，田廬半就荒矣。順治九年，衛主蕭君疏呈招耕，我輩先人蒙霜露、披荊棘，築居而畋厥田焉。越十年，人情翻覆，而衛主力與維持，又得屯長一十三人共相奔理，

15　（清）趙爾巽：《清史稿·志九十五·食貨志》，中華書局，1977年，第3499頁。

十一年而條議以定，版冊留遺，昭昭若前日事也。今日者，里居數百家，煙火相聯，禾麻互映。」[16]據實地調查可知，鳳崗鎮客家人皆是在明、清兩代遷入。統計目前已知的資料，其中的13.6%於明末遷入，77.3%於清朝遷入，54.5%集中在清順治至乾隆年間。正因為如此，可推測在乾隆後期，鳳崗當地已從「田廬半就荒」轉變為「里居數百家」。

3. 響應土著招收佃農而遷入

明清時期，珠江上游地區大量墾荒，造成水土流失，沖積在河口或河沿逐漸形成新的土地資源——沙田。同時，人口逐漸增多，需擴大糧作面積，從而促使沙田的增墾，土著擁田者對勞動力的需求迅速增加，這從客觀上促使東莞客家人的到來。

以虎門鎮陳村、黃村的客家人為例，他們就是歷史上響應土著招收佃農而遷入。「陳村當地方言屬客家語系，村民多姓陳，其祖上於清咸豐二年（1852），從厚街新圍九門山移居到此地立村，原名北柵新村……黃村域內耕地原為北柵陳姓產業。清朝末年，北柵陳姓村民在此地興建土廬，從福建、鶴山、樟木頭等地招收佃農代為耕種，佃農在此繁衍立村，故又名共同村。村民以黃姓居多，主要來自鄰近的大嶺山鎮的高牌、大逕等村，當地方言屬客家語系。」[17]訪談時，一位陳村老村民為我們講述其村歷史：「我們大概是在第一次鴉片戰爭和第二次鴉片戰爭之間立村的。當時北柵是虎門的大村，村民多數姓陳，比較富有。他們的田地很多，包括現在陳村、黃村，甚至大虎山、小虎山那邊都有部分田地。北柵村與鄰近的懷德村常有矛盾，為防止懷德與赤崗村聯合起來對付本村，陳氏計畫多立一條村以壯大自己。當時

16　東莞市文化廣電新聞出版局編：《東莞歷代碑刻選集》，上海古籍出版社，2014年，第317頁。

17　《東莞虎門鎮志》編纂委員會：《東莞市虎門鎮志》，廣東人民出版社，2010年，第88頁。

招人條件有三個：一是必須同姓,因為『同姓三分親』,宗親之間有情分；二是必須是客家人,因客家人宗族觀念強、比較團結；三是懂武術、有文化。最後東莞縣厚街九門山和新安縣觀瀾（今深圳寶安區觀瀾）的陳姓客家人來應招,他們就是我們的祖先。他們來到後在這裡紮根定居,就是現在的北柵新村。」訪談中多名老村民均表示,陳村立村後北柵的廣府陳氏與應招而來的客家人相處和睦。

4.因無法在原居住地立足而遷徙

　　部分客家人因無法在原居住地立足而遷入東莞的,其中家庭衰敗或者陷入絕境是最為常見的因素。

　　如清溪鎮的茅輋與鷓鴣塘兩村的客家人,原籍福建莆田,其先人因戰亂先遷至汀州府清流縣（今寧化縣）石壁村林家城居住。到了文育公（後人稱為岩公）時,他為了避兵亂隱居到梅州,通過寒窗苦讀而獲得功名,並在杭州為官。根據《東莞林氏族譜》的記載,「岩公在朝為官,少理家務,其子尚幼,未諳事務,一切糧錢田塘均付於招郎入贅女婿陳才用打理。岩公身故後,陳便成了招狼入室的強盜,竟將岩公的所有家產全部盜割入其戶,致使岩公子孫無立足之地,被迫遷往大埔、五華、惠東、東莞。」[18]據說這兩村的客家人與今東城街道的火煉樹、橫嶺、牛山以及謝崗鎮的南面、大嶺山鎮的新屋場等村落的部分林氏客家人為同宗關係,可能是遷莞後開枝散葉的結果。

　　又如鳳崗鎮的浸校塘劉氏,也是出於類似的原因遷入。據《浸校塘劉氏族譜》記述,「才公的早逝,年方廿六的妣母廖氏哀腸欲斷（略）才公之子蒼吉尚幼,離熟諳世事之年甚遠,無疑日後的生活營謀難於為繼,舉步維艱。在百般無奈的逆境底下,一對可憐的母子相依為命,含淚告別故鄉親

18　東莞林氏宗親會編：《東莞林氏大族譜》,內部資料,2012年,第306頁。

人，選擇出走的道路，浪跡四方行乞果腹。」[19]遷入現居地後，這戶人家歷經坎坷，最終繁衍成就了如今的一姓一村。

5. 因躲避戰亂等而遷徙

可能是遷入時代較晚且處於相對平靜的社會階段，東莞客家人中因受戰亂直接影響而遷入的相當少見，在文獻研究或者田野調查中尚未發現相關的案例。不過，受戰亂波及而遷入者卻有一定的數量。其中影響最大的，當屬太平天國的若干部屬。

例如，洪秀全族姪洪全福，道光十六年（1836）出生於廣東花縣正徑村（今花山鎮）。他幼年生活於廣西，太平天國運動爆發後跟隨洪秀全轉戰各省，被稱作「三千歲」。太平天國運動失敗後，洪全福逃匿到今東莞鳳崗鎮黃洞村洪屋圍避禍。當時的洪屋圍已有洪姓客家人聚居。據調查，其先人在清朝初年從新安縣布吉遷入東莞鳳崗的榕樹廈村，乾隆五年（1740）又遷至洪屋圍定居。可能是擔心洪全福的身份会使自身招致禍害，已落籍的洪姓客家人普遍排斥他，「洪氏族長不讓其入祠堂」。洪全福只好在村落附近的「象山東邊劈地，蓋了十間房屋，自造一間小祠堂——洪氏宗祠，還購置一批田地，自此成家立室。」[20]由於清朝政府追捕洪秀全余部，洪全福倉皇隻身逃至香港，其後人則留在當地生活。

三、客家人在莞再遷及其原因

歷史上，部分客家人遷入東莞後並非就此定居下來，而是經歷境內再度遷徙。依據文獻研究和田野調查所得，再

19　東莞鳳崗竹塘浸校塘劉氏族譜編委會編：《浸校塘劉氏族譜》，內部
　　資料，2006年，第78頁。

20　黃洞村志編纂委員會編：《東莞市鳳崗鎮黃洞村志》，嶺南美術出版
　　社，2011年，第177頁。

遷不是簡單意義上的「搬家」，而是反映客家族群的發展歷
程，影響客家村落的形成分佈。比如：

　　1.由老圍發展出新圍。由於子孫繁衍致使其原居住地不
敷使用，需在附近另建一處新圍以滿足日常的居住，因此東
莞客家人居住地區產生了眾多「老圍」與「新圍」。老圍通
常位於山坡等高處，新圍通一般位於較為平緩的低處，因此
經常被稱為「上圍」與「下圍」。

　　2.在周邊形成新村落。如黃氏、曾氏兩姓人家於明代遷
入，族群人丁興旺，於是後人逐漸向周圍開枝散葉，形成了
許多新的村落。上述現象，多見於客家人分佈最為集中的樟
木頭、清溪、鳳崗三地。

　　3.向遠處擴散立村。如蔡氏於明崇禎五年（1632）由揭
陽縣河婆遷入東莞樟木頭鎮官倉定居，至清末時已成為一方
望族，在原住地附近形成了柏地、裕豐、金河、石新等新的
村落。隨著人丁日漸興盛，部分族人還遷徙至相距較遠的一
些地方開村，形成了大嶺山鎮的下高田村、東城街道的火煉
樹村和犬眠嶺村以及莞城街道的上嶺村等聚落。

　　4.從山上遷至山下。上文已論及，從外地遷至謝崗、清
溪、樟木頭等地的部分客家人，因初到東莞無田無地而被迫
居住在銀屏山脈一帶。經歷較長時間後，他們才逐步分批遷
往山下。

　　至於促使客家人再遷的因素，經過綜合分析歸納，初步
認為有以下四個：

1. 因土客矛盾而遷徙

　　隨著越來越多的客家人遷來並落地生根，原有的廣府人
與新到的客家人之間出現「土客」對立，最初是爭奪土地、
河流、山林等生存資源，其後雙方在社會其他領域也出現了
競爭。這種競爭，出於排他性，且以佔據各類資源為目的，
必然使得當事的雙方走向長久的相互敵視。調查時，不少報

道人向我們表示，歷史上客家人備受排斥，與土著之間普遍存在著矛盾，規模不一的衝突乃至械鬥時有發生。在村志或族譜中，也常有相關的記載。如《油甘埔村志》：「我仕璘公長子朝秀公及幼子朝良公，初由鳳凰圍遷來油甘埔拓居時，先於新塘埔構廬而居……豈料對面雁田土著，挾其先到為君之淫威，對於後到先祖人等異常歧視，諸多排斥，繼之任意摧殘莊稼，搶掠牲畜，橫蠻非法手段，不一而足……時生衝突，小則口角，大則訴諸武力。」[21]又如《浸校塘劉氏族譜》：「清康熙十二年，妣母廖氏與子蒼吉，安居落籍浸校塘……開基之初，浸校塘原有先於劉氏落籍的陳姓村民，自愧勢單力薄的廖氏母子，常受東道主陳姓人家的欺凌。」[22]

　　當土客矛盾激化到一定程度時，一方可能就要被迫他遷以免不測。客家人由於初來乍到、勢單力薄，所以經常是遷出者。如鳳崗鎮南門村鄒氏，「清朝順治末年（1661），鄒元鏈遷到油甘埔南安（今油甘埔南岸村），生下7個男丁。因受南安當地人（粵語）的歧視，也為了尋找食邑兄弟分家，清朝康熙七年（1668），鄒元鏈從油甘埔南安遷到南門村（今屬官井頭村轄），自成村落，繁衍後代，至今續代約340年。」

2. 為發展壯大而遷徙

　　不論對於廣府人還是客家人而言，土地是他們最基本的生產資料與最重要的生存資源，佔有更多的土地是最為有效的增強本家族實力的方式。落籍東莞數代後，客家人因人口繁衍而變得子孫興旺，但子孫興旺必然導致「地隘人稠」。因此，原居於一處的部分族人必須選擇遷移他處開基立村。

　　撰於道光二十八年（1848）的《賴氏分支移居譜序》中

21　油甘埔村志編纂委員會：《東莞市鳳崗鎮油甘埔村志》，嶺南美術出版社，2006年，第211-212頁。

22　東莞鳳崗竹塘浸校塘劉氏族譜編委會：《浸校塘劉氏族譜》，2006年，第79頁。

説，「子子孫孫世守勿替，非無蕃昌之會，熙熙攘攘，地隘人稠，豈忍久居此土？言念及此，而二三兄弟未免有情，其志大，其謀遠，自必為之向他邦而覘風土，適彼樂郊而擇居為大矣。噫嘻！豈不欲久安長享之基業乎？遷徙備嘗，上可告於宗祖，貽謀圖遠；下可告於子孫，爰斯際也。」[23]應該説，這段文字既符合事實亦極有代表性，道出了當時許多家族分枝的原委。以竹尾田村賴氏為例，「孟奇公不遂其意，又與五子仕俊、仕儀、仕魁、仕信、仕龍遷於莞邑七都，土名浸校塘村右邊插住。仕魁公兄弟與子永高志大，圖謀復遷於土名黃毛嶺居。奈黃姓強迫，無可如何，不得已，便遷於土名老竹尾田村。後永高公幸生二子奕俊、奕才，以助其志、長其謀也。」[24]遷莞後這支賴姓人家歷經發展與分遷，最終發展出數個村落。類似的情況頗為多見，如現居住於油甘埔村的張氏為例。這支張姓遷莞始祖「仕璘公攜家人，於明末清初落居鳳凰圍村。維限於該處食場有限，且姓氏複雜，故為後世繁衍計，朝秀公毅然遷居油甘埔村。蓋因是處曠闊平坦，有山有水，坐北向南，誠落居之理想屋場也。」[25]

3. 為安居樂業而遷徙

上文提及不少客家人曾在銀屏山山脈一帶聚居，然而選擇山居確是無奈之舉，這主要體現在三個方面：一是山上生活條件惡劣。到處荊棘叢生，陡峭難行，生活極為不便，且有傷人的猛獸出沒（如老虎等）。二是受到山賊、土匪的騷擾。因山高林密，易於藏匿，治安形勢十分嚴峻，經常有山賊土匪前來掠劫，使本來就非常貧困的客家人更難以為繼。

23　官井頭村志編纂委員會：《東莞市鳳崗鎮官井頭村志》，嶺南美術出版社，2008年，第26頁。

24　竹尾田村志編纂委員會：《竹尾田村志》，南方出版社，2008年，第40-41頁。

25　竹尾田村志編纂委員會：《竹尾田村志》，南方出版社，2008年，第40—41頁。

三是謀生手段和機會較少，一般只能務農或出售「山貨」、木炭和手工製品來糊口度日。鑒於此，原來居住於在山林間的客家人在經過一段或長或短時間的積累後，均陸續遷至山下，在力所能及的範圍內選擇相對安全穩定的生活環境。加之，在謝崗、清溪等地，客家人和廣府人在交往、交易的過程中增進瞭解，逐步融合，關係趨於緩和，甚至和平共處一村，這在一定程度上為客家人遷居山下提供了社會條件。

4. 因配合水庫建設而遷移

中華人民共和國成立後，為配合水庫建設，東莞部分客家人在境內再度遷移。如1957年12月，位於清溪鎮境內的茅峯水庫動工，庫內淹浸耕地400畝，移民100戶468人。這些人幾乎都是客家人，分屬溫、林、藍、劉姓等姓氏，他們遷至清溪鎮九鄉另立了茅峯新村。1958年6月，為了興建橫崗水庫，庫內淹浸耕地4750畝，移民250戶1299人。原居住於厚街鎮的絨旗墩村的鄧氏族人，部分他遷並另立新村「新聯」；另有一部分則遷至今虎門鎮懷德社區新沙埔村和遠豐村。1958年8月，同沙水庫動工，庫內淹浸耕地2940畝，移民892戶4317人。其中，原居住於大嶺山連平下高田村23戶160人為此他遷建立新村，但仍沿用「下高田」作為村名。

此外，亦有極少數外地客家人因水利工程建設而遷入東莞。如1970年5月，廣東省龍川縣動工修建楓樹壩水庫（即今青龍湖）。據當時廣東省政府的統一安置政策，部分當地村民於1972年從龍川縣楓樹壩鎮遷至今東莞塘廈鎮林村，另立「東方紅」和「太陽升」兩條新村。

四、小結

經過多年辛勤艱苦的勞動與篳路藍縷的創業，客家人逐步紮根東莞並開枝散葉，創造出如今所見的獨特文化與美好家園。關於他們遷入的歷史與遷徙的原因，本文根據初步的田野調查與文獻研究進行粗淺的勾勒與分析，錯謬之處，敬請方家批評指正！

（中山大學人類學系張振江教授對本文所給予莫大幫助，特此致謝！）

附錄：東莞客家人的具體分佈及遷徙情況一覽表

表1　謝崗鎮客家人分佈情況一覽表

鎮（街）	行政村（社區）	自然村（居民小組）	主要姓氏及其來源
謝崗	南面村	上新村、上石鼓、下石鼓、大坡頭、馬公坑、兵營口、謝禾山、黃京坑、新屋下、橫屋背、嚇圍仔	①林姓一支為桂秋公之後裔，桂秋公生於清朝初年（約1644年），祖居廣東興寧縣葉塘鎮勝青村瓦子塘。桂秋公逝世後，其妻攜五子遷居東莞謝崗鎮麻元嶺（今謝崗鎮南面村麻嶺）（《東莞市東城區火煉樹村志》初稿）②劉、羅、闕、李、沙、溫、邱、張姓來源不詳
	大龍村	長江頭、井水龍、大墩一、大墩二、五和井、榕樹嶺、黃毛嶺、新圍仔	①張姓於明中期由梅縣壢林坪遷入②鄧、林、張、羅、溫、黃、何、陳姓來源不詳
	五星村	萬里、上湖、下渡、寨凹	①據村民稱，袁姓從福建寧化遷至江西信豐，由江西信豐先後遷至東莞溫塘、龍川赤光鎮，於1972年5月由龍川赤光鎮遷入②楊姓於1972年5月由龍川縣車田鎮嶂背村遷入③鄡、葉、馮、黃、吳、陳、李、張姓來源不詳

共計：4個行政村（社區）23個自然村（居民小組）

說明：　1.姓氏來源情況主要依據鎮志、村志、族譜及訪談資料。

　　　　2.以下各表皆有類似狀況，不再逐一說明。

表2　樟木頭鎮客家人分佈情況一覽表

鎮（街）	行政村（社區）	自然村（居民小組）	主要姓氏及其來源
樟木頭	樟羅（原名田心洞）	羅屋、劉屋、大圍、新圍、背圍、凹背圍、凹芝頭、塘嘯埔、旗杆嘯、	①劉姓於明萬曆三十一年（1604）從潮州府惠來縣（原居潮州揭陽河婆）移居廣州府東莞縣田心村（即今樟羅）和長山口圍②羅姓於明天啟年間由今東莞縣樟木頭珊珠棚村遷居田心村（即今樟羅）③連姓於清乾隆年間由揭陽田畝龍宮墩遷入，散居背圍、新圍（《東莞市樟木頭鎮志》）
	圩鎮	樟木頭圍、圩一村、圩二村、新村坑、九明村、圩鎮社區居民小組	①黃姓由廣東揭西五雲洞到惠州某豆腐村，再遷到樟木頭圍開基②連姓於清乾隆年間由揭陽田畝龍宮墩遷入九明村、新村坑（《東莞市樟木頭鎮志》）
	柏地（原名百地）	沙井、柏新、柏西、塘子坑、三社、旗嶺	蔡姓於清末由樟木頭官倉遷入（《東莞市樟木頭鎮志》）
	裕豐（原名豐門）	石壁、豐門、椅嶺、刁龍、赤布、赤山、坭坡	蔡姓於清末由樟木頭官倉遷入（《東莞市樟木頭鎮志》）
	金河（原名古坑村）	上南、下南、坭坑、古坑、沙元、沙湖、籬什排、大坑	蔡姓於清末由樟木頭官倉遷入（《東莞市樟木頭鎮志》）
	石新（原名石馬圩）	新圩嘯、鎮江頭、珊珠棚、大埔、大和、七和、元長、石一、石二、石三、石四	①蔡姓於清末由樟木頭官倉遷入②羅姓於潮州府遷入東莞縣珊珠棚村（《東莞市樟木頭鎮志》）
	百果洞（原名白果洞，1994年改稱今名）	無	黃姓於清末由海豐王雲洞遷入廣州府東莞縣樟木頭田心鄉（今樟羅），其後複遷白果洞村立業（《東莞市樟木頭鎮志》）
	官倉	無	蔡姓於明崇禎五年（1632）由揭西縣河婆尖田尾遷至樟木頭官倉窩開基，後又遷官倉河邊立村（《東莞市樟木頭鎮志》）
	樟洋（原名洋四）	第一、第二一、第二二、第三、第四、第四一、第四二、第五一、第五二、第五三、第六一、第六二、第七、第八、第九一、第九二、第十一、第十二、第十三	①吳姓於南宋德祐年間由於廣東大埔縣湖寮同仁遷入，其後裔於明嘉靖年間在洋四銀井開基②賴姓於清順治二年（1645）由廣東大埔縣岩上石行村青哈洞遷入③張姓約於清雍正至乾隆年間由廣東大埔縣湖寮遷來④陳姓於清順治十六年（1659）由福建漳州平和縣遷入廣東莞清溪石田倉背園，四代後遷至樟木頭洋凹黃沙村（《東莞市樟木頭鎮志》）
共計：9個行政村（社區）66個自然村（居民小組）			

表3 樟木頭鎮客家人分佈情況一覽表

所在鎮（街）	所在行政村（社區）	所在自然村（居民小組）	主要姓氏及其來源
清溪	羅馬	羅裙埔（舊稱裸家圍）	劉姓於清康熙年間由廣東潮州府揭西縣河婆圩大埔頭圍遷入（村委會提供資料）
		馬灘	鄧姓於清康熙年間由廣東潮州府揭陽縣河婆圩遷入（《東莞市清溪鎮志》）
		天生湖	孫姓一支於清雍正十二年（1734）由興寧圩下排（今興寧徑南鎮圩下村）遷入（《梅州孫氏族譜》）；另據《東莞市清溪鎮志》，孫姓一支於明天啟早期由興寧遷入；一支於明天啟晚期由紫金縣中心壩遷入。
	荔橫	梁頭圍	張姓於清康熙年間由今東莞清溪鎮新中坑村遷入（《東莞市清溪鎮志》）
		角嶺	張姓於清光緒年間由五華大田遷出，途徑惠陽山徑、草洞短期停留後遷入（《東莞市清溪鎮志》）
	浮崗	浮崗老圍	張姓於明萬曆三十一年（1603）福建漳州平和縣白葉村大片裡坑尾遷入惠州湯化縣田心圍，其後移遷入浮崗老圍（《東莞清溪浮崗圍張氏族譜》）
		浮崗新圍	張姓於明崇禎年間由鄰近的浮崗老圍遷來（《東莞清溪浮崗圍張氏族譜》）
		柏朗（含老圍、新圍）	①溫姓於明萬曆年間由福建漳州平和縣途經陸豐遷入柏朗老圍②張姓於明萬曆年間遷入③黃姓於明萬曆年間由今東莞清溪鎮浮崗柏朗老圍分居於此，建柏朗新圍（以上資料由村委會提供）
		田螺澗	張姓於清乾隆十八年（1753）由鄰近的西村遷入（《東莞市清溪鎮志》）
		光朗	劉姓於明萬曆年間由廣東長樂（五華）遷入（《東莞市清溪鎮志》）
		烏鴉落陽	黃姓、曾姓、余姓、張姓於清咸豐年間由鄰近的崗柏朗村遷入（《東莞市清溪鎮志》）
	松崗	松柏墩	張姓於明崇禎年間由廣東長樂遷入（《東莞市清溪鎮志》）
		西村（原名四村）	①張姓於明崇禎年間由福建平和縣清宵裡黃田村遷入②鄭姓於明成化年間由福建長樂縣遷入（《東莞市清溪鎮志》）
		田心仔	①汪姓於清康熙年間由福建泉州惠安象埔村遷入②李姓於20世紀70年代因修建清溪三坑水庫而遷入（以上資料由村委會提供）
		浮崗	張姓於清乾隆十七年（1752）由今東莞清溪鎮松崗西村遷入（《東莞清溪浮崗圍張氏族譜》）
		上官倉老圍	余姓原籍福建漳州平和縣鐵爐溪鄉，於明萬曆年間遷居廣東陸豐縣新田鄉，約於明天啟三年（1623）再遷入清溪上官倉（《東莞清溪上官倉村餘氏族譜》）
		上官倉新圍	余姓於1912年由鄰近的上官倉老圍分居於此建村（《東莞市清溪鎮志》）
		松本下	①陳姓、余姓於明成化年間遷此定居②蔡姓於明崇禎年間由福建遷居廣東揭西再遷居於此（《東莞市清溪鎮志》）

表4　清溪鎮客家人分佈情況一覽表

所在鎮（街）	所在行政村（社區）	所在自然村（居民小組）	主要姓氏及其來源
清溪	重河	蒲草洞	何、曾、黃、徐、胡等姓氏於明永樂年間陸續由福建遷入（《東莞市清溪鎮志》）
		重木（舊稱董祿村）	楊姓於明萬曆二十六（1599）由廣東陸豐遷入（《東莞市清溪鎮志》）
		楊梅崗	楊姓於明崇禎年間由鄰近的重木村遷入（《東莞市清溪鎮志》）
		油柑坪	楊姓於清雍正年間由今鄰近的重木村遷入（《東莞市清溪鎮志》）
		三椏圳	楊姓於清嘉慶年間由鄰近的重木村遷入（《東莞市清溪鎮志》）
		新圍仔	楊姓於清道光年間由鄰近的重木村遷入（《東莞市清溪鎮志》）
		沙埔	楊姓於清光緒年間由鄰近的重木村遷入（《東莞市清溪鎮志》）
		楊梅坑	楊氏於清咸豐年間由鄰近的大嶺山大灣遷入（《東莞市清溪鎮志》）
	清廈	清溪老圩	有王、盧、葉等多個姓氏，來源不詳
		鹿湖壢	王姓於明嘉靖年間由廣東興寗馬路下遷入（《東莞市清溪鎮志》）
		廈屋村（舊稱大埔圍）	曾姓由廣東五華縣長樂鄉遷至東莞縣七都婆嶺鄉，清乾隆三年（1738）由婆嶺鄉遷入（據《東莞市清溪鎮志》及訪談資料）
	鐵松	深圳仔	黃姓於明宣德年間由廣東長樂遷入東莞縣七都洞清化約，此地後改名為深圳仔（《東莞市清溪鎮志》）
		松本園	黃姓於明萬曆年間由今東莞清溪鎮鐵松深圳仔遷入（《東莞市清溪鎮志》）
		水尾段（曾分上圍、下圍）	①梁姓於明萬曆年間從鄰近的龍眼坑遷入②林姓於明萬曆年間從鄰近的茅筆村遷入（《東莞市清溪鎮志》）
		小近布（原名小近浦）	梁姓於明萬曆年間由今東莞清溪鎮龍眼坑遷入（《東莞市清溪鎮志》）
		鐵矢嶺	李姓於明崇禎年間由梅縣遷入（《東莞市清溪鎮志》）
		缸廠	李姓於清順治年間由鄰近的鐵矢嶺遷入（《東莞市清溪鎮志》）
		鍾圍	鍾姓於清康熙年間由長樂（五華）遷入（《東莞市清溪鎮志》）
		千秋嶺	①恭氏清乾隆年間由惠陽遷入②黃姓於清中葉由今東莞清溪鐵松松本圍遷入（《東莞市清溪鎮志》）
		禾長崗	黃姓於1931年由今東莞清溪鎮鐵松松本圍遷入（《東莞市清溪鎮志》）

所在鎮（街）	所在行政村（社區）	所在自然村（居民小組）	主要姓氏及其來源
清溪	鐵場	鐵場上圍	韓姓於明萬曆年間由福建經惠陽遷入（《東莞市清溪鎮志》）
		鐵場下圍	韓姓於明泰昌元年（1620）由鄰近的上圍村遷入（《東莞市清溪鎮志》）
		西門	韓姓於明泰昌元年（1620）由鄰近的上圍村遷入（《東莞市清溪鎮志》）
		婆嶺（原名何嶺）	曾姓一支於明宣德年間由五華遷入；一支於1644年由廣東五華縣長樂鄉遷入（《東莞市清溪鎮志》）
		牛湖（原名鼇湖，含青麻圍、娥眉月）	李姓於清乾隆十六年（1751）由惠陽縣南坑遷入（《東莞市清溪鎮志》）
		新屋廈	曾姓於明正統年間由今東莞清溪鎮九鄉婆嶺村遷入並立村（《東莞市清溪鎮志》）
		高田唇（含雞棲坑）	曾姓於明弘治年間由今東莞清溪鎮九鄉新屋廈村遷入並立村（《東莞市清溪鎮志》）
		大稔（染）布	李姓於明正德年間由寶安縣龍崗高橋遷入（《東莞市清溪鎮志》）
		金口（原名鉗口賁）	賴姓於明成化年間惠陽縣鎮隆遷入（《東莞市清溪鎮志》）
		竹樹下	黃姓於明弘治年間由鄰近的深圳仔遷入（《東莞市清溪鎮志》）
	大利	香元埔老圍	李姓於明崇禎年間由今鄰近的鐵場村遷入（《東莞市清溪鎮志》）
		利和（舊稱大布圩、利和圩）	李姓於明崇禎年間由長樂縣清化都雙頭大水約老虎畏大人村遷至歸善縣坪地約南坑鄉，同治六年（1867）遷入（《利和李氏族譜》）
		葵湖	余姓於清乾隆十二年（1747）由鄰近的上官倉村遷入（《東莞市清溪鎮志》）
		風吹簾老圍	曾姓於清嘉慶年間由興寧馬山下遷入（《東莞市清溪鎮志》）
		香元埔新圍	李姓於清宣統年間由今鄰近的香元埔老圍村遷入（《東莞市清溪鎮志》）
		風吹簾新圍	曾姓於1912年由鄰近的風吹簾老圍遷入立村（《東莞市清溪鎮志》）
		聚星圍	李氏於民國初期由大布圩、香元埔、大稔布等村分居於此
		茅筆新村	由原居茅筆村的溫姓、林姓、藍姓、劉姓於1957年立村（《東莞市清溪鎮志》）
	青皇	禾場崗（含大喊山村）	①張姓於明萬曆十四年（1587）由潮州府長樂縣大田粘坑村（今五華縣長布鎮粘坑村）遷入東莞縣歸城鄉第四都青塘村 ②江姓於明萬曆年裡由長樂（五華）遷入（《東莞市清溪鎮志》）

所在鎮（街）	所在行政村（社區）	所在自然村（居民小組）	主要姓氏及其來源
清溪	青皇	對面黃屋	①劉姓於明隆慶年間由長樂（五華）遷入②劉姓於明萬曆十四年（1587）由潮州府長樂縣大粘坑村（今五華縣長布鎮粘坑村）遷入③黃姓於清康熙年間由長樂（五華）遷入（《東莞市清溪鎮志》）
		新圍仔	①劉姓於明隆慶年間由長樂（五華）遷入②張姓於明萬曆十四年（1587）、清康熙元年（1662）由長樂（五華）遷入（《東莞市清溪鎮志》）
	三星	呂圍（又名田心崗）	呂姓於清順治年間由鄰近的鐵場村遷入（《東莞市清溪鎮志》）
		百家筆（含沙嶺、筆崗嘴、新圍）	徐姓於清康熙年間由鄰近的清溪老圩遷入（《東莞市清溪鎮志》）
		劉屋圍（原名福星圍）	劉姓於清嘉慶年間由鄰近的羅群埔遷入（《東莞市清溪鎮志》）
		牛路頭	曾姓於清道光年間由鄰近的新屋廈村遷入（《東莞市清溪鎮志》）
		李友堂	李姓於清光緒年間由鄰近的利和村遷入（《東莞市清溪鎮志》）
	廈坭	企嶺下	溫姓、傅姓於清康熙年間由紫金縣遷入（《東莞市清溪鎮志》）
		磨坭圩（含光頭埔）	①溫姓、傅姓由企嶺下村遷入②謝姓於清道光二十年（1845）由博羅縣遷入③葉姓、林姓來源不詳（（《東莞市清溪鎮志》）
		鄭屋園	鄭姓於清康熙年間由鄰近的松崗西村遷入（《東莞市清溪鎮志》）
		花邊嶺	楊姓於清道光年間由今鄰近的重木村遷入（《東莞市清溪鎮志》）
		蚌嶺	曾姓於清道光年間由鄰近的高田唇遷入（《東莞市清溪鎮志》）
		江背（含塘沙圩）	徐姓於清咸豐年間由鄰近的百家筆村遷入（《東莞市清溪鎮志》）
	謝坑	缸窯	鍾姓一支於清光緒年間由今東莞鳳崗鎮洋稠尾遷入，一支於清光緒年間由惠陽山背遷入（《東莞市清溪鎮志》）
	三中	三峰上圍	①聶姓於明萬曆年間由長樂（五華）遷入（《東莞市清溪鎮志》）②卓姓於明末清初由廣東長樂清化弍圖西林墻遷入（《廣東省東莞縣清溪鄉三峰村卓氏族譜》）③另有聶、巫、張、梁、彭、陳、楊等姓氏，來源不詳
		三峰下圍	有謝、魏、陳、黃、賴等姓氏，來源不詳
		蓮塘湖	謝姓於清康熙年間由鄰近的三峰上圍村遷入（《東莞市清溪鎮志》）
		新中坑	張姓於清康熙年間由興寧長樂大田粘坑遷入（《東莞市清溪鎮志》）

所在鎮（街）	所在行政村（社區）	所在自然村（居民小組）	主要姓氏及其來源
清溪	三中	分水坳	黃姓於清乾隆年間由今鄰近的三峰下圍村遷入（《東莞市清溪鎮志》）
		湖篤尾	曾姓於清乾隆年間由今東莞鳳崗田心圍遷入（《東莞市清溪鎮志》）
	清溪圩	連屋	連姓於明萬曆年間由龍川縣大布遷入（《東莞市清溪鎮志》）
		清溪圩	李氏於清康熙年間由歸善坪地約南坑鄉遷入（民國《李氏族譜》）
		鵪鶉藪	黃姓於清乾隆年間由惠陽新圩遷入，另一支由樟木頭圍遷入（《東莞市清溪鎮志》）
		黃屋	黃姓於清乾隆年間由鄰近的柏朗村遷入（《東莞市清溪鎮志》）
		劉屋	劉姓於清嘉慶年間由今東莞塘廈鎮石頭嶺村遷入（《東莞市清溪鎮志》）
		楊屋	楊姓於清同治年間由鄰近的重木村遷入（《東莞市清溪鎮志》）
		企太陽	楊姓於1912年鄰近的三椏圳遷入（《東莞市清溪鎮志》）

共計：17個行政村（社區）91個自然村（居民小組）

表5　鳳崗鎮客家人分佈情況一覽表

所在鎮（街）	所在行政村（社區）	所在自然村（居民小組）	主要姓氏及其來源
鳳崗	鳳德嶺	鳳德嶺	①黃姓於明崇禎十四年（1641）由廣東紫金瑯坑遷入塘瀝樓廈村，又於清乾隆三十一年（1766）由塘瀝樓廈村遷入鳳德嶺②魏姓於清道光年間由五華縣橫陂鎮遷入油甘埔，隨後遷入鳳德嶺③邱姓於清雍正年間由新安縣龍崗沙背壢村遷入④羅姓、李姓、鄒姓於民國初年遷入，蘇姓、劉姓、廖姓於1949年前遷入（《東莞市鳳崗鎮鳳德嶺村志》）
		獅石廈（原名長興圍）	①呂姓於清康熙年間由今東莞清溪鎮鐵場村遷入②黃姓於清初由廣東長樂縣上塘柏坑約遷至惠陽縣淡水黃竹塘，又於清康熙年間由惠陽淡水黃竹塘遷入（《東莞市鳳崗鎮鳳德嶺村志》《油甘埔村志》）
		上村（原名尚村）	①曾姓於清康熙元年（1662）由歸善縣橫崗樓坑遷入②張姓原居福建汀州，先後遷至廣東程鄉縣、長樂縣、歸善縣，又於清康熙年間由歸善縣菜溪鄉遷入③江姓於清乾隆年間由今東莞鳳崗鎮油甘埔蝦公潭村遷入④阮姓於清嘉慶年間由福建上杭縣竹村嶺遷入⑤鄭姓於1949年前遷入（《東莞市鳳崗鎮鳳德嶺村志》）
	官井頭	官井頭	①連姓於明崇禎十三年（1640）由惠東縣南坑約禾苗田村遷入②卓姓原籍香山縣，於明崇禎十六年（1643）由今東莞清溪鎮遷入③鄒姓於清康熙年間由今東莞鳳崗鎮官井頭南門村遷入（《東莞市鳳崗鎮官井頭村志》）
		嶂廈	①周姓於清乾隆五十九年（1794）由興寧、長樂遷入②另有劉姓、羅姓，來源不詳（《東莞市鳳崗鎮官井頭村志》）
		小布	曾姓於清嘉慶十七年（1812）由今東莞鳳崗鎮官井頭西門村遷入（《東莞市鳳崗鎮官井頭村志》）
		細河	曾姓於清中葉由今東莞鳳崗鎮官井頭西門村遷入（《東莞市鳳崗鎮官井頭村志》）
		南門	①鄒姓於清康熙七年（1668）由今東莞清溪鎮油甘埔南安村遷入（《東莞市鳳崗鎮官井頭村志》）
		西門（原名老圍、雍和里）	①曾姓於清康熙十九年（1680）由興寧長樂嘉燕洲遷入②另有張、何、李、楊、余、轟、鍾、曾、鄧、黃（以上據《東莞市鳳崗鎮官井頭村志》）
		黃牛嶺	李姓於清乾隆六十年（1795）遷入（《東莞市鳳崗鎮官井頭村志》）
		庵下龍	李姓於清道光十年（1830）由今東莞鳳崗鎮官井頭西門遷入（《東莞市鳳崗鎮官井頭村志》）

所在鎮（街）	所在行政村（社區）	所在自然村（居民小組）	主要姓氏及其來源
鳳崗	油甘埔	油甘埔	①張姓於清順治年間（一說康熙）由長樂遷入鳳凰圍，再由於鳳凰圍遷入（《東莞市鳳崗鎮志》）②阮姓原居福建上杭縣什嶺村，後遷惠陽坪山三丘田（即今深圳三洲田），於清初遷入（《東莞市鳳崗鎮油甘埔村志》）③江姓於清雍正年間由今東莞鳳崗鎮油甘埔蝦公潭村遷入（《東莞市鳳崗鎮油甘埔村志》）
		蝦公潭	①李姓由長樂玉茶深尾遷至歸善縣長布豬糠圍，清康熙十年（1671）由豬糠圍遷入②黃姓於清初由廣東長樂縣上塘柏田約遷至惠陽縣淡水黃竹塘，於清康熙年間遷今東莞鳳崗鎮鳳德嶺獅石廈，其後又遷至蝦公潭③江姓原居福建汀州府寧化縣石壁村，後先後遷至福建上杭縣、南靖縣，清康熙年間由廣東長樂縣遷入（《東莞市鳳崗鎮油甘埔村志》）
		南岸（原名南安）	鄒姓於明萬曆元年（1573）由五華遷至惠陽坪山均田，於清順治十八年（1661）遷至今東莞鳳崗油甘埔南安村（《東莞市鳳崗鎮油甘埔村志》）
		沙嶺（原名沙嶺背）	賴姓於清嘉慶二十年（1851）由潮州府程鄉縣遷入東莞縣第七都塘瀝洞珊珠坑（今鳳崗鎮官井頭水庫內），土名山豬坑，後改稱龍田村），1958年因修建水庫而遷至鳳崗油甘埔村暫住，1965年遷入沙嶺村居住（《東莞市鳳崗鎮油甘埔村志》）
	什尾田	老圍、新圍（老圍原名永興圍）	①賴氏原居廣東長樂縣小都，一支先後遷至歸善縣果園背、歸善縣田寮，後於清初遷至浸校塘村之右以及塘廈黃毛嶺，又於黃毛嶺遷至今鳳崗鎮什尾田；一支先於清初期從長樂縣小都遷至博羅縣，由博羅縣遷至今鳳崗鎮什尾田老圍，其後兩支同於清乾隆元年築房，次年入夥居住（《什尾田賴氏族譜》）②廖姓原籍福建永定縣，後遷廣東興寧，於清朝時遷至寶安龍崗丙坑村，後於清光緒年間遷至什尾田老圍禾塘背（《什尾田村志》）
	塘瀝	塘瀝（原名塘瀝圩）	①黃姓一支於清中葉由興寧長樂遷入②楊姓於清康熙年間由興寧長樂遷入③何姓原籍福建武平，後遷至廣東紫金縣清溪蒜子圍，後又遷入塘瀝（《東莞市鳳崗鎮塘瀝村志1588—2004》）
		鳳凰圍	①李姓一支原籍廣東長樂紫山，後遷至廣東惠州府歸善邑沙土坪圍，又由沙土坪圍遷入②張姓於清康熙年間由長樂遷入（《東莞市鳳崗鎮塘瀝村志1588—2004》）
		碧湖	①羅姓於明朝末年由長樂遷入②謝姓於明萬曆十六年（1588）由長樂遷入③張姓一支由惠陽打禾江新圩散徑遷入，至今超過400年；一支原籍福建汀州寧化石柞柱，後遷至惠陽麻溪，於清中葉由惠陽麻溪遷入（《東莞市鳳崗鎮塘瀝村志1588—2004》）
		樓廈	①黃姓於清初由今廣東紫金坑遷入②張姓於清中葉由今東莞鳳崗鎮鳳德嶺上村遷入（《東莞市鳳崗鎮塘瀝村志1588—2004》）
		正合	楊姓於清同治年間由今東莞鳳崗鎮塘瀝村遷入立村（《東莞市鳳崗鎮塘瀝村志1588—2004》）
		蘆竹田	①羅姓於明萬曆二十年（1592）由興寧縣遷入②張姓原籍福建汀州寧花石柞柱，後遷至今惠陽麻溪、東莞鳳崗塘瀝碧湖，清中葉由碧湖遷入③廖姓原籍福建永安，清晚期由寶安雁田三洲田遷入（《東莞市鳳崗鎮塘瀝村志1588—2004》）

所在鎮（街）	所在行政村（社區）	所在自然村（居民小組）	主要姓氏及其來源
鳳崗	黃洞	田心	①曾姓於清康熙三十三年（1694）由廣東寶安縣龍崗芋地浦遷入（《東莞市鳳崗鎮志》）②鄭姓於明末清初由寶安縣龍崗坪地遷入今東莞鳳崗鎮黃洞嶺南村、榕樹廈，後於清康熙二十八年（1689）由嶺排圍（即今嶺南村）遷入田心村（《東莞市鳳崗鎮志》）
		嶺南（原名嶺排圍）	①何姓於明嘉靖三十一年（1552）由廣東興寧遷入今東莞鳳崗鎮黃洞田心村，又於明萬曆四十年（1612）集體遷入今鳳崗鎮黃洞嶺南村塘面②劉姓於明萬曆四十年（1612）由廣東鎮平縣金沙遷入嶺南村③鄭姓於明崇禎三年（1630）由今深圳龍崗坪地遷入嶺南村④沈姓於明崇禎八年（1635）由廣東海豐縣遷入嶺南村⑤彭姓於清乾隆四十三年（1778）由廣東潮州府遷入今嶺南村塘面（《東莞市鳳崗鎮黃洞村志》）
		榕樹廈（原名左黃圍）	①鄭姓於明崇禎三年（1630）由東莞塘瀝嶺排圍（今鳳崗鎮黃洞嶺南村）遷入左黃圍②蔡姓於清順治九年（1652）由廣東揭陽縣遷入③洪姓於明末由廣東新安縣布吉遷入。（《東莞市鳳崗鎮黃洞村志》）
		洪武圍	洪姓於清同治三年（1864）由廣東花縣遷入（《東莞市鳳崗鎮黃洞村志》）
		南門山	清晚期立村，主要姓氏為張、謝（《東莞市鳳崗鎮黃洞村志》）
	竹塘	含上圍、下圍、臥龍、紅花圍、兩渡河、浸校塘	①張姓原籍福建武平，於明洪武元年（1368）遷入長樂雙頭，於清順治年間由長樂雙頭遷入（《竹塘竹頭張氏族譜》）②劉姓原籍興寧，前後遷至潮州府揭陽縣河婆、陸豐縣新田黃麻地，於清康熙十二年（1673）由陸豐遷入浸校塘（《浸校塘劉氏族譜》）③賴氏原居廣東長樂黃小都，於清初期先後遷至歸善縣果園背、歸善縣田寮以及今東莞鳳崗鎮竹塘浸校塘村之右（《竹尾田村志》）
	三聯村	排沙圍	房姓原籍福建寧化石壁村，於明末遷入（《東莞市鳳崗鎮志》）
		鶴亮圍	鄭姓原籍福建汀州永定，遷至廣東長樂，於明末由長樂遷入（《東莞市鳳崗鎮志》）
		洋稠尾	不詳
	五聯村	新塘	不詳
		松木崗	廖姓於明隆慶六年由福建汀州上杭遷至廣東寶安鹽田三洲田，後遷入松木崗（《東莞市鳳崗鎮志》）
		秀木橋	不詳
		畔坑	①鄭姓於明弘治十三年（1500）由廣東寶安縣龍崗坪地遷入②鍾姓於清順治年間由廣東長樂遷入。（《東莞市鳳崗鎮志》）
		新興	不詳
共計：9個行政村（社區）41個自然村（居民小組）			

表6　塘廈鎮客家人分佈情況一覽表

所在鎮（街）	所在行政村（社區）	所在自然村（居民小組）	主要姓氏及其來源
塘廈（原名塘頭廈）	林村	東方紅（原名虎口村）	因修建廣東河源龍川縣建楓樹壩水庫，駱氏與謝氏於1972年遷入（訪談資料）
		太陽升（原名虎口村）	因修建廣東河源龍川縣建楓樹壩水庫，駱氏於1972年遷入（訪談資料）
		電光	①李姓約於1905年由黃江長龍上流洞遷入電光村，1958年因修建電光水庫，與同村賴氏、羅氏、周氏、林氏遷至塘廈振興圍長莆村。次年遷回電光村舊址附近壩墾下（今電光村）定居②蔡姓由樟木頭裕豐遷入，1958年因水庫修建回遷樟木頭，於1960年又遷回電光村新址（根據訪談整理）③賴姓於1953年由樟木頭樟洋遷入④羅姓由惠東縣遷入，具體時間不詳⑤馮姓於1964　年由河源紫金縣遷入⑥周姓於1953年由惠東縣良化遷入⑦林姓於1949年前由東莞謝崗大龍遷入（訪談資料）
塘廈	龍背嶺	龍背嶺	葉姓於清光緒二十五年（1899）由東莞黃江長山口村遷入（訪談資料）
		牛眠埔老圍	張姓於清乾隆二十二年（1757）由東莞黃江下流洞村遷入（據訪談資料整理），祖先來自五華，之後遷至廣東深圳市境內的黃背嶺，十六世祖張潤選再遷到東莞榴洞，二十世祖張有祥再遷至東莞塘頭廈（現稱塘廈鎮）牛眠埔村"（《從塘頭廈到燕南圍：我的母親張偉瑛》）
		牛眠埔新圍	1911年（一說1912年）由牛眠埔老圍人張馨和創立，又名永安村（《從塘頭廈到燕南圍：我的母親張偉瑛》）
	振興圍	長莆	①劉姓於清末從寶安縣布吉區馬安堂遷入（訪談資料）②張姓來源不詳
	蓮湖	石頭嶺	林姓於清末分別由廣東興寧縣、寶安縣和東莞縣清溪羅群埔遷入（《東莞市塘廈鎮志》）

共計：4個行政村（社區）8個自然村（居民小組）

表7　黃江鎮客家人分佈情況一覽表

所在鎮（街）	所在行政村（社區）	所在自然村（居民小組）	主要姓氏及其來源
黃江	長龍	竹山下	明嘉靖二十九年（1550）立村，葉氏因戰亂而南遷，由今河北、福建等地遷入（《黃江鎮志》稿本）
		老圍	不詳
		嚇圍（原名福興圍）	曾氏、葉氏於清乾隆三十五年（1771）從福建、梅州、五華、興寧等地遷入定居（《黃江鎮志》稿本）
		長安圩	原居於老圍、嚇圍村民於1911年在此建房經商（《黃江鎮志》稿本）
		黃書角（原名黃獅角）	張氏於清末從五華縣遷至下流洞，再遷入黃書角（《黃江鎮志》稿本）
		上流洞	李、曾、江氏於清初先後於梅縣、興寧、長樂等地遷入（《黃江鎮志》稿本）
		下流洞	張氏於清初從河北輾轉到福建上杭、梅州、興寧，後遷入此地（《黃江鎮志》稿本）
	三新	黃牛埔（原名永興圍，1958年因修建黃牛埔水庫而遷至今址）	李姓原籍為今福建省龍華市上杭縣，後遷廣東梅縣大埔，於清乾隆四十五年（1780）遷入立村。另有張、陳、蔡、範等姓氏（《黃江鎮志》稿本）
		黃江	張、陳、巫氏前後遷入（《黃江鎮志》稿本）
		黃京坑（原名黃猄坑）	於清康熙五十一年（1712）立村，蘇氏最早遷入，其次為陳、張、巫、黃、葉等姓氏（《黃江鎮志》稿本）
	梅塘	田心、星光、大冚、舊村	不詳
共計：3個行政村（社區）14個自然村（居民小組）			

表8　大嶺山鎮客家人分佈情況一覽表

所在鎮（街）	所在行政村（社區）	所在自然村（居民小組）	主要姓氏及其來源
大嶺山	連平	計嶺	李氏於清初由廣東龍川縣老隆遷入（《東莞市大嶺山鎮志》）
		畔山	張氏於清乾隆元年（1736）由東莞厚街羅探埔（今不存）遷入（《東莞市大嶺山鎮志》）
		新屋場	鍾氏於清嘉慶年間由東莞厚街狗門山（《東莞市大嶺山鎮志》）
		連平	王氏由廣東興寧縣遷入，曾氏由廣東紫金縣遷入（《東莞市大嶺山鎮志》）
		上高田	歐陽氏於清初由東莞厚街白泥井遷此立村（《東莞市大嶺山鎮志》）
		大石板	黃氏由東莞厚街大遲村遷入（《東莞市大嶺山鎮志》）
		下高田	蔡氏於清光緒年間由東莞樟木頭官倉村移入（《東莞市大嶺山鎮志》）
	大嶺	下油古嶺	①廖氏於清順治元年（1644）從廣東惠陽沙堆遷入上油古嶺②劉氏於清乾隆十八年（1753）由東莞厚街新圍、九門山遷入，定居大王嶺、上下油古嶺③李氏於清乾隆四十三年（1778）由東莞厚街新圍張家山遷入油古嶺（《東莞市大嶺山鎮志》）
		上油古嶺	
		大王嶺	
		蠶窯	張氏、林氏於清康熙四十二年（1703）由廣東惠州君子營遷入（《東莞市大嶺山鎮志》）
	農場	第一、第二、上場	不詳
	大環	無	①吳氏於清乾隆元年（1736）從廣東龍川縣鐵場鎮遷入②劉氏於清嘉慶年間從寶安縣烏石岩村羅姿遷入（《東莞市大嶺山鎮志》）
	舊飛鵝	無	不詳
	下高田	無	1959年，因建設同沙水庫，連平下高田村23户160人遷移至今居住地（大地）建新村，並組成獨立行政村，仍沿用原下高田作村名（大嶺山鎮官網）

共計：6個行政村（社區）17個自然村（居民小組）

表9　東城街道客家人分佈情況一覽表

所在鎮（街）	所在行政村（社區）	所在自然村（居民小組）	主要姓氏及其來源
東城	火煉樹	火煉樹	①羅姓一支約於清朝同治十三年（1874），由東莞樟木頭田心村羅屋圍遷到東莞城南郊背夫山東北面山坡立村（今東莞東城區火煉樹村）；一支約於同治九年（1870）由今東莞黃江鎮長山口村（即今長龍村）遷入；一支約於清光緒九年（1883）由今東莞謝崗鎮大龍社區九洞村遷入；一支於1924年由今東莞清溪鎮重河下塘村遷入②蔡姓一支於清同治九年（1870）由今東莞樟木頭鎮官倉村遷入；一支於清同治末年或光緒初期由今東莞樟木頭鎮筋竹排村遷入；一支於清光緒年間由今東莞南城街道始地社區錢屋村遷入；一支於清末由今東莞樟木頭鎮官倉村遷入；一支於清末由今東莞樟木頭鎮柏地村遷入；一支於民國時期東莞樟木頭鎮筋竹排村遷入；一支於1936年由今廣東增城市增江鎮西山社區霞餘村遷入；一支於1958年由今東莞南城街道勝和社區圍鎮村蔡屋圍遷入③林氏一支約於清同治元年（1862）由東莞謝崗鎮南面村禾檀崗遷入④溫姓原居地為今東莞謝崗鎮南面村，後遷居今樟木頭鎮古坑村，於1911年遷入火煉樹⑤陳姓於民國時期從外地遷入⑥黃姓於抗日戰爭期間從惠陽縣陳江村遷入⑦萬姓於1952年由廣東五華縣落戶火煉樹分田地（《東莞市東城街道火煉樹村志》初稿）
	牛山	橫坑	①據村民稱，成姓於清朝末年由廣東興寧甘屋村遷入②李姓、張姓來源不詳③卓姓於清朝末年由東莞清溪遷入（《東莞市東城區志》）
		積善里	張姓於清朝初期由廣東龍川縣獅子寨遷入（《東莞市東城區志》）。
		老圍	據村民稱，李姓由興寧均什澗遷入，至今13代人
		老鴉山	張姓於清朝初期由廣東龍川縣獅子寨遷入（《東莞市東城區志》）
		梁家（原名梁家莊）	梁姓於清朝末年由今東莞南城街道始地社區遷入（《東莞市東城區志》）
		牛頭（原名鼇頭，1951年改作今名）	劉姓祖籍興寧，約於清嘉慶年間由廣東惠陽縣布仔鄉塘肚村遷至今東莞大嶺山鎮大王嶺村，後約於清嘉慶二十五年（1820）遷來東莞縣楊梅鄉鼇溪村；19世紀末部分村民轉移到鼇頭嶺山坡下建立新村場，並改名為鼇頭村（《鼇頭村劉氏族譜》）
		仁厚里	不詳
		上山門	①宋姓一支於清朝末年由廣東惠陽縣淡水鎮遷入（《東莞市東城區志》）②蕭姓於1927年由東莞大嶺山林場村遷入（《東莞市東城區志》）③葉、陳、張、李、吳姓來源不詳
		新村	①成姓於清朝末年由廣東嘉應州遷入（《東莞市東城區志》）②卓姓於清朝末年由東莞清溪遷入（《東莞市東城區志》）③劉、林、李姓來源不詳
		新錫邊	①姚姓於1958年由東莞同沙林場小洞村遷入（《東莞市東城區志》）②謝、駱、庾、黃姓來源不詳
		余慶里	①張姓於清朝初期由廣東龍川縣獅子寨遷入（《東莞市東城區志》）②李姓來源不詳
		鍾屋圍	①據村民稱，李氏來源較多，其中有來自東莞厚街大逕②郭姓於1947年由廣東增城縣遷入（《東莞市東城區志》）

所在鎮 （街）	所在行 政村 （社區）	所在自然村 （居民小組）	主要姓氏及其來源
東城	立新	橫嶺	①楊氏於1911年由東莞清溪楊梅村遷入（另據該村村長稱，楊氏有一支因修建同沙水庫於1958年遷入）②據該村村長稱，林氏約在一百年前由謝崗南面村遷入③范、李、張、賴、陳、朱、溫、曾、羅、鍾姓來源不詳
		犬眠嶺	蔡姓於1911年由東莞樟木頭石馬村遷入（《東莞市東城區志》）；另據該村村長稱，蔡氏約於100年前從樟木頭豐門、石馬村、官倉等地陸續遷入
	同沙	下圍	①陳姓於光緒初期（約1875-1880）分別從寶安觀瀾、東莞塘頭廈遷入（《東莞市同沙村志》）②鍾姓來源不詳③廖姓於清朝末年從廣東寶安縣遷入（《東莞市東城區志》）
共計：4個行政村（社區）16個自然村（居民小組）			

表10　莞城街道客家人分佈情況一覽表

所在鎮 （街）	所在行 政村 （社區）	所在自然村 （居民小組）	主要姓氏及其來源
莞城	鴻裕	上嶺	據村長稱，蔡姓約在光緒十一年（1886）由今東莞樟木頭鎮黃皮坑遷入
共計：1個行政村（社區）1個自然村（居民小組）			

表11　南城區客家人分佈情況一覽表

所在鎮（街）	所在行政村（社區）	所在自然村（居民小組）	主要姓氏及其來源
南城	雅園	雅園（原名鴨形嶺）	①張姓一支於清道光十七年（1837）由龍川縣獅子寨梅村遷入缺口司下山門村，同治元年（1862）再遷入鴨形嶺；另一支由惠州君子營遷入龍旺埔，再遷入鴨形嶺②吳姓於清代光緒元年（1875）由今東莞樟木頭鎮勒什圍遷入③程姓於1957年由五華縣新橋鎮程屋村遷入（《東莞市南城區志》）
	蛤地	青竹筍	①李姓族人於清同治四年（1865）由五華縣遷入龍旺阜，再遷居青竹筍（《南城探源》）
		龍旺埔	黃氏於清同治十年（1871）由福建遷入（《南城探源》）
		蛤地	①黃姓於清光緒初年（1875）由惠陽菁莨湖遷入②李姓於清光緒二十九年（1903），分別由惠陽鋪仔和東莞上山門遷入（《南城探源》）
		大進步（大圳埔）	李姓於清光緒二十九年（1903）由惠陽遷入（《南城探源》）
		新板嶺（西平生產大隊於1969年將小板嶺村劃歸蛤地生產大隊，稱"新板嶺"，又稱"板嶺仔"、"梁家仔"）	梁姓於清同治二年（1863）由寮步兩頭塘遷入（《南城探源》）
		立新（因修建水濂山水庫而搬遷的連丁、大埔於1966年合併為立新村）	李姓來源不詳
		新農村（因修建水濂山水庫，龍旺埔黃姓村民另建龍旺埔村，其他姓氏村民建立新居民點，稱"新農村"）	①楊姓於清光緒四年（1878）由清溪篤木村（注：應為重木村）遷入，1960年遷至路下村（新農村）②廖姓於清光緒八年（1882）有增城縣廖村遷入龍旺埔，1960年遷至路下村（新農村）③鍾姓於清光緒十一年（1885）由增城縣遷入，1960年遷至路下村（新農村）④潘姓於清光緒三十一年（1905）由增城勒布電山遷入，1960年遷至路下村（新農村）⑤黃姓來源不詳（《南城探源》）
		前屋錢（錢屋前）	李姓來源不詳

所在鎮（街）	所在行政村（社區）	所在自然村（居民小組）	主要姓氏及其來源
	水濂	西湖	①魏姓於清道光十五年（1835年）由五華縣長樂村遷入（《東莞市南城區志》）②成姓來歷不詳。
		大雁塘	宋姓一支於清乾隆十二年（1747）遷居東莞縣缺口司上山門村，道光末年（1850）由上山門遷入；一支於清乾隆年間由長樂移居惠州府歸善縣淡水禾裡壩村，於清咸豐六年（1856）由禾裡壩村遷入（《南城探源》）
		鄧屋	①據村中老人稱，其先世為河南南陽人，後遷至珠璣巷、長樂縣伯公潭（堂），再遷入鄧屋
		九里潭	李、黃姓來源不詳
		瓜田嶺	周、羅姓來源不詳
		老圍	①村民稱張姓一支來自東莞牛山②村民稱李姓來自厚街大迥屋尾、大迥古村以及厚街新圍
	西平	陂頭	①張姓約在明代中後期由亨美村遷入定居（《南城探源》）②吳姓、黃姓來源不詳
		上手（上手巾嶺村）	張姓於清同治二年（1863）由清溪牛湖遷入（《東莞市南城區志》）
		下手（下手巾嶺村）	①張姓一支於清代同治二年（1863）由惠陽君子營遷入，另一支於清光緒十年（1884）由清溪摸泥墟遷入（《東莞市南城區志》）②李姓來源不詳
		水澗頭	張姓一支於清光緒九年（1883）由東莞清溪遷入水澗頭村，另一支於同年由東莞清溪牛湖遷入（《東莞市南城區志》）
		彭眼	張姓來源不詳
共計：4個行政村（社區）19個自然村（居民小組）			

表12 厚街鎮客家人分佈情況一覽表

所在鎮（街）	所在行政村（社區）	所在自然村（居民小組）	主要姓氏及其來源
厚街	新圍	新圍、高排、新圍仔、高排仔、九名山、白坭井、新村、南蛇坑、山咀頭	①李姓於清康熙六年（1667）由五華縣五榮樓村（大逕村志則言洋田樓下村）遷入新圍羅坦埔②戴姓於清康熙六年（1667）由五華縣五榮樓村遷入新圍高排（《東莞市厚街鎮志》）③陳、歐陽、鍾、廖、劉、卓、譚、彭、林姓來源不詳（《東莞市厚街鎮志》）
	大逕	大逕	①黃姓於清康熙初年由龍川縣洋貝遷入立村（《大逕村志》）②李姓於清康熙年間由今五華縣遷入
		屋尾	清乾隆七年（1742）李姓從興寧縣葉南筠竹村遷入立村
		石馬	李姓於清康熙年間由厚街新圍羅坦埔遷入立村（《大逕村志》）
		古村（原名鼓村）	李姓一支於清雍正年間由今五華遷入立村；一支於清乾隆年間由今東莞厚街新圍遷入（《大逕村志》）
		江頭（原名崗頭）	①李姓於由大沙麻輋遷入②彭姓於同治年間由今東莞清溪鎮田心遷入③周、黃、梁、成、余、溫以投靠親友而聚居，遷入年份不詳（《大逕村志》）
		汪潭（原名黃潭）	黃姓於清康熙年間由惠東鴨仔灘帽子嶺遷入立村（《大逕村志》）
共計：2個行政村（社區）15個自然村（居民小組）			

深圳廖氏源流及村莊分布簡況

廖虹雷

深圳市本土文化藝術研究會

廖顯軍

深圳廖氏宗親會

深圳廖氏宗親會　天下廖氏一家親

【導讀】：深圳廖氏祖先是河南南陽叔安公後裔，先後從江西寧都、福建汀州輾轉入粵，再遷徙寶安入籍，屬 "武威堂" "世彩堂" ，系崇德公、花公後世。

深圳市前身為寶安縣，晉成帝咸和六年（公元331年）置縣（《晉書·地理志》），寶安縣又古稱新安縣。1840年鴉片戰爭前，新安縣轄香港地區，故香港廖氏與深圳廖氏同宗共邑，習俗無異。

1992年，寶安縣882個自然村戶籍人口（不包括光明華僑畜牧場、縣城及各圩鎮，因經濟特區成立而不計羅湖、福田、鹽田區）共計127個姓氏……廖姓分布的行政村有29個（《寶安縣志》，廣東人民出版社，1997年）。2013年初，深圳廖氏宗親會（籌）在首任會長廖遠耿策劃下，由第二任會長廖錦洪率領廖顯軍、廖德興、廖彪、廖虹雷和廖小帆等幾位副會長、秘書長、顧問，陸續走訪數月10多個廖姓村莊，發現深圳市廖姓村莊實際上是45個。深圳廖氏村莊先後立村，皆因歷史上逃避戰亂和自然災害。據各村族譜記載，最早遷入寶安縣定居的廖氏，為元泰定帝年間（1325年）的龍華鎮清湖村和元順帝至正十年（1350年）上水圍（今香港新界），其他大多數的廖姓村莊均在明清時期遷至寶安，尤其是清康熙年間"遷海復界"，受朝廷輕徭薄賦，政策優惠，而落戶寶安，墾殖荒地，建立家園。

深圳廖氏祖先是河南南陽叔安公後裔，先後從江西寧都、福建汀州輾轉入粵，再遷徙寶安入籍，屬"武威堂""世彩堂"，系崇德公、花公後世。

一、深圳廖姓村落與源流

深圳於1979年1月23日撤縣建市，1980年8月26日建立全國首個經濟特區。深圳市涵蓋原寶安縣的2020平方公里面積（後經衛星重新勘測為1952.84平方公里）。轄有羅湖、福田、南山、鹽田、寶安、龍崗6個行政區和光明、龍華、坪山、大鵬4個新區。2010年11月第六次全國人口普查，公布深圳市有1036萬常住人口。

根據《寶安縣志》記載和我宗親會實地走訪，全市純屬姓廖的村莊和廖姓與其他姓氏混雜的自然村有：龍華新區清湖村、橫朗村，觀瀾街道松元下村、新田村、馬瀝村老圍、樟坑徑村、田寮村、大水坑村、新塘村；寶安區石岩街道羅租村、黎光村，沙井街道萬豐村；龍崗區布吉街道下水徑村，橫崗街道大康村、馬游崗村，龍崗街道龍崗村；坪山新區坪地街道六聯村、年豐村、渡頭圍，坪山街道坪環村、牛角壟村、杜崗嶺村、穀倉下村、青草林村、黃竹坑黃二村、碧嶺上沙村、下沙村、安田村、沙績村、新作坡村、永盈陂村、榕樹背村、沙屯村、碧嶺圍、湯坑（今沙湖）村、坑梓街道沙田村；大鵬新區大鵬街道王母村，葵涌街道三溪村、徑心村（今搬至圩鎮）、壩光白沙灣村、產頭村、高源村，南澳街道東涌村；鹽田區三洲田村；羅湖區南湖街道湖南圍 (龍華清湖廖姓分支，因1980年羅湖口岸建設全村拆遷)等45 個。廖姓原居民據不完全統計為3萬多人。隨著特區建設發 展，全國各地落戶深圳居住的人口比原居民增長30多倍，其 中從江西、河南、廣西、湖南、四川及廣東的梅州、惠州、 江門、韶關、肇慶、河源、汕頭、汕尾在深圳工作居住的廖 姓宗親4萬人(僅五華籍有1萬多人)，因此深圳市目前廖氏宗 親約7萬人左右。

二、深圳較著名的廖氏村落有如下10個

1. 清湖廖氏

清湖村位於龍華新區龍華街道東北部，為純廖姓村莊， 至今約680多年歷史。該支廖氏來自廣東龍門縣功武鎮，開 基始祖明德公，為南宋增城縣令廖堅公六世孫。

廖堅，於宋寶慶三年（1197年）任增城縣令，歷任九 載，遂定籍西林都（今龍門）。四世金鳳為抗元英雄，卒贈 太尉。至六世明德公娶李、楊氏，約元朝泰定帝二年（1325 年）遷清湖落籍主圍，至今690多年來已發展32代，1300多 人口。明德公與李氏葬於龍門，楊氏葬於清湖。源出唐朝時 江西寧都崇德一派，故屬“武威”郡，祠為“崇德”堂。

世系為：崇德—蘭芝—光堯—德隱—友福—昌信—廖 仁—福一—師元—德榮—文一—六五—宗仁—廉郎—明郎— 廖堅—榮公—大九郎—金鳳—剩甫—明德—光道、光迪。

2, 三洲田廖氏

三洲田村，原屬寶安縣坪山約，今屬鹽田區轄區。北鄰 龍崗，南接鹽田沙頭角。地處梧桐山脈系。由上圍、下圍、 南坑和阮屋等七個村組成，是廖、賴、林、鍾、阮、陳等7

姓的聚集地。

　　廖氏開基祖信公，為福建花公（徹系）十七代孫，約於明隆慶六年（1572年），從福建永定縣上塔洪山寺，與堂弟采公一同遷來。

　　三洲田是反清"庚子首義革命"的地方，革命失敗後，慘遭清廷血腥屠村，房屋被鏟平，村民四處逃避。辛亥革命成功後，1912年孫中山特派副官到三洲田撫恤犧牲的義軍家屬，每人發200元白銀慰問金，重建三洲田村，另撥3000元白銀給三洲田興建校舍，以作紀念。1925年孫中山逝世後，孫科親筆題寫"庚子首義中山紀念學校"匾額；1933年12月12日廣東省國民政府批准建立"三洲田庚子革命紀念亭"。1958年因建水庫需要，廖姓村民將所有村舍、山地、農田全部無償獻給了國家。

　　三洲田村如今沉浸在水庫底下。從三洲田遷出去的村莊有：大康村、碧嶺嘉績，觀瀾馬墊，南山區西麗光前村及東莞爐竹田、古樓嶺、松木崗、小塘村等。

　　世系：花公—昌公—徹公—百一郎—百七郎—萬一郎—五四郎—祖壽—伯淳—良儉—仲祥—文禮—人敏—日金—瑚公—立琦—信公李氏

3. 新田廖氏

　　新田村，今為龍華新區觀瀾街道新田社區。新田村廖氏開基始祖沛公，是三洲田信公祖父瑚公的弟弟，同屬花公15代（徹房），約於明朝中後期，從福建永定上塔村遷來，至今約五百年，發展至31代。另有一支據說由山子吓（大康）遷來，約有三、四百人。

　　世系：花公—昌公—徹公—百一郎——百七郎—萬一郎—五四郎—祖壽—伯淳—良儉—仲祥—文禮—人敏—日金—沛公

4. 羅租廖氏

羅租村位於寶安區石岩街道的陽台山下，該村廖氏先祖是福建花公敏房思明系，開基祖長玉（法玉）公，為花公24代，思明14代，約於清康熙十年（1672年）從長樂縣（今五華）大都鎮棟梁坑遷來立村，至今繁衍至13代(花公37世)，除世代居住本村的人外，遠居海外馬來西亞、美國、香港和內地的"羅租廖姓"共有1100人。

世系：花公—昌公—敏公—三十三郎—仲遠—安叔—四十六郎—德源—敬齋—思明—有誠—榮甫—文貴—朝新—志膺—法裕—顯榮—珠—祖臣—廷恕—待征—鏡—崇一—長玉—雲宗、雲會、雲通、雲伍。

5. 黎光廖氏

黎光村古稱泥崗村，緊鄰寶安區石岩街道羅租村東面，開基祖維新，清中期從興寧遷來烏石岩陽台山下落籍開村。

世系：花公—昌公—敏公—三十三郎—仲遠—安叔—四十六郎—德源—敬齋—思明—有誠—榮崇—文顯—朝信—彗—佋—仕章—以良—言急—軒—維新

6. 渡頭廖氏

渡頭村位於坪山新區坪地街道東北部，與惠州市惠陽縣新圩鎮相鄰。廖氏開基祖為鼎雲公，約於清中期從興寧遷來，妣劉、張氏。發展有12代。

世系：花公—昌公—敏公—三十三郎—仲遠—安叔—四十六郎—德源—敬齋—思溫—宗信—仲安—法興—迪公—十三郎—十滿郎—法清—安公—維學—鼎雲

7. 碧嶺廖氏（9條自然村）

（1）新作陂村廖氏開基祖是明亮公，順治八年（1651

年）從興寧縣新圩鎮藍布村遷來。至今有14、15代，達900多人口。

世系：花公—昌公—敏公—三十三郎—仲遠—安叔—四十六郎—德源—敬齋—思明—志誠—遂良—謳公—颷昌—仲信—振—明亮

（2）上沙村廖氏開基祖粵文公，於1651年從興寧石崖遷來，今約有600人。

（3）榕樹背村廖氏開基祖雲浩，從坪地純梓遷來，約有180人。

（4）永盈陂廖氏開基祖德志，從五華遷來，約230人。

（5）安田村廖氏開基祖欽和，遷來約200年，有500人

（6）下沙村開基祖慧德，1651年從興寧遷來，約有200人。

（7）沙屯：從龍崗南約遷碧嶺沙屯，約70人。三洲田遷沙屯，有7人。廖賓從三洲田遷沙屯，有25人

（8）嘉績圍開基祖如超，約清中期從三洲田遷來，至今有十代，約有300人。世系：花公—昌公—徹公—百一郎—百七郎—萬一郎—五四郎—祖壽—伯淳—良儉—仲祥—文禮—人敏—日金—瑚公—立琦—信—應科—仕弘—賡舜—廷裕—永權—如超

（9）牛角壟廖氏開基祖振芳，於清中期從興寧遷淡水再到牛角壟。世系：花公—昌公—敏公—三十三郎—仲遠—安叔—四十六郎—德源—敬齋—思明—志誠—遂良—謳公—颷昌—仲義—鎮—宗寬—文朝—積—可雲—振芳、振清—天麟—文秀—子德—嘉玟、嘉琮

8. 馬游崗廖氏

馬游崗位於龍崗區橫崗街道大康村口，背有一小河，流新陂塘至龍崗河。現分兩個小村為馬五村、馬六村，村前今有老街。有廖、何、李、羅、顏等姓。廖氏開基祖為因由

公，妣李氏，屬花公十六世；約於清初由福建永定上塔洪山寺遷來，發展至今為花公31世，應龍公祠和賡獻祠，約有200人。世系：花公—昌公—徹公—百一郎—百七郎—萬一郎—五四郎—祖壽—伯淳—良儉—仲祥—文禮—人政—日瑢—望公—因由—顯—應龍—仕俊—賡獻、賡翰、賡瑜、賡琅、賡佑。

9. 大康廖氏

龍崗區橫崗街道大康村，舊稱山子吓。大康一名源於清朝時期的大康約，民國時有大康學校，故新中國成立後稱為大康村。

大康廖氏開基祖為采公，立籍上圍，開基處為上圍"伯公"，地方今已建廠。約於明末時采公與信公一同遷來，至今約400多年，現大康廖氏子孫發展至花公33代，有七個自然村組成，除上圍屬采公外，其餘均為信公後裔：老圍（福田）、鳳山（老全盛）、大萬、下中、上中、龍村、莘塘。鳳山、下中屬欽友公後裔：福田、大萬、上中。龍村、莘塘為賡聖公子孫，全村約有2000多人口。

世系：花公—昌公—徹公—百一郎—百七郎—萬一郎—五四郎—祖壽—伯淳—良儉—仲祥—文禮—人敏—日金—瑚公—立琦—信—立常—采

10. 觀瀾廖氏

（1）馬壢村位於龍華新區觀瀾街道。馬壢村廖氏從三洲田村遷來，屬三洲田賡賢公長子伯亮後裔。

（2）大水坑廖氏據説從坪山沙壢村遷來，世系待查。

三、深圳廖氏在歷史中做出的貢獻

深圳地處珠江口，扼守往來廣州的咽喉水道；它位於南海之濱，屯門和赤灣港曾是海上絲綢之路重要驛站。明洪武年間建立南頭和大鵬兩座古城，素為軍事要塞。明洪武元年（1368年）二月征南將軍廖永忠由海道直取廣州，寶安廖氏宗親隨廣東都元帥何真在赤灣港（今南山區），候迎明軍，朱元璋不費一槍一彈收穫嶺南，保鄉民免生靈塗炭。清光緒二十五年（1899年）三、四月，香港"新界"錦田、元朗、上水、大埔等村數千武裝民眾進行"反展拓香港界址"的鬥爭，同年五月，英軍強占深圳、布吉，廖氏宗親和當地人民奮起抗擊，迫使英軍於十一月二十二日退至深圳河以南，挫敗英帝國主義擴大"新界"的陰謀。光緒二十六年(1900年)閏八月十三日，孫中山領導三洲田起義，打響反清的第一槍，起義軍奮戰月餘，動搖了清朝政府。起義中三洲田人廖慶發（起義軍先鋒官）和義軍骨幹廖毓坤、廖仁玉、廖官秀、廖金姐、廖三、廖雲秀、廖觀嬌、廖萼樓、廖鳳、廖德富和廖紀秀等12位義士壯烈犧牲。在抗日戰爭和解放戰爭中，我坪山碧嶺村、田心村、橫崗大康村、石岩羅租村、黎光村（解放前夕，中共寶安縣委在此召開會議，史稱"黎光會議"）、龍華清湖、橫朗村及觀瀾馬壢村是東江縱隊和粵贛湘邊游擊隊的革命根據地。為革命犧牲而銘刻在坪山、龍華、深圳3座紀念碑的就有廖九(碧嶺村人)、廖運祥(葵涌高原人)、廖清平、廖春明、廖添勝和廖明光(均為觀瀾馬壢人)、廖疆仔(坪山田心村人)、廖玉容(女，坪地屯梓村人)、廖國思(坪山穀倉下村人)、廖少生(大康新塘村人)、廖淑儀(女，大康村人)、廖瑞光(坪山沙壆村人)、廖皆友(石岩羅租村人)、廖壽(坪山碧嶺新沙村人)、廖英(女，龍華人)、廖進(葵涌溪涌村人)、廖興友(又名廖興有，龍華清湖村人)等18位烈士。

　　新中國成立後，廖氏宗親又在各條戰線、各個部門做出貢獻。特別是改革開放後，當地的廖氏和來自全國各地的廖氏宗親為深圳經濟特區建設添磚加瓦，流血流汗，貢獻力

量。歷年來，在深圳市各級政府機關擔任廳局級以上幹部18
人、處級以上幹部50多人，教授、專家、學者以及國有企業
總經理、民營企業董事長一大批。讓深圳廖氏宗親引以為豪
的有深圳嘉田有限公司董事長廖慶生先生和實業家廖瓊山、
廖光明、廖健忠、廖宇波、廖治平、廖宇東、廖文中、廖文
標、廖告清等宗親。

四、深圳市廖氏宗親會（籌）熱心宗親工作

為加強深圳廖氏宗親的聯誼和交流，團結廖氏宗親，更
好地為深圳政治文明、社會文明和生態文明建設服務，2005
年成立了深圳宗親會（籌）（以下簡稱我會）。幾年來，在
探索有中國特色的廖氏宗親會活動模式，做了如下幾項工
作：

1. 成功籌辦召開了世界廖氏宗親總會首次代表大會

2006年9月受"總會"委托，由我會積極籌辦召開世界
廖氏宗親首次代表大會。經過多方艱難努力，聯繫和接待
了全國各省、市、縣及一些國外700多位廖氏宗親，在嘉寶
田大酒店成功召開代表大會。會議一致通過了重建廖王廟，
由"總會"與河南省唐河縣湖陽鎮簽訂了購買廖山 20 畝山
地建廖王廟的協議書。會後全國各地廖氏宗親雨後春筍般，
紛紛成立宗親會、研究會。充分顯現了中國太平盛世下廖氏
興旺發達的大好景象。

2. 積極參加各地宗親會成立和建新祠堂慶典活動

首先是參加"總會"召開的多次座談會和"武威廖氏"、
中國廖氏歷史文化研究會會議等活動。其次，參加了陸河縣
廖氏、五華縣塘純村廖氏、惠來縣廖壯福兄、陸豐縣廖俊偉
兄和深圳市石岩鎮廖氏等五處祠堂新建落成慶典。參加香港

上水鄉廖萬石堂六十年大祭和2011年春祭活動。還參加了廣州市和潮汕地區宗親會的成立活動。

　　積極發動中國廖氏宗親參於四川省汶川地震廖氏宗親受災的賑災活動。

　　我會按"總會"廖澤雲會長意見，發動國內廖氏宗親賑災，并向災區廖氏宗親寄發慰問信和捐贈慰問金。

3. 加強與台灣張廖簡宗親會聯繫

　　該會秘書長廖善求曾多次來深圳市和宗親座談，共商加強台海兩岸宗親聯誼事宜，均熱情接待。2009年我會組團30多人到台灣參拜3個廖氏祖先大祠堂，分別送了3塊牌匾給3個祠堂留念，受到了當地宗親的熱烈歡迎。

4. 積極參於修建廖王廟、崇德公祠、花公墓

　　我會和梅州市廖氏宗親會是第二次帶頭重修花公墓的發起人。為花公墓捐資約7萬元。我會不遺餘力地參於重建廖王廟，一連4年為重建廖王廟，每年農曆二月二十八日均組團數十人參加祭廖王，為廟王廟重建捐獻40多萬元。我會帶頭重建江西省寧都縣廖氏江南始祖崇德公祠和墓，由首屆宗親副會長廖錦洪任重建理事長，廖漢標、廖遠耿任顧問。我會捐資一百多萬元，使崇德公祠和墓重建順利完成。

深圳坪山打醮

楊耀林

深圳歷史博物館前總館長

　　1989年12月下旬至1990年2月底，深圳博物館黃崇岳、文本亨、楊耀林諸人，會同坪山鎮政府工作人員何國雄、潘靜友、麥、何兩小夥子以及各村民委員會派出的嚮導，對坪山鎮客家民俗進行調查。

　　坪山鎮共有110多個自然村落，30多個姓氏。依次重點調查了馬西村張氏、大萬村曾氏、金龜老圍村、金形村丘氏、鹹水湖村劉氏、江邊村黃氏和鄧氏、嶺腳村何氏、三洋湖村戴氏、曾氏、三河村江氏、長壽村巫氏、石井李家村李氏、石坡頭文氏、橫嶺村駱氏、沙壆村陳氏、穀倉下村和牛角壟村廖氏、大王圍村葉氏、橫塘村高氏、三家村石井村彭氏、果園背麥氏、竹園村黃、曾、沈、張四姓、石樓圍村羅氏、樓角村林氏等。共23個自然村、22個姓氏。此外還調查了坑梓鎮田段心村和新橋圍黃氏。

　　在此，我們將坪山客家民俗調查資料中有關譚大仙信仰及坪山打醮的民俗活動內容做整理介紹。

　　在自然經濟時代，農村祈雨、消災祈福、酬神、驅鬼和撫慰忙靈的安龍、打醮民俗活動極為普遍，所調查的23個自然村落中，就有譚公醮、關公醮、牛王爺醮，大萬世居、三洋湖的大王伯公安龍，幾乎每個村落都有安龍和參加聯村的打醮活動。

　　譚公廟位於坪山墟東北面與三洋湖村之間。中華人民共和國成立前譚公廟建築規模宏偉，連左右偏房不下20間，20世紀50年代破除迷信被拆毀。1988年，鄰近村莊各姓氏善男信女出力耗資重修一新，新建的廟房三開間、二進一天井。上堂正中安放譚大仙神像，兩側各有關帝、觀音、天后及其它神像，多神合一，香煙繚繞。在廟左前側的大榕樹下，安有土地伯公神位。

　　坪山遠近村民均信奉傳說中的譚大仙，平時家中不寧，到廟中燒把香，添盞油，乾鮮果品供奉拜祭，曰"許願"；化難消災，辦牲三酬謝，曰"還福"。

　　每年農曆四月初八為譚公誕，舊時，坪山鎮所屬四面八方村民擁來譚公廟，帶來拜祭牲三，燒香磕頭後，舉行一系列的活動。其中最有趣的是"燒炮台"。將銅線綁在毛筆杆大小的竹竿上，如同箭鏃，稱之為"炮台"，放入火藥炮筒裏，發炮打上天空，跌落後眾人蜂擁而上，拼命搶奪，搶到者將會得到好運，倘若一個銅線或"炮台"杆分成兩半，分別被兩人所得，那麼就用厘鼎來稱，若有重輕必然導致打架。被訪問者三洋湖村的戴喬（78歲）和江邊村黃天來（78歲）青少年時均親身參加過搶炮台活動。

　　民國及其以前的坪山打醮，關帝、譚仙和山大王三神合祀，打醮活動在坪山墟關帝廟前舉行。關帝廟現已不復存在了，舊址在糧所附近。正常年景下十年一大醮，三年一小醮。如本鄉遇到天災人禍或瘟疫，坪山鄉鄉長及各村長者商議設醮。醮主一般由鄉長擔任，所需銀兩由鄉公所支付。如果醮主是由四鄉八鄰的鄉紳抽籤產生，需負責籌集資金，牽頭到各家領取。窮人出不起錢，則捐米、黃豆之類的實物。

　　醮會在關帝廟前搭起大棚，將譚公神像，山大王神像請來，關帝居中，譚公像安左，山大王像安右，每個神像前置一張神案，擺上各家辦的牲三。不請法師，請一個福、祿、壽俱全或好命者（五男二女）的人主持。打醮開始，由醮主主持祭奠儀式。祭桌上擺滿精美的果脯酒饌。醮主"攬榜",即將一張寫著祈求神靈庇佑合家平安、生子祈福之類的吉祥辭和參醮戶主名單的黃表,在關帝神像前念畢焚化,鄉民隨之伏地叩拜。

深圳博物館《深圳民俗文化》展覽中的"坪山打醮"場景

醮會活動有賭博,醮場賭博抽水,所得款項用於補貼辦醮開支。搭有三台戲台,在當時坪山墟中的鹽行、谷行和伯公祠前各搭一戲棚。下午五時後,在關爺廟前做大戲,各個棚中亦做各種戲曲,如從外地請來的線吊戲,皮影戲等。

打醮宰肥豬,架起大鍋煮大塊肉,分給醮民帶回家中,醮主分得豬腿或豬頭。未分完的肉和米飯相拌,晚間分拋灑在村頭屋尾和大路旁邊給野鬼吃,名曰"送小鬼"。現在當地還流行著一句俗語"打醮惹鬼"。

大醮期間,各村挑選英俊男女青少年扮演"八仙"、西游記中的唐僧師徒和紅孩兒等,走村串戶游行。當年(1988年)78歲的江邊村黃天來就扮過"景仔",並打鼓。大鬧三天三夜。

深圳坪山打醮習俗不復存在了,唯有大鵬東山寺仍然保留"太平清醮"活動。順便提及的是,原本驅除瘟疫的"瘟醮"或"儺"的大鵬清醮,轉換成為追悼英烈五年一醮、為期7天的醮會。大鵬清醮無論佛、道、儒集於一體,兼收並蓄,道具有製作各種紙扎祭品,活動內容有神祇巡游、放生、吃齋,也有大魚大肉的"將軍宴"。2007年,大鵬清醮被收錄為省級非物質文化遺產名錄,同時申報國家級非物質文化遺產名錄。

敬悼蘇師景坡瑩輝教授
（1915-2011）

蘇慶華
馬來亞大學

　　2011年12月，余赴福建泉州參加由泉州市人民政府、華僑大學及香港大學主辦的"饒宗頤與華學國際學術研討會"，碰見與會的台灣南華大學文學系敦煌學專家鄭阿財教授，急忙向他詢問久未見面的業師蘇瑩輝教授近況。不料他竟捎來噩訊，謂景坡師已於今年（2011年）6月間駕鶴西歸了。余聞之不禁黯然神傷，久久不能自已！

　　業師蘇瑩輝教授，生於1915年，江蘇丹徒縣人，字景坡（因景仰東坡居士故也）。1940年畢業於無錫國學專修學校，同年入雲南大理民族文化書院經子書院子學系。1942年，任職重慶中央圖書館。1943年到敦煌藝術研究所工作。1949年他離開大陸赴台灣，曾任台北中央博物館圖書館聯管處編輯、編纂。1966年他到馬來西亞任職於吉隆坡馬來亞大學中文系直至1980年。[1]同年6月他赴香港於珠海書院文史研究所講學，約三年餘後離職返回台灣。自1983年起，他出任台北故宮博物館研究員、顧問。最終因年事已高而自任上退下來，賦閒家居頤養天年。2011年6月17日景坡師逝世

1　景坡師自1966年起，出任馬來亞大學中文系講師職。1973年6月起他被擢升為副教授，直至1980年6月榮休離馬。

於台北，享壽九十餘高齡。

　　由於早年曾供職於國立敦煌藝術研究所，景坡師對於敦煌石窟有過直接之接觸，並收集了大量的原始資料，為他此後的研究工作打下雄厚的基礎。[2]著名東西方交通史學家方豪教授嘗於《敦煌論集‧序》中，盛贊景坡師"於瓜沙之建置与沿革，〔……〕雕刻之特徵，壁畫之源流，與夫寫經卷之統計，瞭若指掌，蓋非如先生之寢於石室，饋於石室，歷年餘之久者，[3]曷克有此？故當其《敦煌學概要》於民國五十三年與世人之共見也，一時治斯學者無不人手一冊，以其源源本本，詳實簡明，為前所未有也"。[4]

　　景坡師是卓有成就的敦煌學專家，尤其長於敦煌佛教藝術。他著有：《敦煌學概要》（台灣中華叢書編審委員會出版，1960年版）、《敦煌論集》（台灣學生書局，1969年版）、《敦煌論集續篇》（台灣學生書局，1983年版），《敦煌》中、日文雙語圖文版（台北藝文印書館，1977年版）[5]　及先後發表"論敦煌本史傳變文與中國俗文學"（刊台灣《圖書館學報》第6卷，1964

2　參引自林家平、寧強、羅華慶著《中國敦煌學史》，北京語言學院出版社，1992年，頁684。

3　華按：景坡師曾應國立敦煌藝術研究所之聘，度隴而西，在敦煌千佛洞居留了一年多。謝愛萍博士追憶景坡師於馬大中文系課堂中，曾親口告訴當時仍為本科生的他們："中國解放的時候，我（景坡師）正在敦煌研究敦煌的資料。那裡的風很大，我每次吃的饅頭都含有沙粒，生活極為艱苦。而當我完成研究出來時，看到的是'變天'了，已是中共統治的時代。"【引自〈謝愛萍訪談〉，楊清龍主編《馬來亞大學中文系50週年紀念特刊》（圖史資料彙編），吉隆坡：馬來亞大學中文系畢業生協會‧馬大中文系聯合出版，2013年，頁218。】

4　方豪的〈序文〉寫於民國五十七年（1968年），引文見蘇瑩輝著《敦煌論集》，台灣學生書局，1969年8月初版。

5　該書乃由蘇瑩輝撰、日人余直夫譯。1972年，蘇氏受香港《中外畫報》之邀，撰寫"細說敦煌"長篇連載，共完成了一十八輯之相關圖文報導。全文刊完後，在台灣藝文印書館嚴一萍敦促下，以《敦煌》為書名，將中文和日譯本合訂成冊於1977年出版。

年）、"論
敦煌本望江南
雜曲四首之
寫作年代"
（刊新加坡
《新社學報》
第5期，1973
年）、"《敦
煌曲》評介"
（刊香港中
文大學《中國
文化研究所學

圖1　1979/80年中文系本科班級合照，前排左
　　起為鄭良樹師、蘇瑩輝師及楊清龍師。
　　後排左4即筆者蘇慶華。

報》7卷1期，1974年）、"從敦煌古寫本文書中看雅俗
作品的相互關係"（刊台灣《國立中央圖書館館刊》11
卷2期，1978年）、"敦煌文化傳自東方略論"（刊《藝
壇》141期，1979年）等相關論文多篇。[6]其中，他曾因撰
寫《敦煌曲》評介，而得與敦煌研究名家饒宗頤教授和法
國漢學家戴密微（Paul Demieville）教授書函往還論學，
使其深感榮耀，而於我輩面前多次提及此事。

　　林家平、寧強、羅華慶於他們合著的《中國敦煌學史》
一書中即指出：在台灣、香港的敦煌藝術研究者中，蘇瑩輝
和饒宗頤的成績比較突出。蘇瑩輝的《敦煌學概要》（1960
年版）對敦煌藝術有較多的論述，並刊印了一些敦煌藝術圖
片資料。而在其《敦煌論集》（1969年版）中，則收集了
作者歷年撰寫的敦煌學論文32篇，其中4篇是關於石窟藝術
的，即〈敦煌石室和敦煌千佛洞〉、〈敦煌的壁畫藝術〉、
〈敦煌石室壁畫發現對中國繪畫之影响〉、〈中國彩塑藝術
之特徵〉。他們認為："（蘇氏）這番對中國傳統藝術的深

6　以上書目資料乃參考、整理自張錫厚著《敦煌文學源流》，北京：
　　作家出版社，2000年，頁556，558，572-575。

刻認識，對我們今天的敦煌藝術繼承與創新很有啟發性"。[7]

　　此外，他們亦於該書〈瓜沙歸義軍歷史研究〉章節中，肯定了"台、港地區有關這個問題的研究，取得了顯著的成績"，並指出："其中卓有建樹的，首推蘇瑩輝"。該書續稱："他（即蘇瑩輝）在瓜沙歸義軍歷史研究方面，共計發表了十多篇論文，對這個專題的諸方面都作了探索"。[8]其中，《曹元忠卒年考》一文發表於《大陸雜誌》（第7卷9期，1955年）"對曹元忠繼任歸義軍節度使的經過作了詳細考證；並大量利用敦煌文獻和莫高窟供養人的題記，就曹元忠的卒年問題，對正史記載和羅振玉、王國維、張大千諸家在此問題上的論點作了對比，考其得失"。

　　而發表於1964年"第二屆亞洲史學年會"上之《瓜沙史事系年》一文，則"以年代為經，將各人之事蹟（包括著作、寫經、供養題名等）分系於下，遇有史籍疏誤或前人著述偽舛者，則據實物資料加以訂正。總之，這是一篇較為系統的研究瓜沙歸義軍史實的論文，是對羅振玉、向達同類研究論文的一個深入。此外，蘇瑩輝還有：《論索勳、張承奉節度沙州歸義軍之起訖年》、《張淮深於光啟三年求授旌節辨別》、《論張義潮收復河隴州郡之年代》、《論晚唐統治瓜、沙二州的張、索、李三姓政事始末》、《瓜、沙曹氏兼事宋、遼顛末》等論文，（作者均）付出了大量心血，取得了卓越成績"！[9]該書復於〈莫高窟碑刻研究〉章節中，再度肯定"台、港地區學者們於）這方面的研究，有所建樹。（其中），主要有蘇瑩輝和陳祚龍的有益探索"。

　　早在1940年代，景坡師已於《西北文化》周刊上發表

7　引自林家平、寧強、羅華慶著前揭書，北京語言學院出版社，1992年，頁672。

8　引自林家平、寧強、羅華慶著前揭書，北京語言學院出版社，1992年，頁684。

9　引自林家平、寧強、羅華慶著前揭書，北京語言學院出版社，1992年，頁684-685。

了《跋敦煌岷州廟經幢殘石》一文，並引述印度学者之研
究加以論證云：“殘石上之婆羅謎文乃論‘像生’者。魏晉
之際，中亞一帶盛行‘像生’之說，此經幢足資證明”。其
後，他又相繼於《大陸雜誌》（第4卷10期，1951年）發表
了《跋莫高窟造像及功德題名石刻拓本》；於《大陸雜誌》
（第20卷7期，1952年）發表了《敦煌新　出泰始十一年樂生
碑跋》；及於《大陸雜誌》（第36卷10 期，1967年）發表了
《敦煌霍家碑時代考》諸文，均為景坡師有關敦煌碑刻研究
之重頭篇什。[10]

　　1966年10月，景坡師自台灣抵馬來西亞，受聘為馬來亞
大學中文系講師。他在系里講授目錄學、中國文學史、漢魏
六朝文選、唐宋文選等課程。其中，令同學們印象最深刻和
感覺最精彩的部分，乃其所專長的敦煌學、敦煌藝術和敦煌
變文內容之講授。[11]

　　在這期間，景坡師亦嘗多次受邀出席會議和講學，包
括：參加“國際佛教藝術會議”（1969年）、赴星洲南洋大
學中國語言學系作“敦煌研究專題演講”（1975年12月）
、赴法國巴黎出席敦煌學會會議（1976年9月）及赴巴黎參
加“第一屆敦煌及西域文獻會議”（1979年10月）。

　　景坡師為人謙和、訥於言。方豪教授於景坡師著《敦煌
論集‧序》中即指出：“（他）為人樸實，治學嚴謹，學人
也，亦君子也；（與之）相交以還，益深欽敬。雖訥訥不善

---

10 引自林家平、寧強、羅華慶著前揭書，北京語言學院出版社， 1992
　　年，頁685。

11 慶華謹按：景坡師於課堂中談到莫高窟壁畫和經卷繪畫時，更是精
　　彩絕倫、滔滔不絕。他不但為吾輩談其所精專的莫高窟、榆林二窟
　　壁畫 “白畫與手譜”，且示以張大千親自鉤摹之手足、面龐複印摹
　　本。對此課題屬門外漢的我，僅記得老師對張大千在敦煌鉤摹大宗
　　畫稿中的歷代手譜曾予以高度的評價，並隨口拋出 “畫人難畫手；
　　畫獸難畫走” 這兩句畫家術語，迄今仍令我難忘。

言辭，而真摯誠篤"。[12]猶記得，大二那年我在景坡師指導下撰寫題為〈古詩十九首的主題思想與藝術特色〉之畢業論文。面臨相關參考資料十分匱乏的窘境，余懷着戰戰兢兢的心情向蘇老師求援。景坡師不但沒有責怪之意，倒反和顏悅色的施予援手——通過各方管道，幫我搜集刊載於國內外學報的論文。最終，我的這篇畢業論文在老師的鼓勵和細心指導下順利完成，並考取頗佳的成績。景坡師平時不苟言笑，教學之餘總是埋頭讀書、寫作。偶爾有學生到其辦公室來討教，則放下手頭的工作，態度祥和　　、細聲地與彼等討論功課。雖然，個人記憶中倒有幾件與景坡師相關、令人印象深刻的"趣事"。茲分別略述於下，與大家分享：

其一、景坡師向來辦起事來慢條斯理，但卻於寄投書函時求其快速無誤。先生每每於中午十二時前即連走帶跑的從其位處數層樓高（我們戲稱為"雲頂"）的研究室急速走下樓，然後趨往總圖書館前的郵箱方向，準時將其所欲郵寄的信件投入其中，以便讓郵差把它和其他信件及時於中午搜集時段帶走。

其二、每當下課前幾分鐘，景坡師總是不停地看其腕上戴着的手錶。這事令同學們頗感好奇，卻無由揭開心中的謎底。一日下課後，我即尾隨先生快速的腳步由"雲頂"跑下樓，經過一小段長廊、直達另一棟朝向教育學院前的馬路口。但見老師急忙登上師母開來接他回家的私房車，尚來不及坐好、將車門關上，車子即被開走、揚長而去！親睹眼前這一幕，終於解開了一直以來令我感好奇且不解的"謎底"。然則，先生每每於下課前為"趕搭車子"而於無意間露顯之"不自在"焦慮神情，迄今猶歷歷在目。[13]

其三、一如其他傳統讀書人，景坡師似乎在研究學問之

12　引自方豪前揭書序文，見蘇瑩輝著《敦煌論集》，台灣學生書局，1969年8月初版。

13　話雖如此，除了性子頗為急躁外，蘇師母在照料景坡師日常起居生活的方方面面，倒還是細心體貼的。

餘，平日鮮少涉及打理家務。先生於1980年退休、即將離開馬大轉赴香港珠海書院講學之際，忙於收拾在宿舍積累了十餘年的藏書和行李。而師母卻恰巧於此時不得不啟程飛往美國，準備於近一个月內安排嫁女事宜。因擔心景坡師不擅烹煮菜餚，她於臨行前給老師醃製了一大塊鹹凍豬肉外，還烹煮了一大鍋的紅燒牛肉放入冰箱冷藏，以備老師將鹹凍肉切片連同白蘿蔔熬湯，同時將紅燒牛肉弄熱後，即可上桌進食。

看到此情形，我於心不忍，便自薦留宿老師家，除了幫忙收拾行李外，主要為了照料老人家一日三餐的飲食烹飪。景坡師建議分工，由他擔負為咱二人準備早餐——煎蛋、在麵包上塗牛油和沖泡“好利克”飲料的工作；其餘每日兩餐則由我負責。結果老先生因不善控制瓦斯的火勢，導致煎出來的雞蛋被燒焦成“黑蛋”。最後，他只好放棄準備早餐，

圖2　蘇瑩輝師墨寶（戊午1978年，贈与慶華）

讓我獨自承擔三餐的烹飪工作。至於到市場購買蔬果肉類的工作，則由時任中文系書記的翁紹鳳小姐代勞。偶爾，我還燒煮了簡單的三菜一湯，讓到訪老師的朋友一起用餐。

相處近一个月，協力整理書籍、把書裝箱期間，師徒

圖3　1997年中文系畢業生協會舉辦晚宴，向幾位前中文系老師致敬。左起為蘇瑩輝，中協主席陳廣才，傅吾康，熊遠賓（馬大中文系第一屆畢業生）。

倆感情融洽。頗受老師青睞的我，除了獲贈他老書寫的"羅馬昔有東西帝，如來初無南北宗"甲骨文對聯條幅，暨其臨羅雪堂集契文"入明出幽，知來告往，踐言立行，安命樂天"揮就之墨寶；我竟有幸聆聽到老師以江蘇鄉音吟唱的詩仙李白《將進酒》詩篇。[14]

憶及（1980年）當晚的情景，猶歷歷在目，仿佛耳際邊隨即响起了昔日老師低沉且略帶悲戚之吟唱聲："君不見，黃河之水天上來，奔流到海不復回……"。那裊裊餘音，繚繞一室，不絕於耳。聞之能不令人動容，而倍感惆悵？！

1997年，馬大中文系畢業生協會為了倡導尊師重道精神而舉辦"獻愛傳薪之夜"，向包括景坡師在內的5名前任中文系教授致敬。[15]在蘇師母陪同下，景坡師遠自台灣趕 來吉隆坡赴會。這是老師自1980年离休以來，於17年後再度踏上馬來西亞的土地與系友們歡聚一堂，宴席氛圍令人感到無比溫馨和親切！

猶憶當晚與老師碰面時，我緊握住老師的雙手，久久不

14　華按：猶記得當天晚飯過後，閒聊之餘，老師似若有所感，隨即吟唱起李白 《將進酒》詩篇來。基於老師平日不苟言笑且訥於言的內向性格，這一稀罕聆聞老師吟唱的機遇竟讓我也給碰上了，真令我喜出望外，迄今仍難以忘懷！

15　這五位老師分別是：景坡師、傅吾康師、洪天賜師、鄭良樹師和陳應德師。

忍放開。這，也是我最後一次與景坡師的相見。韶光易逝，
距與恩師於1997年的見面，不覺又過了近二十載光景！追懷
夙昔，仿佛昨日。厄訊傳來，令身處千里以外的我，不免感
傷不已！執筆想寫篇悼念恩師的文字，卻怎麼也無法成章。
待心情平伏後，我終於提起禿筆撰此蕪文敬悼景坡師，願老
師一路好走，安息天國！

　　　　　　　　2018年3月12日第五次改訂稿

赤柱歷史考察

蕭國健教授

珠海學院香港歷史文化研究中心主任

　　赤柱，是香港最南的地區，早在四百多年前已建有村落，明朝的輿地圖亦繪有赤柱的名稱。「赤柱」一名的由來有多種傳說：一說在古代這裡有一棵巨大的木棉樹，當木棉花開的時候，嫣紅一片，樹下的村落便以「赤紅的木柱」取名，稱為赤柱。另一說赤柱半島山崗的泥土，在朝暉照映下便會顯得鮮紅燦爛，航海者以此為航標，稱為赤柱。又有謂該地曾為盜賊盤據，故稱「賊住」，蜑語為「赤柱」。

　　赤柱在香港早期歷史上是一個重要鄉鎮，一八四一年香港政府第二號憲報便稱赤柱為香港島的首府，當年已有人口二千人。赤柱原居民多來自福建及廣東沿海地區，有潮府、鶴佬、客家及漁民聚居。

一、舊赤柱警署

　　是香港政府法定古蹟之一，建於一八五九年。它是香港最早建成的六所警署之一，由於其餘五所已先後拆卸，所以它現在成了香港最古老的警署。該處現被南區政務處借用，而警署則在附近另建新址。

二、軍人墳場

　　位於黃麻角道，接近聖士提反海灘，墳場內埋有二次大戰時為保衛香港而犧牲的盟軍戰士，墳場內花木栽培顯見心思，是赤柱著名的名勝紀念地。

三、劏人排

在聖士提反海灘，是一塊露出海面的礁石，相傳在清朝時港島一帶的死囚或海盜被捕後，被判死刑便在這裡正法，所以有此名稱。

四、黃麻角村

今赤柱砲台所在地，一八四九年，村民徐亞保在此地刺殺兩名調戲村婦的英兵，事件震動中外，香港政府懸紅五百元緝捕徐亞保及其餘有關村民，徐亞保被捕後被判處遞解出境。在黃麻角建立的赤柱砲台，在二次大戰時曾發生激烈的攻防戰，一九四一年十二月二十四日，日軍動員左右兩翼及輕型裝甲車中隊千多人與砲兵兩中隊攻擊赤柱砲台，駐守砲台的英國、加拿大籍士兵一千七百多名及五百名砲兵奮力抵抗，日軍久攻不下，施行夜襲亦不成功，數百日軍戰斃，為盟軍重大勝利，但翌日香港總督下令投降。據說，日軍佔領砲台後施行大屠殺，並將屍體埋放大潭灣。赤柱砲台現在是軍事禁區，但每年有一天開放日，公開讓市民參觀。

五、天后廟

是香港南區歷史最古的廟宇，廟內有一座鑄於清朝乾隆三十二年（一七六七年）的銅鐘，記載了當年村民陳信澤與灣泊赤柱的漁民合資建廟的經過。據說當年擇此地建天后廟，原因是赤柱村形象蟹，蟹是橫行的，這樣令到當地極不安寧，於是村民找到蟹眼的位置建築天后廟鎮壓，從此赤柱村民得以安靖。天后廟規模本來十分宏偉，可惜在一九六二年颱風溫黛襲港時遭受破壞，重修後已失去舊日風采。赤柱天后廟現存文物十分豐富，除乾隆時鑄的銅鐘外，尚有同時期鑄造的九十八公斤重鐵秤鉈，嘉慶廿四年（一八一九年）的門匾、木聯、鐵香爐。廟正殿供奉的神祇亦算全港最多，除天后外，又有十多位民間奉祀的神像，一年四季參拜的善信可隨意祈福。廟左壁牆上張掛有一塊老虎皮，這隻老虎原是一隻體重二百四十磅，高三呎，長六呎一吋的龐然大物，一九四二年日治時期在赤柱警署前被印籍日警羅亞星所殺，日軍為討好村民，將老虎皮供奉於天后廟。每年的農曆三月廿三天后誕，廟前空地都會搭棚演戲，為赤柱村一大盛事。

六、北帝廟

　　位於赤柱灣西岸岩石上，規模雖然細小，但座向極佳，可俯瞰赤柱灣全景，是「赤柱觀濤」的最有利位置。廟宇初建於清朝嘉慶十年（一八〇五年），由在赤柱灣作業的潮州籍漁民倡建。另一個說法是廟是由海盜張保仔所建，用以監視赤柱灣的情況。相傳廟內神壇下有一秘密通道，連接春坎角的張保仔洞，張保仔投降後通道被清廷所封。該廟現在仍保存了建廟時善信所贈的雲板。但其餘歷史文物則已蕩然無存。每年的農曆三月初三北帝誕香火鼎盛，為赤柱的一大盛事。以前每當神誕時，村民在海灘上演傀儡戲助興，香燭元寶奉拜之後，更有搶花炮的活動，搶得花炮的人必大事慶祝，場面十分熱鬧。

七、大王宮、土地廟、水僊廟

　　赤柱村內除了兩間歷史悠久的天后及北帝廟外，尚有由赤柱街坊會代華人廟宇委員會管理的大王宮、土地廟、水僊廟，這些小廟雖無歷史文物考證建立年代，但從其奉祀神祇及位置分佈，可以察覺赤柱至今仍保留有濃厚的中國鄉村宗教氣氛。

香港歷史文化研究中心
2017年9月-2018年5月 活動報告

甲、2017-18年講座系列

（一）與香港歷史博物館合辦香港歷史文化講座系列

主題：二十世紀上葉港粵地區的文化與生活

1) 07/10/2017　〈香港戰前私人電話：科技演變、
　　　　　　　　　專營權風波、本地化和長途電話〉
　　馬冠堯先生　　退休工程師、香港大學房地產及建設系
　　　　　　　　　兼任副教授

2) 14/10/2017　〈日軍在港防務及盟軍對港戰略
　　　　　　　　　1942-1945〉
　　鄺智文博士　　香港浸會大學歷史系助理教授

3) 21/10/2017　〈戰前香港在華人世界的角色與地位〉
　　丁新豹教授　　香港中文大學歷史系客席教授

4) 28/10/2017　〈從樊仙和華光崇拜看神靈信仰與
　　　　　　　　　生活變遷〉
　　危丁明博士　　珠海學院香港歷史文化研究中心副研究員

5) 04/11/2017　〈民國時期悦城龍母廟的進香文化〉
　　潘淑華博士　　香港中文大學歷史系副教授

（二）與保良局歷史博物館合辦「保世除暴·良民感恩」歷史講座系列

　　2017年11月18日至12月9日與保良局歷史博物館、長春社文化古蹟資源中心合辦「香港歷史講座系列」

　　蕭國健教授主講「香港的開埠與保良局的成立」

　　黃競聰博士及梁惠娟館長主講「保良局領婚制度與華人婚姻傳統」

　　游子安教授主講「港澳地區善堂與關帝信仰---從保良局祀神說起」

　　張為群博士主講「南來文人與保良局對聯---實地講解與導賞」

乙、文化考察活動

1) 11/11/2017 蕭國健教授帶領赤柱歷史文化考察 - 懲教

處博物館及赤柱舊墟

2)　　03-03-2018本校舉辦之「新春二重奏」邀請本中心主任蕭國健教授帶領參觀屯門區青龍頭及掃管笏古蹟文物。

丙、與「新界西長者學苑聯網」合辦講座及考察

2017年11月13日「沙田歷史與文化」
2017年11月14日 沙田曾大屋

丁、出版刊物

蕭國健、游子安主編《鑪峰古今──香港歷史文化論集2017》，2018年6月。

戊、學術研討會

2018年3月9-10日，珠海學院香港歷史文化研究中心與
嗇色園合辦「首屆華南地區歷史民俗與非遺」國際學術研討會

編後語

　　本書是《鑪峰古今——香港歷史文化論集》系列的第六部。收進專題論文、學人傳略、地區考察共11篇文章。論集涵蓋的題材既廣且深，內容充實：沙田自1910至1970年代之歷史變遷、殖民地時期鯉魚門地區的防禦工事、香港科學工藝教育的濫觴、冷戰初期兩岸的僑教政策、扶乩對圓玄學院早期所起的關鍵作用；以及多篇有關廣東地區歷史來稿，廣州喪葬儀式與空間的重構、客家人遷徙東莞歷史及原因、深圳廖氏源流、深圳坪山打醮等等。還有一篇追念蘇瑩輝教授的傳略，瑩輝教授與本校甚有淵源，1980至1982年其間曾在香港珠海書院文史研究所擔任客座教授，任教「敦煌學導論」等科目。

　　2018年適逢本中心成立十周年。今年春季，珠海學院香港歷史文化研究中心與嗇色園合辦「華南地區歷史民俗與非遺」國際學術研討會，與會專家來自廣東、北京、天津、台灣、日本、馬來西亞、英國與香港地區學者及博物館館長等，進行交流，商討如何傳承及展示非遺各項目，並發表學術報告。會議前後，深圳與東莞博物館，及來自馬來亞的朋友，都踴躍來稿，讓本書更形豐贍，在此衷心感謝各位朋友的支持。

　　《鑪峰古今──香港歷史文化論集》每年結集一部，園地開放，歡迎投稿，以推動更多朋友探索本地史與華南社會文化的興趣。

游子安
珠海學院香港歷史文化研究中心副主任
2018年5月4日